The Art of Insurgency

The Art of Insurgency

*American Military Policy
and the Failure of Strategy
in Southeast Asia*

DONALD W. HAMILTON
Foreword by Cecil B. Currey

 PRAEGER

Westport, Connecticut
London

Library of Congress Cataloging-in-Publication Data

Hamilton, Donald W., 1959–
    The art of insurgency : American military policy and the failure
of strategy in Southeast Asia / Donald W. Hamilton ; foreword by
Cecil B. Currey.
        p.   cm.
    Includes bibliographical references and index.
    ISBN 0–275–95734–9 (alk. paper)
    1. Counterinsurgency.   2. United States—Military policy.
3. Vietnam—History—1945–1975.   4. Philippines—
History—1946–1986.   5. Malaya—History—Malayan Emergency,
1948–1960.   I. Title.
U241.H36   1998
355.02′18—dc20   96–44178

British Library Cataloguing in Publication Data is available.

Library of Congress Catalog Card Number: 96–44178
ISBN: 0–275–95734–9

First published in 1998

Praeger Publishers, 88 Post Road West, Westport, CT 06881
An imprint of Greenwood Publishing Group, Inc.

Printed in the United States of America

The paper used in this book complies with the
Permanent Paper Standard issued by the National
Information Standards Organization (Z39.48–1984).

10 9 8 7 6 5 4 3 2

Copyright Acknowledgments

The author and publisher gratefully acknowledge permission for use of the following material:

Excerpts from Douglas Pike, *Viet Cong* (Cambridge, Mass.: M.I.T. Press, 1966). Courtesy of M.I.T.
Press.

Excerpts from Robert Thompson, *Defeating Communist Insurgency* (New York: Frederick A. Praeger,
1966). Courtesy of Isabel Oliphant.

For

Stephanie Ruth, Joshua Lawrence, and Brian Alexander

Contents

Illustrations

Foreword

Writing about Vietnam has been around since the earliest days of American involvement there, a veritable cottage industry. There are literally thousands of books that discuss one aspect or another of that conflict. While many of them are both interesting and illuminating, most are not particularly helpful in deriving knowledge of why the American enterprise there failed so badly.

The concentrated analysis and study of the conflict is not as old and has had a much thinner production. There were, of course, the writings of theoreticians/practitioners of the art of People's Wars of National Liberation—old-line revolutionaries such as Regis Debray, Mao Tse-tung, Che Guevara, Ho Chi Minh, Truong Chinh, Vo Nguyen Giap, and others. Despite the fact that it was once popular to own copies of their works, few of those in authority actually ever read them, and even fewer understood them.

There were other books, few and far between, that made their way into print that actually tried to pinpoint the problems that were causing such an upheaval in our armed forces as they struggled in Southeast Asia. My own list of the most essential of those writings includes:

Robert E. Osgood, *Limited War* (1957). One of the earliest studies that tried to understand the nature of conflicts that did not involve massed armies and divisional movements to contact with an enemy. Osgood pointed out the necessity for a different approach to such warfare.

Robert Taber, *The War of the Flea: A Study of Guerrilla Warfare, Theory, and Practice* (1965). An insightful author, Taber wrote that "the specifically modern aspect of guerrilla warfare is in its use as a tool of political revolution—the single sure method by which an unarmed population can overcome mechanized armies, or, failing to overcome them, can stalemate them and make them irrelevant" (pp. 131–32).

J. A. Pustay, *Counterinsurgency Warfare* (1965). An early and earnest effort to understand irregular warfare and how to defeat its proponents.

John J. McCuen, *The Art of Counter-Revolutionary War: The Strategy of Counterinsurgency* (1966). Another early work—we had been in Vietnam in large numbers only since April 1965—that took a serious look at the problems inherent in guerrilla counterinsurgent conflicts.

Julian Paget, *Counterinsurgency Operations: Techniques of Guerrilla Warfare* (1967). Used for a time by the U.S. military, this was a practical guide to combating irregular troops.

William R. Corson, *The Betrayal* (1968). A Marine lieutenant colonel who wrote of the Corps' Combined Action Platoon program in I Corps, and how that fairly successful approach to pacification was ultimately dismantled.

William J. Lederer, *Our Own Worst Enemy* (1968). Lederer wrote of the corruption and sleaze that accompanied America's presence in Vietnam and the incomprehensible wastage of our logistical shipments.

Carl F. Bernard, *The War in Vietnam: Observations and Reflections of a Province Senior Advisor* (USACGSC, paper, 1969). An Army lieutenant colonel, Bernard saw keenly one of the major problems caused by the direction U.S. forces took in Vietnam: "The U.S. continues to concentrate the bulk of . . . resources and military might on controlling the terrain and looking for massed enemy formations. The VC continues to concentrate its talents on controlling the people. Each succeeds." No one listened to this sensitive and brilliant officer.

Ward Just, *Military Men* (1970). A scathing indictment of the higher echelon of rank within the American military establishment.

John T. McAlister, Jr., *Vietnam: The Origins of Revolution* (1970). This author, among other things, lamented the vast ignorance Americans had of the history and culture of Vietnam. Nor could we talk with people we were supposedly there to help. With few exceptions, we had no linguistic experts capable of speaking with their Vietnamese political or military counterparts. McAlister told how it was not until his senior year in college at Yale in 1957, that he prevailed upon the faculty there to institute the nation's first university-level course in the Vietnamese language—only eight years before two Marine battalions swarmed ashore on the beaches of Da Nang. That first course had three students!

Even as late as 1968 the military had little linguistic capability. Thousands of officers and enlisted men could now "order a meal in a restaurant or tell somebody where to carry a bundle." Only a few, however, could "discuss the nuances of politics and security with the peasants let alone the generals" (p. viii). And those who could were ignored. In Vietnam we were as mute as Balaam's ass.

Michael T. Klare, *War Without End: American Planning for the Next Vietnams* (1972). While the war still raged, this author wrote of the endless complications derived from our strife in Vietnam and of the implications for the future.

Edward L. King, *The Death of the Army* (1972). An Army lieutenant colonel who despaired over the lack of progress of the war in Vietnam and what participation there had done to the cohesiveness, morale, and readiness of the U.S. military.

Edward Lansdale, *In the Midst of Wars: An American's Mission to Southeast Asia* (1972). A major general in the Air Force and a sometime CIA agent, he was America's most successful and knowledgeable expert on counterguerrilla strategies, who once proclaimed that "no responsible government, responsive to the needs of its own people can *ever* be overthrown." His work in the Philippines and his early days in Vietnam lent credence to his observation. Despite his real world experience he had long been ignored by those in power.

Stuart Loory, *Defeated: Inside America's Military Machine* (1973). This work delved deeply into the deterioration of morale within the military during the 1960s and early 1970s. The root cause of that decline was caused, he believed, by our involvement in Vietnam.

William L. Hauser, *America's Army in Crisis: A Study in Civil-Military Relations* (1973). An Army lieutenant colonel at the time he wrote this book of mild criticism and a *defender* of the system, he still felt impelled to say that "widespread allegations of manipulation of statistical indicators, unseemly pursuit of rank and decorations, and 'ticket-punching' careerism—even if some of the critics appeared to have come into court with unclean hands—are too damning to be ignored" (p. 185).

Jeffrey S. Milstein, *Dynamics of the Vietnam War: A Quantitative Analysis and Predictive Computer Simulation* (1974). An operational research and systems analysis (ORSA) approach to understanding the situation in Vietnam. It received little attention.

Maureen Mylander, *The Generals: Making It, Military Style* (1974). Having interviewed dozens of men holding flag rank, she lamented that "to become a general, and particularly to become a high-ranking one, an

officer must conform, avoid error, shun controversy, and forego dissent."
Such a system did not bode well for its own health.

Douglas Kinnard, *The War Managers* (1977). A retired brigadier
general who had served in Vietnam, he asked "Why didn't the military
leaders at the top speak out?" (p. 116). Why didn't he? According to his
book, nearly 70 percent of army generals who served in Vietnam were
uncertain what the objectives of that combat were. Over 50 percent
believed the United States should not have participated in the conflict.
An even 61 percent believed that McNamara's famous "statistical
indicators of success" were nonsense (pp. 25, 154, 164). Yet the Green
Machine rolled on.

Richard Gabriel and Paul Savage, *Crisis in Command:
Mismanagement in the Army* (1978). Both were Army Reserve field-
grade officers who criticized a system that turned those who bear the
burden of combat against their own self-seeking, high-ranking officers,
who either did not or would not share the dangers of contact with the
enemy.

Cincinnatus [Cecil B. Currey], *Self-Destruction: The Disintegration
and Decay of the United States Army During the Vietnam Era* (1981). A
controversial book written when I was an Army Reserve lieutenant
colonel. I believed then, and do so still today, that the military disaster in
Vietnam grew out of ineptitude at the top, and that the Army made too
many mistakes in its years in Vietnam. If those same errors are not to be
repeated in some future conflict (and some were, in Panama and in
Grenada), their sources need to be identified, understood, and corrected.
At some point, I wrote then, for reasons believed to be good, America's
army will once again be sent into battle. The outcome will be unfortunate
if the Army closes its eyes to the lessons of Vietnam and again
experiences a debacle (Preface, passim).

Andrew F. Krepinevich, Jr., *The Army and Vietnam* (1986). A solid
and thoughtful description of the problems faced by the Army in
Southeast Asia and how those self-inflicted wounds came about.

Others might differ with some of my selections and would create a
different list. This, however, is mine. And, despite their worth, most of
them missed the essential mark. They detailed the collapse of morale, or
the end of unit cohesiveness, or the scandals uncovered, or analyzed
tactics used, or criticized the lack of knowledge about Vietnam. There
was too little analysis in almost all of them of the nature of insurgency
itself. Only one or two actually looked at the conflict in Vietnam and
tried to analyze it for what it was—to extrapolate its essential character
and to distill its essence—and so to come to a full and complete
understanding of what we faced there.

We began with such confidence. It would all be over soon. In 1966 General William Childs Westmoreland commented spiritedly: "We're going to out-guerrilla the guerrilla and out-ambush the ambush" (*Life*, 11 November 1966). He was wrong. Clearly we did not achieve his goal. And just as clearly, the United States lost the conflict in Vietnam. In the aftermath there was no surge of investigation to learn what had gone wrong. Sir Robert Thompson spoke for many observers when he wrote: "The lessons of the past in Vietnam and elsewhere have just not been learnt" (*No Exit from Vietnam* [1969], p.129–30).

Although much has been made of it and doctrines written to explain it, even the Army's decades-long concentration on low-intensity conflict (LIC) has not brought about a sufficient awareness. A lieutenant colonel instructor of mine at the U.S. Army Command and General Staff College once said to me that "My God, man, in the latter years of the Vietnamese experience the Army was almost unusable. It had a fantastic breakdown in cohesion. Discipline was . . . absolutely shot. We didn't have a unit in the U.S. Army by late 1972 or early 1973 that really was at all usable. . . . Despite what the army officially claims, the lessons learned and the expertise gained in Vietnam all took place at a higher level of intensity. So today they talk about how to use helicopters, how to use armor, how communications are employed, how to resupply in the jungle, and so forth and so on."

He continued. "Unfortunately, none of these things have any relevance in a real low-intensive situation. They fought a mid-intensity war and called it a low-intensity one. . . . So what the Army doesn't understand even yet is that it lost the war at a level it doesn't even *see*. What we did and what we learned . . . sure as hell won't help us win another Vietnam-type conflict. . . . The worst problem is that it will only be another couple of years before anybody with real insight into what went wrong in Vietnam will be out of business" (1977).

This book gives us a chance finally actually to do so. It is high time, for even President George W. Bush assured us that "We have learned the lessons of Vietnam." He was incorrect. Those lessons were not grasped in their entirety nor understood in their particularity until Donald W. Hamilton set them forth in this book. Drawing from men as disparate as Jomini, Clausewitz, Liddell Hart, Sun Tzu, and dozens of lesser-known authors, and adding his own keen insight, Hamilton demonstrates that the Army's understanding and definition of "insurgency" has changed little since 1962—more than thirty years ago—despite the Vietnam experience.

The military's understanding of insurgency was flawed in the beginning and has remained so until now. Hamilton's book corrects this defect. Thus Hamilton's first important assumption, that the American military has no valid concept of insurgency that is either singular or clear. His second essential assumption is that the global security of the United States after 1945 demanded a formal doctrinal approach to the nature of insurgency itself rather than using incomplete and catch-as-catch-can measures year upon year. Thirdly, Hamilton insists correctly that there was not one but two insurgencies in Vietnam after 1945, both of which had a negative influence on U.S. military policy. Failure to understand these three factors, he concludes, has meant confusion for scholars and disaster for policymakers.

In noteworthy fashion, Hamilton discusses insurgency as a "method" and as a "type" of warfare. His analysis is clearly superior to anything yet written. I have been studying the Vietnam conflict for twenty-two years. Without any reservations, I believe this to be the best book I have yet seen on this subject, and I have read most of them.

Professor Hamilton, who currently teaches at Mesa College in Arizona and is an Army Reserve officer, has worked on this text in his civilian capacity for twelve long years, correcting, adding, polishing. He sets forth a splendid analysis of insurgency itself, followed by brief and adequate examinations of the insurgencies in the Philippines and in Malaya following World War II. He then discusses the American involvement in Vietnam and tells why it was flawed from the beginning. His conclusion is a sobering one—we have not yet learned to deal properly with such uprisings: "Third World subversive insurgent regimes have little to fear from a post-Vietnam America, and even less to fear from a post–Gulf War America."

Since at least 1973 the Army has contented itself with the old German explanation of why that country lost its contest with the Allies in The Great War. Their Army was "stabbed in the back" by unrest at home and by political interference. Many Americans have resorted to the same answer about Vietnam. The record set by the U.S. military in listening to more complicated explanations has not been a good one. It has inevitably reacted defensively. It has assailed the motives and character of those who have criticized it. It now has another opportunity to listen, to study, to make necessary changes. If the Army remains unwilling to accommodate itself to the lessons set forth by Professor Hamilton, then as a nation we have little hope that in the next real conflict we will do any better than we did in Vietnam.

Cecil B. Currey
Lutz, Florida

Preface

For nearly fifteen years now I have been pursuing questions related to the elusive concept of *insurgency war*, the past twelve of which I have spent writing this book. I always try to keep in my own mind, as I try to impart to my students, that answers are often less important than the sharpening of questions. Too frequently, particularly in an American society which expects ever decreasing response time, we look for the quick and fast answer before we have defined the real question. It is almost as if immediate response proves one's worth in knowledge, and therefore the validity of the question posed. This process in turn leads to a cycle of immediate responses based on inaccurate questions. What is worse, the results become a series of false conclusions stacked on top of one another. Many of those things that might otherwise be explained appear as "phenomena," and because our ability to problem solve is faulty, we continually add to what astronomer Dr. Carl Sagan might have referred to as our "demon haunted world." More than not, such conclusions pass for wisdom—a truly unfortunate occurrence in a society that must learn to clearly redefine many of its important questions today if its own future is to continue as productively as much of its past has.

One of these important questions surrounds the concept of insurgency. It is not an overemphasis to state that just how we come to understand strategic concepts of insurgency will either strengthen or weaken our nation in the future. We might surmise from the ancient Chinese philosopher and strategist Sun Tzu, that war, though political in nature, does not need to be destructive in policy, whether foreign or domestic. Yes, insurgency has its violent overtones, just as all forms of warfare have. Truly understanding war, however, allows a nation to design its outcome and manipulate its purpose and use. For this to happen with insurgency it must then be perceived as viable strategy. But why insurgency?

Although this is not the place for a detailed discussion of the concepts of nation-building, it is important to note that those nations not interested in nation-building need to get out of the business of being a nation. This actuality results in two particular contemporary problems for Americans. First, the United States has a long history of reacting to war, even being surprised by it. Understanding insurgency means having to develop a more subtle posture, becoming more "proactive" without being militaristic. It means a foreign policy that can strategically influence nation-building in a direct fashion without appearing to do so overtly. Insurgency is strategy that does not need to be destructive, but, through understanding, time, and patience, can be used as a tool for building and reinventing. Second, insurgency has relevance which is primarily equated historically with nation-states that have not only achieved dominance throughout their own particular world, but have also achieved an apparent conclusion to their own state of existence, be that of the Roman Republic during the first century B.C., or the United States at the end of the twentieth century A.D. Examples of such magnitude are good because they offer us a clearer glimpse into the actual process of insurgency at other, less tangible, levels. I do not mean to be so morose as to intimate that the American way of life (whatever that may be) is coming to an end, because such life is cultural and therefore a symptom of the society, or the nation-state as a whole, and is always in a state of generational flux. Insurgency has little to do with cultural transitions, and exists in spite of any generational flux. This is an essential point because we must understand that insurgency is not a symptom, but rather a driving force in the collective self-determinism associated with nation-building.

What I speak more completely about is what social thinker Alvin Toffler might refer to as *wave theory*, essentially the idea that global transformation is linked between, and within, all societies. These waves are representative of different levels of societal transition that are occurring simultaneously and directly affect the collective self-determinism of each society. The one thing I believe to be consistent with such societal transitions—for example, that which might be represented by clashes occurring between and within *Second Wave* (industrial-based) and *Third Wave* (information-based) societies—is that insurgencies are the most likely political-military conflict to occur under such conditions. The fact that Americans are moving through this transition today is what makes understanding the strategic design of insurgency more relevant than ever before. Moreover, not only is America dealing with this political-military occurrence, but many of its contemporary and future allies are as well. Unfortunately, the real complexity may not be with understanding insurgency, but in being able to manipulate its design.

While many factors emerge as to the reasons for a decay in collective self-determinism at the height of a nation's own progress, none are more critical than those relevant to insurgency. Let me explain. When the kind of political environment exists that makes possible insurgencies, usually ambivalence, forming out of antipathy, fear, or a combination of the two, permeates the collective consciousness of the people. Insurgency as a way to achieve political satisfaction, particularly for a minority organization looking to evolve in power, will strike both from within and from without a nation. This, in turn, often hastens the decay of that nation's collective self-determinism. Nations are always attempting to answer questions about where to proceed, especially when the society has apparently achieved an end, and usually when the perceived threat to the national interest is least. This is when collective self-determinism no longer has the meaning it once did. When that self-determinism shifts within a nation, when revitalizing the nation-state appears to provoke a change in course that is not perceived as evolutionary, then the prospects for confronting insurgency rises.

American's should look at their experience in Vietnam as an opportunity to discover something about politics and war that many nations before them were seemingly unable to envisage. If anything, the experience in Vietnam has bought the United States time as a nation, time which is naturally running down. Americans are perhaps now reaching a point of critical understanding about the lessons of Vietnam as related to contemporary foreign and domestic policy, yet, are still in the midst of trying to determine just which lessons are the most significant. Understanding more precisely what insurgency is, its theoretical and applied importance, will help develop a relevance in its meaning, and, perhaps, alter the significance of lessons from the Vietnam past. Doing so is critical, and the responsibility falls equally upon the shoulders of both the American military and civilian political body.

The lessons from Vietnam are more easily seen in a political-military context because of the nature of the war itself, something that was more revolutionary/civil in design, and emphasized warring conflict between people who believed themselves to be oppressed and disenfranchised. Because of my background as a military officer, and because I have been a student of warfare most of my life, I more naturally gravitate toward an understanding of military strategy and tactics. With this said, I do believe an equally aggressive study concerning the civilian political community and its relationship to insurgency war must also be undertaken. My work is primarily focused on understanding insurgency as a *method* and *type* of warmaking. By no means do I intend this book to be another of those "last words" on the subject. However, I do hope it stimulates a desire on the part of Americans to ask better questions about just what insurgency means to the quality of their future as a nation. I have tried to make this study as readable as possible, both in length and in construction. Because of the general confusion which has evolved over the notion of insurgency war in the post-Vietnam era, my task has been a daunting one at best.

The inspiration for this work belongs to two particular people, namely Sir Robert Thompson, who has recently passed from us, and to Cecil B. Currey, who I trust is tending to his ranch in Montana. First, Sir Robert. His prolific output in the late 1960s, after success and failure in the realm of understanding insurgency, was a great stimulant to me. His writings are the most accurate, most overlooked, and least understood works to come from the American-Vietnam period. Being overlooked may have something to do with the fact that these works are not American, but British. Being misunderstood today is probably related to the same difficulties he had in being understood by the American advisory group in Saigon during the early 1960s. This is too bad because his words also represent some of the clearest and most important on the subject of insurgency war. I encourage all Americans to read his books, overlooking the dated political language we all eventually succumb to, and listen to his message. The message is timeless for those societies interested in perpetuating themselves as a nation-sate.

Now to Cecil Currey. I would like to thank Professor Cecil B. Currey, a man who has given his life to service as a scholar-soldier. His brilliant writings have helped me directly and indirectly in the writing of this book. His seminal work, entitled *Self-Destruction*, has forged a path for many scholar-soldiers to walk. A number of works within the military during the post-Vietnam years attempted to make honest appraisal and recommendation, and to all of them the American people are indebted. Although Cecil Currey may not have been the first to walk point in this battle against ignorance, and in some cases deception, he may very well have been the first to succeed, certainly in the post-Vietnam American military. Such accomplishment did not come easy, and was only possible because Cecil Currey was not merely provocative in his observations and analysis, but correct. Such is the path—it has always been the path—that represents honor and integrity, truth and reality, one that only the "spiritual warrior" can understand and follow. I am forever grateful to

Cecil Currey, for his valuable suggestions and comments in private about my own work, and I am honored that he would find time to write a foreword to this book.

A work of this scope and complexity was not completed without the help of a number of people over several years, a larger number unfortunately than the space here allows for. However, I would be remiss not to mention a few of the key people that have professionally and personally offered their time. The seeds for my work began germination during graduate school, and several of my professors were particularly kind to me in their patience, understanding, encouragement, and mentoring.

Dr. Paul G. Hubbard represents a tradition of mentoring and scholarly stewardship in the highest order, a man whose solid principles and ideals continue to influence me to this day. His life-long dedication to learning history has been an inspiration to all who have had the pleasure to work with him. When much of my work appeared impossible to convey, his honest, penetrating questions directed me, and his unswerving belief in my ability to accomplish the task always drove me.

Dr. L. Christian Smith is an American folk historian in the truest since. Clearness of thought, enthusiasm, wit, and wisdom were the things he conveyed to me. He is a man who brings depth and integrity to the meaning of teaching and learning. His confidence in my abilities was also a major influence in my pursuing this work. Through Chris I have been better able to accept the genius of what it means to simplify the complex, and to make the important obvious, not trivial.

Dr. Sheldon W. Simon, a political scientist who possesses a remarkable genius for his subject, has conveyed much of his own personal insight and wisdom to me. A scholar, analyst, and tenor of the first order, Dr. Simon encouraged me to evolve in my thinking about insurgency warfare, to go beyond historical perspective and discover a vision for pursuing contemporary and future policy change. To me, this is the true purpose of history, to be the vehicle for meaningful change.

Though these men did not always agree with all of my observations all of the time, they never attempted to crush creative inspiration, and especially what creative inspiration leads to. I would like to express my heartfelt thanks to these three men who have provided so much for me in such a short period of time, indeed a clearness that has significantly added to the attributes of this work.

I also wish to thank the many research librarians and archivists from the Center for Military History, the Military History Institute, the National Archives, and the Imperial War Museum, among various university libraries, who have lent their time and help. Special mention must be given to Ms. Greta Marlatt of the U.S. Naval Postgraduate School, a true genius in the art of deciphering government documents. Her knowledge and skill as a research librarian was a tremendous asset in helping me locate much of the necessary reference material used in this work.

Two people have aided me, both in their correspondence and their conversation. Mrs. Isabel Oliphant, the daughter of Sir Robert Thompson, has helped me in obtaining valuable insights into her father's personality and life. This has led to the obtaining of detailed information about Sir Robert not readily available, particularly here in the United States. I also wish to thank Mrs. Margaret Patti for her patience in the reading of several passages of my manuscript. I have benefited from enlightening conversation about her husband's exploits, both in the Army and in Vietnam. The integrity of the book has been helped by her honest and candid suggestions.

I am also indebted to several people at the college, both in the history department and in the CTL. Mr. James N. Tipton has unceasingly given of his time in fixing broken software and in giving the book clearer illustrations than I could have provided. Mrs. Anne H. Vandeventer creates wonderful artwork, and three of her maps appear in this book. Dr. John Kennedy Ohl, a tremendous scholar, historian, and author, has given my work a thorough reading, and has discussed many of my ideas with me in their historical context, and on more than one occasion. He has made many valuable suggestions and recommendations to me about content. Though we have not come to agreement on all things, the stimulation and encouragement from him are always appreciated. He is a colleague who I am pleased to call a friend.

I would also like to thank Praeger Publishers for knowing the significance of this subject, and the meaning it has for the future of our society. Their production of other works belies their earnest desire to help educate. I appreciate all of those people at the Greenwood Publishing Group who have aided me in the presentation and production of this book. I would especially like to thank Mr. Dan Eades who believed that this book could make a valuable contribution to the literature on the subject, and who served as senior editor for most of the project. Also, a big thanks goes to Mr. Jason Azze, for his painstaking attention to detail and to getting the design of this book correct.

Finally, I wish to thank my wife Stephanie Ruth, and our two boys, Joshua Lawrence and Brian Alexander. Without their devotion and steadfast patience I likely would not have made it through the number of computer breakdowns, lost notes, and countless hours of research. For several years my wife has endured my continued work on this subject, and yet we have managed to stay married, remain productive, and continue raising two wonderful boys. The world has not come to an end, and for all we know, the universe continues to expand. I am pursuing work on another book and no one appears to be vacating the premises—certainly a good sign. Such is true love. My family has done everything possible to make this challenging experience easier for me. To these three magnificent people I dedicate this work.

And, of course, this one last obligatory note. All of the ideas presented in this book have been inspired by a vast array of people and events. However, any perceived problems with interpretation or inadequacies about my research must fall squarely on my shoulders. I apologize ahead of time if I have offended anyone mentioned in these pages or otherwise. It was not my intention to do so, only to bring some light to a subject that has remained unlit for so long.

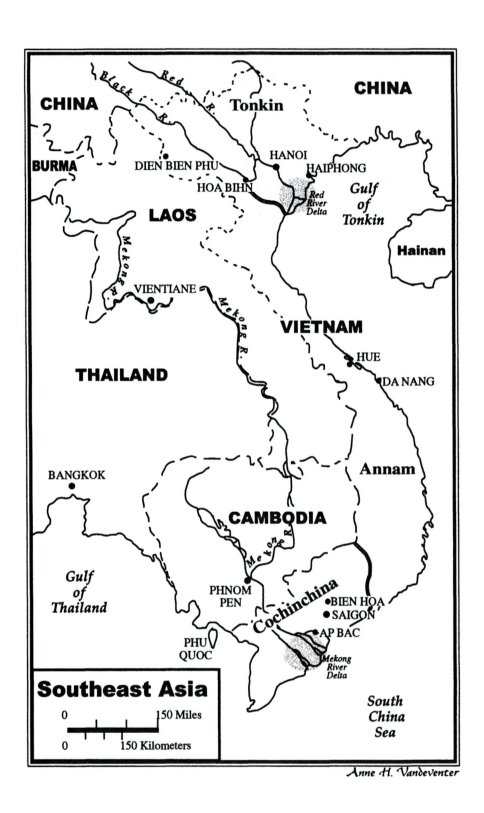

CHINA

CHINA

BURMA

Black R. *Red R.*

Tonkin

DIEN BIEN PHU

HANOI

HAIPHONG

HOA BIHN

Red River Delta

Gulf of Tonkin

LAOS

Mekong R.

Hainan

VIENTIANE

Mekong R.

VIETNAM

THAILAND

HUE

DA NANG

BANGKOK

Annam

CAMBODIA

Mekong R.

Gulf of Thailand

PHNOM PEN

Cochinchina

BIEN HOA

SAIGON

AP BAC

PHU QUOC

Mekong River Delta

South China Sea

Southeast Asia

0   150 Miles

0   150 Kilometers

Anne H. Vandeventer

Insurgency and American Military Doctrine: An Introduction

In the years following the American Civil War, young military tacticians being taught the finer points of battlefield theory at the U.S. Military Academy at West Point borrowed heavily from the treatise of that century's most prominent and well recognized military theorist. Antoine Henri de Jomini, not Carl von Clausewitz, held center stage by the middle to late nineteenth-century in nearly all military circles. His renowned treatise, *Summary of the Principles of the Art of War*, published in 1838, was the foundation for teaching strategy at West Point and would continue to have a "profound effect on military thought in America."[1] Translated from the French, copies of the book rode in the saddlebags of American officers from both sides during the Civil War. While some erroneously consider much of his strategic theory to be antiquated today, the fundamental precepts advanced by Jomini nearly two centuries ago are used time and again as a basis for modern strategic criticism.[2] For our purposes, it is critical to explore, albeit briefly, Jomini's words as they pertain to our study of insurgency war. No other nineteenth-century strategist, including Clausewitz, proves more insightful about the process and development of war.

Throughout his *Summary*, Jomini discusses concepts of warfare in near holistic terms. From his Article VII, entitled "Wars of Opinion," Jomini outlines the subtle complexities of the violent side of human experience, and he provides the following terms for our use: *intestine and civil*, *intestine and foreign*, and *foreign or exterior*.[3] Though his words are somewhat dated, the concepts imparted are crystalline. With further examination, it becomes clear that Jomini has elucidated upon what we might refer to today as the three types of warmaking: *revolutionary/civil, revolutionary/foreign,* and *foreign/exterior.* Despite these terms being of a minimalist quality, it can be quite plainly stated that all strategic aspects related to warmaking emanate from these three basic concepts. It is also clear Jomini understood that nothing tactical in war is so unique as to not fall within the parameters of one of these three categories. While it is often dangerous to categorize, I think the reader will agree that some compartmentalization can help ease the pursuit of a tangible war doctrine. Certainly, Jomini's evaluation and explanation about the nuances of each particular category is worth continuous rereading. From such study one begins to understand the reason for Jomini's significant impact upon students of warfare, an impact that irrefutably lasts to this day. Jomini possessed the ability to synthesize information about war beyond the theoretical nature, penetrating its very design. Today, the political-military establishment is well served to forge doctrine based upon these three concepts about war. In truth, nearly everything written or "doctrinalized" about warfare must adhere to these basic principles. And so they do. Thus, it is strange that one of the key conundrums about warfare Jomini represents in his treatise is today either avoided or forgotten. A concept that might seem simple at first takes on further complexity with each subsequent reading.

As the concepts of war are broken down into manageable pieces, the reader will discover the existence of what appears to be another category of strategic thought. Revolutions, civil wars, and conflicts between foreign nations are explained. While Jomini carefully illuminates the subtleties of each category, he overlaps or embeds modified concepts about revolutionary/civil strife in his Article VIII, entitled "National Wars." This is where the student of Jomini is left with a formidable question: Are national wars really a separate category or merely a transition point, the glue that holds the other three parts together? While revolution is dealt with in Article VII, civil war is developed throughout Article IX, "Civil Wars, and Wars of Religion," where Jomini explains such conflict as "intestine wars, . . . not connected with a foreign quarrel."[4] So what is Jomini alluding to in his article on national wars?

We do know that Jomini's personal experience with irregular warfare, particularly when compared to Clausewitz's, was considerable.[5] Jomini clearly saw the severe consequences that partisans, guerrillas, and terrorists brought upon Napoleon's army of occupation. For certain reasons Jomini treats the subject of irregular warfare with caution, well aware of the disruptive effect such political-military struggles have on the grand strategic design of regular armed forces. "National wars," he thought, "are the most formidable of all."

This name can only be applied to such [wars] as are waged against a united people, or a great majority of them, filled with a noble ardor and determined to sustain their independence.

The spectacle of a spontaneous uprising of a nation is rarely seen; and, though there be in it something grand and noble which commands our admiration, the consequences are so terrible that, for the sake of humanity, we ought to hope never to see it.[6]

The above passage is significant for several reasons. First, it becomes apparent that Jomini makes a clear distinction between wars of opinion and national wars.[7] In his article "Wars of Opinion," Jomini addresses the concept of revolution, providing several historical and contemporary examples from the period. It would appear, then, from an initial glance at his article "National Wars," Jomini simply embellishes upon these concepts. But this is not the case, since we know both civil war and revolution are discussed elsewhere. Though national wars may be revolutionary in nature, Jomini does not explain them as revolutionary wars in the typical sense of revolution. From his years alongside Napoleon, particularly while in Spain and later in Russia, Jomini learned about wars fought against colonial regimes. In essence, such wars are typically fought by the indigenous majority (i.e., those who are colonized), against the non-indigenous minority (i.e., the colonial regime). But he also transposed his thinking to wars fought by an indigenous minority against an indigenous majority, or conflicts waged against a "united people" from within. Beyond a coup d'etat or simple rebellion, these are conflicts which take on a far more sinister character. In order to succeed, such groups must become highly organized, coercive, and fanatical in their intent, and they do not need a majority in order to develop to their apex. If such a political organization can be seen as something which exists outside the bounds of revolution or civil war—as perhaps a seed of *insurgency*—then we must understand that development of the organization by itself means success. The more protracted the struggle, the better opportunity for further growth. Moreover, when such groups do develop highly politicized structures, they become nearly impossible to destroy. The resulting conflict is neither revolution nor civil war. As part of his concept of national wars, Jomini writes of the strategic makeup of events that lead a government or a subversive organization to wage such a conflict. Although Jomini never used the term insurgency, he expressed some of its most basic principles under the heading "National Wars." His words still ring prophetic:

If success be possible in such a [national] war, the following general course will be most likely to insure it,—viz.: make a display of a mass of troops proportioned to the obstacles and resistance likely to be encountered, calm the popular passions in every possible way, exhaust them by time and patience, display courtesy, gentleness, and severity united, and, particularly, deal justly.[8]

Sir Basil Henry Liddell Hart, a British army captain who became one of the most important strategic thinkers of the twentieth century, recognized the significance such wars posed to the nuclear era. He stated consistently that, in the post-1945 period, "campaigns of this . . . [insurgency] kind are the more likely to continue because it is the only kind of war that fits the conditions of the modern age."[9] From his lifetime as a student of warfare, it is unlikely that Liddell Hart made mention of such a concept lightheartedly. In fact, his reasoning was quite clear—that if peace was to be preserved, one needed to prepare earnestly for this "subversive" form of conflict.

Today, the modern age is represented by population explosions, decaying natural resources, a decreasing Third World, and a loss of Superpower polarity, which has in turn brought about the hasty proliferation of catastrophic weapons. Scholars and soldiers alike believe there remains a critical need for the development of an insurgency doctrine, one that can be effectively employed in a number of global security matters facing Western nations, indeed civilization at large. The danger is that many believe such a doctrine already exists. It does not.

For the purpose of identifying such a doctrine, the term *insurgency* applies in this study to a broader and more complete set of circumstances than one traditionally accepted. Some readers may seek the key to *insurgency doctrine* solely among the concepts put forth by Mao Tse-tung and encompassed in his writings on communist revolution. Some believe that answers to questions about insurgency can be found in the earlier manuscripts of Jomini and Clausewitz, or perhaps the ancient Chinese works of Sun Tzu. Still others do not believe that insurgency war is a valid strategic or tactical concept at all. Nevertheless, in spite of the confusion and disagreement over insurgency, the development of doctrine that is meant to counter insurgency has ensued among Western nations. Such *counterinsurgency doctrine* is attributable to any number of theorists, not simply those listed above, and embodies a wide range of concepts and definitions, from *pacification* to *low-intensity conflict* to *operations other than war.*

On the surface, the current U.S. military concept of *operations other than war* appears to be a far cry from earlier concepts defined by the military for use during the struggle in Vietnam.[10] Army documents are now produced with greater flare, color, and illustration than ever before. They are concise, precise, and readable. It would seem that the American military learned a great deal from that earlier period and incorporated its experiences into thoughtful, progressive documents, providing an edge to U.S. combat forces who might be employed to fight in future irregular wars, something often represented by the term low-intensity conflict. However, one would expect newer concepts to demonstrate greater wisdom than concepts defined in the early years of America's involvement in Vietnam and, subsequently, in the early years of developing an understanding of insurgency war. In 1962 the official army definition for insurgency was:

> A condition of subversive political activity, civil rebellion, revolt, or insurrection against a duly constituted government or occupying power wherein irregular forces are formed and engage in actions which may include guerrilla warfare, that are designed to weaken or overthrow that government or occupying power.[11]

As a part of this definition, the term *counterinsurgency* was described as "the entire scope of actions (military, police, political, economic, psychological, etc.) taken by or in conjunction with the existing government of a nation to counteract, contain, or defeat an insurgency."[12]

It was some five years after U.S. troops were removed from Vietnam that the U.S. Army Intelligence Center and School produced a work which placed the idea of subversive insurgency within the parameters of low-intensity conflict. A more realistic approach, it explained ideas about *counterinsurgency* within the framework of insurgency and not as a unique and separate tactical concept. Low-intensity conflict, as perhaps insurgency doctrine, then represents something that "lacks the observed logic of the conventional battle-field . . . [where] the commander and his staff might be left frustratedly clutching at a very fluid and unstable condition, defying the usual logical evaluation; thereby, obstructing standard counter-efforts."[13]

In the early 1980s, the U.S. military settled on a document which officially merged the term *insurgency* with the phrase *low-intensity conflict*:

> Low intensity conflict is a limited politico-military struggle to achieve political, social, economic, or psychological objectives. It is often protracted and ranges from diplomatic, economic, and psycho-social pressures through terrorism and insurgency. Low intensity conflict is generally

confined to a geographic area and is often characterized by constraints on the weaponry, tactics, and the level of violence.[14]

Strategists writing the army's document on insurgency warfare, TRADOC PAM 525-44, *Low Intensity Conflict*, borrowed heavily, if not completely, from earlier versions. After a thorough reading, it is not difficult to recognize that the TRADOC document is simply a more streamlined version of like documents on *counterinsurgency* published nearly thirty years before.[15] The contemporary follow-on, Joint Pub 3-07, *Joint Doctrine for Military Operations Other Than War*, differs little in its effort to thoroughly explain insurgency warfare, and does nothing to question previous army experiences and assumptions. There is a common belief promulgated among those in the military that everything is all right and under control in understanding the dangers of insurgency war. One cannot possibly believe that it is all right for these contemporary documents to be in the forefront of doctrinal development while also realizing that they are a simple restatement of *counterinsurgency theories* as understood and practiced during America's experience in Vietnam. Not only does much of the terminology go undefined, but many of the terms used contradict one another. Subsequently, the doctrine reflects much of the same misunderstandings about insurgency war today as it did then. This study takes the position that insurgency war must first be strategically and tactically understood before it can be effectively countered. In other words, the enemy must be seen before he can be fought; one must be able to accurately plan before he can train. Despite popular belief, the U.S. military remains on the wrong track in its understanding of insurgency war.

Three general assertions are made in this study. The first assertion has already been stated, simply that a valid concept of insurgency war does not exist today in a singular or clear manner within U.S. military doctrine. Although many analysts use the term *insurgency*, they often confuse it with other concepts, both like and dissimilar. The intention is that in discussing a wide range of works about insurgency war, it will be possible to develop a succinct definition which better identifies insurgency warfare in clear strategic, as well as tactical terms.

With a clearer evolutionary background, this study turns to its second assertion, that the global security picture for the United States after 1945 demanded a formal doctrinal approach to insurgency war, not *counterinsurgency* theories. Those theories produced by the United States during that period were never more than marginally effective in their conventional and unconventional military response to guerrilla operations. Most *counter-guerrilla* operations were mainstreamed into the conventional fighting force of the U.S. military effort in Vietnam and did not represent a complete understanding of the subversive threat posed by the existing insurgency. Because the response was first and last a military response it was doomed to fail. The distrust and confusion between military commanders and policymakers during the most critical periods illustrates the residue of this failure. It can also be seen today in the ongoing debate among Americans who blame their failed experience in Vietnam on policy, those who blame it on military strategy, and those who blame it on both. Some have gone so far as to say that the United States was "misled by the revolutionary model," and therefore "fought the wrong war."[16] Although flaws existed in developing counterinsurgency theory, these flaws were not part of a misdiagnosis of the strategic problem in Vietnam. Rather, such flaws were indicative of not having a complete understanding of insurgent strategy from the beginning and thus maintaining a defensive or reactionary posture toward combating subversive insurgent threats. A clear understanding of both the theory, and the realities of insurgency war, as well as the events that took place early in America's involvement with Vietnam, reveal that the United States was not at all misled by a revolutionary model of warfare, but misunderstood its insurgency parameters and how to effectively wage war against such a threat. Today there exist two schools of strategic thought related to Vietnam War analysis. One might be represented as the *insurgency school*, and the other as the *conventional school*. By delving into the U.S.-Vietnam past, this study reaches conclusions that are at odds with the conventional thinker who believes that the conflict was always misrepresented as an insurgency, and that North Vietnam always intended to distract forces in the south from their real intention, which was victory through conventional war.[17]

A third assertion of this study contends that there was not simply one, but two separate insurgencies in Vietnam after 1945. Both insurgencies negatively affected the conduct of the U.S. advisory effort and its political and military alliances and unnecessarily resulted in increased American military commitments. Consequently, the U.S. failure to defend South Vietnam from the subversive insurgency occurred much earlier than the generally accepted time period of 1960 to 1965.

Still, among those in the *insurgency school* there is a continued split. Confusion reigns among many analysts within this school who believe the war in Vietnam represented a series of different types of struggles superimposed upon one another over a period of two or more decades.[18] Some hold the belief that a revolutionary model of insurgency war existed but disagree over the parameters which fueled the subversive movement in South Vietnam after 1954. Emerging are those analysts who look toward the unresolved socioeconomic problems within Vietnam's rural provinces, while others find answers in the political organizational models of the Vietnamese communists. Douglas Pike has viewed the problems in Vietnam as being part of three different interwoven struggles: the overreaching political struggle, the insurgency, and the quasi-conventional, big-unit war, a war that masked the genuine insurgency, which simply continued unabated after 1965.[19] While Pike's view is intriguing, it, and others like it, can also lead to distinct strategic misperceptions about how complete the insurgency in South Vietnam really was before 1965, in fact, before 1960.

Then there is the fundamental concept of *insurgency* itself, still represented by many analysts as being a political-military *phenomenon*. As defined in the conflict model presented in Chapter 1, insurgency warfare can clearly be placed into the conflict hierarchy as a separate and consistent element of warfare, an element that nations and societies, both weak and strong, have dealt with throughout history. Thus, insurgency is not viewed in this study as being a *phenomenon* of any sort, particularly since there is nothing unusual about its existence. Perhaps the only *phenomenon* is that nations and societies do not seem to get measurably better in defying, or consorting with, insurgencies as part of common policy. In relationship to this study, the definition of insurgency war developed in the first chapter should help to better explain just why the insurgency in South Vietnam was more all-encompassing than previously thought, particularly in light of America's security and foreign policy outlook.

In addition, this study attempts to point out the larger unlearned lessons proffered by the U.S.-Vietnam conflict. As such, it will attempt to view the circumstances of American involvement in Vietnam from a defined strategic perspective. The analysis will proceed through a rationale of parameters about insurgency war. Thus, a clear definition of insurgency is necessary before it is possible to place into context the failure of American military and political strategies for South Vietnam. The conflict in Vietnam, with its historical implications for the United States both militarily and politically, remains the single best model for study of insurgent strategy in the post-1945 era. As Bard E. O'Neill points out, the challenge of truly understanding insurgency war must be directly confronted: "Abdication of responsibility, reliance on oversimplification, and avoidance of painstaking analysis will eventually exact their costs. For the scholar it will mean intellectual confusion; for the policymaker it spells potential disaster."[20]

NOTES

1. Maurice Matloff, ed., *American Military History* (Washington, D.C.: GPO, 1969), 149; Russell F. Weigley, *The American Way of War* (New York: The Macmillan Company, 1973), 83. For further treatment of Jomini, his life and his principles on military strategy, as well as his effect on American military theory, see: Crane Brinton, Gordon A. Craig, and Felix Gilbert, "Jomini," in *Makers of Modern Strategy*, ed. Edward Meade Earle (Princeton, N.J.: Princeton University Press, 1966), 77–92; Michael Howard, "Jomini and the Classical Tradition in Military Thought," in *The Theory and Practice of War*, ed. Michael Howard (New York: Frederick A. Praeger, 1965), 3–20; John Shy, "Jomini," in *Makers of Modern Strategy: From Machiavelli to the Nuclear Age*, ed. Peter Paret (Princeton, N.J.: Princeton University Press, 1986), 143–85. For a less flattering view of Jomini, see John R. Elting, "Jomini: Disciple of Napoleon?" *Military Affairs* 28 (spring 1964): 17–26. On affect of U.S. Army during the Civil War, see Russell F. Weigley, *History of the United States Army* (New York: The Macmillan Company, 1967), passim.

2. Shy, "Jomini," 178.

3. Baron Henri de Jomini, *The Art of War*, trans. G. H. Mendell and W. P. Craighill (Philadelphia: J. B. Lippincott and Company, 1862), 25–29 and passim.

4. Ibid., 35. In other words, Jomini makes the claim, well accepted today, that revolutions are non-indigenous to a nation and its people, while civil war remains an indigenous struggle.

5. Robert B. Asprey, *War in the Shadows: The Guerrilla in History* (Garden City, N.Y.: Doubleday and Company, 1975), 1:150. It is clear that much of the decided confusion over insurgency war within the American military (as perhaps it is in other militaries), can be traced in large measure to a near complete acceptance of the Clausewitzian interpretation of war. In spite of all the things that are significant about his treatise, Clausewitz devoted little space to the subject of "irregular" warfare. The closest form of comparison made by Clausewitz appears to be his "five points" from the chapter entitled, "People in Arms," (Book Six). And, even in these instances, he relates nothing of the obvious experiences Napoleon had with guerrilla war in Spain and Russia, avoiding the decided political ramifications of each event. In fairness, Clausewitz never wished that his incomplete treatise be published. See Carl von Clausewitz, *On War*, edited and translated by Michael Howard and Peter Paret (Princeton, N.J.: Princeton University Press, 1976), 480 and passim.

6. Jomini, *The Art of War*, 29–30.

7. "Although wars of opinion, national wars, and civil wars are sometimes confounded, they differ enough to require separate notice." Ibid., 25.

8. Ibid., 33.

9. B. H. Liddell Hart, foreword to Mao Tse-tung and Che Guevara, *Guerrilla Warfare*, trans. Samuel B. Griffith (London: Cassell, 1962), xi. Also, see B. H. Liddell Hart, *Strategy* (New York: Praeger, 1967), 361–70.

10. Reference is made to the most recently published U.S. military document, entitled U.S. Joint Pub 3-07, *Joint Doctrine for Military Operations Other Than War* (Washington, D.C.: GPO, 16 June 1995) esp. sec. III-15, "Support to Insurgency." For further treatment, see S. L. Arnold and David T Stahl, "A Power Projection Army in Operations Other Than War," *Parameters* 23 (winter 1993): 4–26.

11. "Cold War Terminology," *Army Information Digest* 17 (June 1962): 54. It should be noted that the army definition for insurgency was the accepted military-wide definition for U.S. forces. Cf. U.S. Marine Corps, *FMFM-21 Operations against Guerrilla Forces* (Washington, D.C.: GPO, 1962), 1.

12. Joint Chiefs of Staff, *A Dictionary of United States Military Terms* (Washington, D.C.: Public Affairs Press, 1963), s.v. "counterinsurgency."

13. Department of the Army (U.S., D.A.), U.S. Army Intelligence Center and School, *The USAICS Handbook on Urban Terrorism*, sup. rev., 033171-1 (Fort Huachuca, Az.: USAICS, June 1978), 378–79.

14. U.S., D.A., TRADOC PAM 525-44, *U.S. Operational Concept for Low-Intensity Conflict* (Washington, D.C.: GPO, 1988), 2.

15. See, for example, U.S., D.A., *FM 31-15 Operations against Irregular Forces* (Washington, D.C.: GPO, 1961); U.S., D.A., *FM 31-16 Counterguerrilla Operations* (Washington, D.C.: GPO, 1963); U.S., D.A., *FM 31-21 Guerrilla Warfare and Special Forces Operations*, (Washington, D.C.: GPO, 1961); works cited in n. 11, this chapter. For other discussions about LIC during the period of doctrinal development, see Richard Shultz, "Strategy Lessons from an Unconventional War: The U.S. Experience in Vietnam," and David W. Tarr, "The Strategic Environment, U.S. National Security and the Nature of Low Intensity Conflict," in *Nonnuclear Conflicts in the Nuclear Age*, ed. Sam C. Sarkesian (Westport, Conn.: Praeger Publishers, 1980).

16. Harry G. Summers, "Vietnam Reconsidered," *The New Republic* (12 July 1987): 25. Also see the popularly published book by Summers, *On Strategy: A Critical Analysis of the Vietnam War* (Novato, Ca.: Presidio Press, 1982). Reflecting on Summers' views, Robert Komer disagrees, stating dryly that Summers "was a representative of a school of thought that did not understand either the constraints on limited war in the nuclear age or that what we were fighting was somewhat different from the conventional kind of war." Robert W. Komer, "Commentary," in *The Second Indochina War: Proceedings of a Symposium Held at Airlie, Virginia 7–9 November 1984*, ed. John Schlight (Washington, D.C.: CMH, 1986), 161.

17. See for instance, Lt. Col. James R. Ward, "Vietnam: Insurgency or War?" *Military Review* 69 (January 1989): 16–18; Maj. Edward J. Filbert, "The Roots of U.S. Counterinsurgency Doctrine," *Military Review* 68 (January 1988): 50–61; cf. Harry G. Summers, Jr., "A Strategic Perception of the Vietnam War," *Parameters* 13 (June 1983): 42–44; Summers, *On Strategy*, 3–4 and passim. Since the Gulf War of 1991, American military thinking appears to be even more mired in this conventional aberration of strategic analysis over Vietnam. Summers

continues the argument in his *On Strategy II: A Critical Analysis of the Gulf War* (New York: Dell Publishing, 1992), 7–21 and passim.

18. Komer, "Commentary," 161–62 and passim.

19. Douglas Pike, "Conduct of the Vietnam War: Strategic Factors, 1965–1968," in Schlight, *The Second Indochina War*, 100–6.

20. Bard E. O'Neill, "Insurgent Strategies: An Examination of Four Approaches," in *American Defense Policy*, ed. John E. Endicott and Roy W. Stafford, Jr. (Baltimore, Md.: The Johns Hopkins University Press, 1977), 173. In this article, O'Neill provides one of the clearest arguments of insurgency war in "non-Maoist," grand political terms. His succinct analization of insurgency is carried over to his more recent effort, a provocative look at various processes of insurgency and related conflict hierarchy, entitled *Insurgency and Terrorism: Inside Modern Revolutionary Warfare* (New York: Brassey's, Inc., 1990). Works of this nature are too few, and those that do exist are usually overlooked.

CHAPTER 1

Explaining Insurgency

In an academic treatment on the evolution of counterinsurgency doctrine in the U.S. Army, Stephan L. Bowman writes that "one of the problems of the doctrine-makers was the matter of exact definitions. At times it seemed there were as many definitions as there were official sources to put the definitions into print."[1] In a like tone, Douglas Pike does not confine such criticism to the military:

> Equally scandalous . . . was the total failure of the American academic community to contribute to knowledge and understanding of the enemy and his strategy. . . . With no basis of knowledge, their counsel was rooted in error; in the field their advice was dismissed, as it should have been, as worthless. During the Vietnam War, virtually nothing was produced by the American academic community on the strategic thinking of the Vietnamese Communists. There should have been a flood of such studies.[2]

Before discussing American involvement in Vietnam, and its search for a counterinsurgency doctrine, attention must be given to a definition of insurgency. Without a clear understanding of insurgency there is little chance that it can be countered, or more precisely, defeated. With an accurate definition of insurgency in hand, it will hopefully be clear that defeating an insurgency may not always be the appropriate goal, but that becoming the insurgency might be. The desire is to be able to explain the process and existence of insurgency, not simply in political terms, but both as a *method* and as a *type* of war. Insurgency can therefore better be represented as a strategic tool for policymaking. Against this definition and understanding it will be possible to more accurately place irregular warfare events in the American military past and more clearly explore American military thinking in Vietnam.

Numerous writings about irregular warfare found their way into print after 1945, both of an official government nature and of a less formal journalistic nature. When calls for a formal, unconventional war doctrine echoed throughout the country at the beginning of the 1960s, U.S. military leaders, politicians, and academics alike responded with a flurry of effort. These existing studies representing insurgency warfare, however, look primarily at the political and social consequences and do not accurately explain insurgency as a separate facet in war making or as a separate strategic thought. Under these terms, any definition of insurgency war must appear incomplete. Typically the term *insurgency* is intertwined and often confused with other terms. A list of the more prominent transpositions would include the following: *subversion, coup d'etat, terrorism, guerrilla war, revolution,* and even *civil war*. In any number of works related to these subjects, the word *insurgency* might be used as a substitute. It is often alluded to without explanation, or provided as a means to explain individuals that engage in such activities (i.e., *insurgents*). That all of these terms invoke different concepts is clear from the most elementary definitions found in political-military doctrine. Just why the term *insurgency* is blended together with others in so many separate works is not fully understood. It is certain, however, that this careless usage represents a lack of respect for the term's roots.

An English translation of the Latin word *insurgere*, occurred as early as 1765.[3] Many authors found uses for the term in writings ranging from poetry to psychological analysis. Insurgency came to be commonly recognized as having to do with "internal political revolution" perpetrated by a certain group publicly acknowledged as being "nonbelligerent." Along similar lines two centuries later, Jack C. Plano states that an insurgency is "a revolt against an established government not reaching the proportions of a full-scale revolution. Under international law, an insurgency is a rebellion not recognized as a belligerency or civil war."[4] Going further, Roger Scruton notes that *insurgency* is a term used in international law that describes an uprising against a constituted government that falls short of revolution, rebellion, or civil war.[5]

Through many years of continuous refinement and redefinition on the subject of unconventional war, insurgency is still loosely represented as participation in the larger scope of internal political revolution. In many respects, the same could be said for such terms as *guerrilla war, subversion, rebellion,* and *civil war*.[6] In the end, it would appear that all of these terms simply merge with each other, having no significant individual qualities. To appreciate the confusion that surrounds the term *insurgency*, it might be helpful to cite from an array of recent examples.

Official U.S. Army doctrine from the early 1960s best typifies the broad catch-all that the term *insurgency* came to be. One particular manual published by the Army Special Warfare School was intended to train Special Forces advisors en route to Vietnam. Entitled the *Counter-insurgency Planning Guide*, and published in 1963, this manual acted principally as a tactical overview for advisors who needed help in producing operations orders and reports in a variety of unconventional formats not commonly dealt with in previous military experiences.[7] However, the guide contains no definition of insurgency war, implying that the military was not in any hurry to revise its then current understanding of the term outside conventional force application. That the most current military definition is almost no different indicates that perhaps little emphasis has been placed on producing a valid understanding of insurgency. Though the military was apparently void of contention over the issue of insurgency during that critical period, a large international community that was indeed concerned produced a large plethora of works.

A work written in 1964 by David Galula, entitled *Counter-Insurgency Warfare*, received much attention by an American government anxious to understand its then current plight in Southeast Asia. It appeared to be one of the first Western works to establish a hierarchy that attempted to explain insurgency as a separate concept, a part of political revolution and war. Galula lists three stages to this hierarchy: revolution, plot (coup d'etat), and insurgency. These terms embody the elements of "revolutionary war," which Galula explains as an "explosive upheaval," an accident which might better be explained after the fact. All that can really be ascertained in the early stages of an insurgency is that a revolutionary situation exists. "On the other hand," Galula points out,

> . . . an insurgency is a protracted struggle conducted methodically, step by step, in order to attain specific intermediate objectives leading finally to the overthrow of the existing order (China, 1927–49; Greece, 1945–50; Indochina, 1945–54; Malaya, 1948–60; Algeria, 1954–62). To be sure, it can no more be predicted than a revolution; in fact, its beginnings are so vague that to determine exactly when an insurgency starts is a difficult legal, political, and historical problem. . . . An insurgency is usually slow to develop and is not an accident, for in an insurgency leaders appear and then the masses are made to move.[8]

Some may take exception with Galula's explanation of the hierarchy, and to some degree with the examples he gives of insurgency war (certainly the experiences in China and Greece after World War II have been labeled everything from revolution to civil war). But, to Galula, "insurgency is civil war."[9] It is never quite clear whether he means that insurgency replaces the notion of civil war, or if he believes that insurgency is a part of a growing discontent that leads to civil war. Although Galula explains in great detail the role of the counterinsurgent against a successful insurgency, he never expands upon the definition of insurgency. Therefore, the reader is left to speculate on just how insurgency differs from a protracted revolutionary war, or, for that matter, how rebellion differs from revolution. Galula, in the end, makes no real distinction between insurgency war and these other concepts, apparently using it in place of the phrase *revolutionary war*.

In 1967, Julian Paget subscribed more closely to the Latin derivative of *insurgency* in his book, *Counter-Insurgency Operations*, stating simply that insurgency describes a kind of armed rebellion against a government. Here, the "rebels have the support or acquiescence of a substantial part of the populace; the methods that they adopt to achieve their aim of overthrowing the Government may include guerrilla warfare, but insurgents may equally well resort to civil disobedience, sabotage or terrorist tactics."[10]

Even ideas that referred to a kind of *pure insurgency* made their way into formal definition. In a work entirely devoted to the subject, Andrew Scott and his coauthors write:

> The term insurgency in this volume refers to efforts to obtain political goals by an organized and primarily indigenous group (or groups) using protracted, irregular warfare and allied political techniques. This definition excludes sudden coups, short-lived outbreaks of violence, or invasion by non-indigenous guerrilla forces.[11]

Accordingly, a distinction is drawn between insurgency and irregular warfare. "The term irregular warfare refers only to military activities . . . insurgency is irregular warfare plus politics."[12]

In their discussion, Scott and his coauthors develop the idea of insurgency around two principal themes: "protracted war strategy" and "indigenous movements"—two facets they say are "unexplainable." There is no real way, they assert, of determining just when a conflict becomes protracted, and, in turn, they indicate no specific way to determine how great a degree of outside intervention is compatible with a group being considered primarily indigenous. Yet according to the authors, without these two ingredients, there can be no insurgency. Insurgency is thus reduced to a revolutionary political and social "phenomena."[13]

Prior to the development of the U.S. Army's Low-Intensity Conflict (LIC) Doctrine of the early 1980s, Brigadier Frank Kitson of the British military had written a unique tactical exposition on insurgency war in 1971 entitled *Low Intensity Operations*. He breaks insurgency into two distinct parts. The first part represents pure tactics and is called "The Handling of Information." The second part, entitled "Direction, Units and Equipment," explains the logistical details needed for effectively countering an insurgency. Although no singular definition is provided for insurgency, Kitson acknowledges that many of his ideas stem from the tactical precepts yielded by Mao Tse-tung.

According to Kitson, as a final phase in the overall scope of revolutionary guerrilla war,

> . . . armed insurgents come out into the open and fight the forces of the government by conventional methods, but in the earliest stages the war is fought by people who strike at a time and place of their own choosing and then disappear. Sometimes their disappearance is achieved by the physical process of movement into an area of thick cover such as a jungle, and at other times by merging into the population.[14]

Kitson's treatment of the tactical aspects is representative of a time when the term *insurgency* was accepted as a kind of phenomenon, shrouded from Western strategists. These strategists were criticized for operating with fixed beliefs about conventional warfare, and, in the two decades following World War II, were sent scrambling to make sense of this new kind of war for the "atomic age."[15] Ever since the Truman Doctrine, and the idea that "limited war" was not only feasible but necessary, the United States has searched for ways to design just such a limited strategic response to global security concerns.

However, by the mid-1950s the idea of overt military response had not met with great success, particularly on the Asian mainland. The American-led defense of Korea ended in stalemate, and the French debacle at Dien Bien Phu was proof that large conventional military actions were far too costly in men and materiel for the proposed gains. It was believed that for global strategy to succeed in turning away the communist revolutionary tide in Asia, the response needed to be more subtle, more covert, and more focused on the reasons for such apparent sweeping successes by Third World communist nations.

Mao Tse-tung was seen as one who had mastered the phenomenon called insurgency. His rise to power, his establishment of a communist China, and the revolutionary political influence he maintained throughout Asia appeared as testimony. As well, the phenomena of insurgency was seen to be spreading regionally: to Laos, Cambodia, Thailand, Malaya, the Philippines, and Vietnam. It was also spreading globally: to Algeria, Greece, Angola, and Cuba.

Samuel B. Griffith, in the early 1960s, provided the first truly significant Western interpretation of works by the ancient Chinese military and political philosopher Sun Tzu.[16] Mao spoke of, and alluded to, Sun Tzu on numerous occasions throughout his writings. For many strategists and scholars, the study of works like Sun Tzu's was viewed as vital in helping to solve the puzzle of communist uprisings and subversive political successes throughout Asia.

When Mao was discovered, in the early 1960s, to be the preeminent architect of guerrilla strategy, few wanted to see beyond his ambiguous terminology and communist dogma. Such phrases as "controlled terror," "winning over the hearts and minds," and "people's war" were relatively new to modern war vocabulary and caught the imagination of most military and political scholars. It is key to recognize that the majority of those writing on insurgency war during that period, particularly those trying to represent both political and military experiences, pay unabashed homage to Mao Tse-tung by adopting much of his terminology in their own works.

Indeed, Mao's discussions about revolutionary guerrilla war are believed by many to be critical to understanding Western misperceptions about insurgency warfare. However, Mao's works represent to a large and terribly narrow extent, the terminology of the "people's war," not a more eclectic understanding of insurgency. The varying degrees of political indoctrination embodied in all of his writings make it difficult to draw on the underlying strategic value. Therefore, while an explanation of revolutionary guerrilla war using Mao's terminology may be acceptable, using the same terminology to explain the strategic design of insurgency, particularly in its larger context, is not. Douglas Pike refers to several aspects about the Vietnam war which support Mao's ideas of revolutionary guerrilla war. In his important book on the Viet Cong, Pike develops the concept that revolutionary guerrilla war is a unique form of warfare, not to be confused with older concepts such as irregular war, civil war, revolutionary war, rebellion, partisan activity, and so on. He states:

> Revolutionary guerrilla warfare as practiced in Vietnam was a way of life. Its aim was to establish a totally new social order, thus differing from insurgencies whose objective is either statehood or change of government. . . . It was an important product, revolution from the outside; its stock in trade, the grievance, was often artificially created; its goal of liberation, a deception.[17]

Thus, it would appear that ideas about guerrilla war embrace a number of factors associated with revolution, and Pike's definition clearly attempts to bridge a gap between old and modern concepts about guerrilla war.[18] Pike, combining these terms in Maoist fashion, is representing what he calls "acknowledged strategy," superb as an "antidote to modern arms and in harmony with the world's temper, efficiently harnessing social forces already loosened."[19] In answering questions about "limited war" strategy, Pike seeks to divide insurgency into two categories: (1) The political change which is still insurgency and (2) the social upheaval Mao purported to be "revolutionary guerrilla war."

But even when using the term in its most ambiguous sense, one must still ask the question: Does an insurgency have the charismatic power, in the end, to change the social order of things after an established government has fallen? Certainly it does, because that is the fundamental nature of political revolution. By taking this then to extremes, one realizes that if such governments are to fall to insurgent forces, it is because the support and will of the population allows such change to take place, in fact helps it along. Without the support of the people there is no revolutionary intent, therefore no insurgency. Insurgency can, in and of itself, be social upheaval, and can be sponsored internally, externally, or both simultaneously.

It is not so far-fetched to see almost complete social change following quickly on the heels of the defeat of an existing authoritarian regime by an insurgency. Previous examples of insurgency support this claim. An insurgency, even considered in the sense of Pike's "revolutionary guerrilla war," has the capability of turning into a revolution, a civil war, or multiple insurgencies. Careful analysis of sources predating Pike's work that appear allied to his reasoning reveals little which would lead to a dismissal of insurgency as a practical means to prosecute social, as well as authoritarian change.[20] Indeed, insurgencies are grand deceptions, publicly declaring on one hand to be a nonbelligerent movement, while gaining power that could be used to perpetrate political revolution on the other.

In a more concise manner, but similarly to Pike, Chalmers Johnson also addresses the subject of revolutionary guerrilla war:

> Guerrilla warfare is a form of warfare in the technical sense in which all war involves the use of armed men to annihilate the men and arms of an enemy. The initiation of a revolutionary guerrilla war thus requires that an armed band of men take to the field and launch attacks against a regime's forces. . . .
>
> The essence of guerrilla strategy is to entrap the status quo forces in the swamp of an overwhelmingly hostile population, and to organize this population to serve a coherent, long-range program of military conquest in which the defending force's strengths are turned to weaknesses.[21]

In similar fashion, Sam Sarkesian defines revolutionary guerrilla warfare as "the forcible attempt by a politically organized group to gain control or change the structure and/or policies of the government, using unconventional warfare integrated with political and social mobilization, resting on the premise that the people are both the targets and the actors."[22]

In both Johnson's and Sarkesian's definitions we see an attempt to correlate the concepts of insurgency and revolutionary guerrilla war. The ideas of a "revolutionary guerrilla war," and a "people's revolutionary war" cause immediate confusion because of the terms themselves. While revolution may be the end strategic value, guerrilla war is the tactical force that carries the insurgency forth amongst the people. This implies that revolutionary upheaval must be the result of any insurgency. If, however, an insurgency may also exist simply to acquire political recognition within the predominant political and social framework, then its intent would not necessarily be political or social revolution. The phrase "people's revolutionary war" implies revolution from the outset of subversive activity. While an insurgency may eventually focus on political and social revolution, it might in the beginning only focus on political and social inclusion.

That Sarkesian, Johnson, and Pike are all students of Mao Tse-tung's works about revolutionary guerrilla war is obvious, as it is with many of those quoted in our preceding examples. But there is no mysticism to Maoist guerrilla philosophy. As W. W. Rostow points out: "It is historically inaccurate and psychologically dangerous to think that [Mao] created the strategy and tactics of guerrilla war. . . . Guerrilla warfare is not a form of military and psychological magic created by the Communists."[23] It becomes obvious after reviewing works by Mao Tse-tung, as well as various secondary sources which analyze doctrinal virtues based on Mao's writings, that he only partially addresses the specific concept of insurgency.

As an antidote to the various misconceptions he saw developing in the mid-1960s, Sir Robert Grainger Ker Thompson observes that, in spite of their "grandiloquent and misleading titles," an insurgency is not a people's revolutionary war. Citing government intelligence figures, Thompson indicates that by 1965 the number of insurgents and their supporters active in South Vietnam never exceeded 1 percent of the total population. With this in mind, he concludes that the insurgency was not qualified to be a people's revolutionary war, but only a "revolutionary form of warfare designed to enable a very small ruthless minority to gain control over the people."[24]

Robert Thompson's practical views about insurgency warfare, particularly from that period, remain the most definitive.[25] Refreshingly, Thompson refrains from mixing terminology, and, although he does not provide a specific definition of insurgency war, his illustrations of insurgency tendencies and peculiarities better explain an important strategic concept that otherwise appears useless.

A first objective must then be to reach a more precise understanding of insurgency without confusing terminology. From this, and in a modern spirit of *insurgere*, comes a working definition and explanation of insurgency war:

> *Insurgency* is a political-military conflict waged against a specific faction(s), implementing irregular military actions in support of a unified political outcome, short of revolution and civil war.
>
> While regular military forces may be employed, irregular operations rooted in political subversion, selective terrorism, and guerrilla operations, play an integral, if not primary, role in the outcome. Political subversion, selective terrorism, and guerrilla operations are then tactics that, when combined, may or may not represent an insurgency.
>
> Insurgency is a strategic political development that implements these tactics as a means to sustain itself until further development can occur. Consequently, an insurgency, as a *type* of war, may lead to and be part of a large conventional conflict, revolution, or civil war. Insurgency, as a *method* of war, implies the attempt to use violence and irregular forms of warfare against a particular faction(s) for the express purpose of political-military gain, which may later lead to inclusion with, or the overthrow of, existing regimes.
>
> The object of insurgency is to force political-social upheaval, in an organized fashion, for the express purpose of validating a cause, and there-fore justifying its violent means. Insurgencies do not have the capacity to be a revolution or a civil war, but with staying power and continued sup-port can ignite either.

Therefore, an insurgency is neither revolution nor civil war. As well, there are three major elements identified as tools used in an insurgency: political subversion, selective terrorism, and guerrilla operations (see Figure 1.1). Any other aspect, political or military, that might be attributed to an insurgency will likely fall under one of these three major tactical elements.

Thompson has stated with consistency that the first phase of an insurgency always begins with subversive activity. He goes so far as to state that "insurgency is a measure both of the success and of the failure of subversion."[26] If the subversion is successful enough to continue the insurgency, but not successful enough to achieve the objective by subversion alone, then the insurgency moves to a second phase: open insurgency or the armed struggle. The second phase consists of the use of guerrilla operations combined with terrorist activities and will typically result in a protracted struggle.

Figure 1.1
Insurgency Model of Tactical Elements

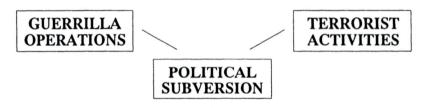

When Thompson spoke about insurgency, he spoke directly about communist insurgency, and thus communist subversion. From his experiences in both war and politics, in Malaya and in Vietnam, one might believe that he was led to this understanding for obvious reasons. And possibly, not unlike many others of the time, Thompson believed that insurgency was a unique tool of the communists, and therefore fashioned to a unique communist design. Many analysts who have since pulled ideas from Thompson have also pulled from him this peculiar error.

However, the working definition provided here does not perceive insurgency as being of any particular origin nor specifically fashioned out of any political dogma. Insurgency possesses certain universal qualities that set it apart as a separate strategic concept from revolution and civil war.[27] While revolution is non-indigenous and civil war is indigenous, insurgencies can be either (see Figure 1.2).

Figure 1.2
Conflict Model

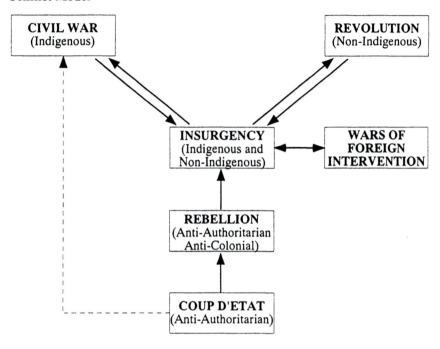

Source: This model is partially based on a model provided in United States Department of the Army, U.S. Army Intelligence Center and School, *The USAICS Handbook on Urban Terrorism*, sup. rev., 03317-1 (Fort Huachuca, AZ: USAICS, June 1978), 380.

TYPOLOGY OF INSURGENCY

While political subversion, selective terrorism, and guerrilla operations are all key elements in an insurgency, political subversion is unquestionably the one element that must exist for the other two elements to have any unified effect. As well, the extent of the political organization of the subversives will likely predict how competent and effective the entire insurgency will turn out to be. The heart of an insurgency is thus the political capability of the subversives, the quality of their organization, and the extent of the roots they set down. To establish a valid insurgency, the subversive organization must acquire the necessary resources and support from both internal and external factions. Just how well this support is managed will determine whether a second phase will be required, or is even possible.

Political subversion attempts to accomplish four specific things: first, to build and test the political infrastructure needed to wage a successful insurgency; second, to generate political clout both internally and externally; third, to support a second phase of open insurgency; and fourth, if it intends to go beyond insurgency war, to plan for government after revolution or civil war is achieved. Those insurgencies resulting in either revolution or civil war represent some of the most skilled and resourceful political organizations. These groups will not appear fanatical in their actions, only ardent in their resolve. While such intent seems "revolutionary" to outsiders, it is purely "evolutionary" to the insurgent. It is this outlook which provide the potential for success, and is the catalyst for all growth.

The crossover to violence is accomplished during the early stages of an insurgency by the use of terrorism. This is the heavy-handed persuasion used by the political subversives as a means of drawing closer attention to their cause; and, when truly selective, it is capable of removing strategic targets that prove to be an obstruction. Indiscriminate terrorism has never been the friend of an insurgent movement. But when implemented correctly and with precision, the results usually favor the subversive political body. Thompson indicates that even in a "pre-insurgency" time of murder and terrorism, the "normal processes of law and order will fail to cope with the situation; the police are unable to effect arrests for lack of witnesses, or the crime itself may not even be reported."[28] A strong history and willingness on the part of the subversives to perform vendetta and reprisal killings typically silences the majority of the public.

If the government is internally crippled or substantially unsupported and weak, the insurgency will not need to progress to the second phase. A government of this hobbled nature will succumb to insurgent pressure. It is important to note here that this still does not qualify the insurgency as revolution. While an insurgency may usurp authority if the government falls, assumption of responsibility may not have been the actual intent of the original subversion. The insurgents may get hold of governmental reins before they are actually willing or even capable of successfully governing.[29] These subversives will usually weaken and fall to other factions. Knowing the difference between an actual "revolution" and a failed insurgency may be critical to the foreign policy intentions of an outside government interested in attaining stability in such a country or region. Such misinterpretation could easily lead to false recognition or a false application of force.

A potential merry-go-round of insurgencies can exist under such a state. It is probable that this kind of transfer of power, violent or otherwise, would appear to be a coup d'etat or internal rebellion. But because the subversive activity is seeking change from outside the existing government, it cannot be a coup d'etat. Because the insurgency is more highly organized and seeks long-term objectives through a protracted struggle, it cannot be considered an internal rebellion (see Figure 1.2). But both a coup d'etat and a rebellion differ from an insurgency in a larger sense. While both forms of internal struggle are commonly trying to restore an earlier social and political order, an insurgency commonly seeks to transform power, preempting any attempt to restore old orders.[30]

Revolution and civil war are other matters. Since the object of an insurgency is not necessarily the establishment of a new state—the ousting of either external colonial factions or internal civil antagonists—the attempt must then be for the subversives to strengthen their cause. This is done through the use of guerrilla operations in the second phase (see Figure 1.3). During this period, selective terrorist activities may heighten, and political subversives will continue to expand their control in populated areas where support will strengthen guerrilla operations. Because the insurgents expect a protracted struggle, a careful search for *base areas* is undertaken.

Two types of base areas exist—one controlled by the guerrillas, the other by the political subversives. The first is the *jungle* base area which provides the guerrillas with sanctuary, supplies, and war materiel—in essence, a logistics base for military support.[31] The other base of support comes from the population and is controlled by the insurgent political organization and its terrorist arm. The purpose of these base areas is to sustain recruiting efforts and supply lines for the duration of the protracted struggle.

Insurgent political strength in the rural setting comes from the links maintained with organized *cells* previously established in the large cities and towns. While this *rural* form of operation may be more desirable, another form of insurgency may establish and maintain organized cells within the urban population center. This type of insurgent operation is seen less frequently because of the inherent dangers placed upon movement, concentration, and communication between the subversive cells. No insurgency can successfully grow beyond phase one if it remains solely within an urban environment.

Figure 1.3
Phases of Insurgency

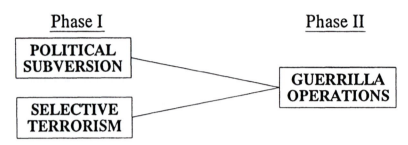

Two specific functions are performed by the subversive insurgent cells. First, they must maintain a continual flow of propaganda, often supported by terrorist activity. This would typically include the assassination of formidable political figures who might turn elements in the population against the insurgency.[32] A second function is to keep the guerrillas supplied with war materiel and technical support not available in the rural setting, and, perhaps most importantly, with intelligence information about government plans, movements, and strengths.[33]

During the subversive phase, much of this planting of base areas is accomplished. Finding these insurgent base areas then becomes a game that the government forces feel obliged to play during the first phase. For the insurgents, success during a second phase depends on how harmoniously its guerrilla operations and its political organization work together. If thorough planning was done by the insurgents, the government may be in for an unwelcome protracted struggle.[34]

The second phase, guerrilla operations, has two stages. During the initial stage the guerrilla units begin operating in conjunction with terrorist units, both in the rural and urban settings. Guerrilla operations in this first stage are diversionary and are employed in consort with terrorist actions in and around government army centers. Often the government confuses the actions of insurgent terrorist with these of guerrilla forces during this period.

When the guerrilla units begin operations on their own in the second stage, they direct their operations specifically at military targets of opportunity. This excludes activity that can be perpetrated by terrorist units, particularly assassinations and the bombing of civilian targets. The guerrilla forces at this second stage are usually engaged in the kind of warfare that they perform best—tactics which include hit-and-run, search and destroy, and ambush patrols against government army units.

Strategy on the part of the insurgent guerrilla force becomes evident during this stage. Its intent to exploit the rural villages in a manner that allows them to encircle the cities, its supporters serving the singular purpose of "rendering an as yet undefeated army [grounded in its urban power base] powerless to save the country."[35] Growing loss of confidence about the government's will rises among the people. A destructive but ineffective military, a surge in inflation and economic disturbance, an overall inability to gain external assistance for internal problems, and an inability to provide capable future governing are all failures that the subversive insurgents hope the common people will begin to perceive as being irreversible within the current government.

PRIMARY AND SECONDARY INSURGENCY

During the later stage of guerrilla operations, the type of insurgency being conducted against the government can easily be identified. The insurgents must make the decision to follow either a *primary* or a *secondary* course of strategy.[36] Primary insurgency seeks military victory by maintaining pressure through guerrilla operations but avoiding any major set-piece battle with government forces.[37] The intent is to wear down government forces through a protracted conflict that relies upon isolated fights at the guerrillas' own choice of place and time. By keeping the initiative away from the government for an extended period, the hope is that demoralization will establish itself among government officials. With no feasible way in which to win a decisive victory, the government, it is expected, will negotiate a cease-fire with insurgent forces, accepting a "neutralist solution as a means of ending the war."[38]

Secondary insurgency seeks victory by way of changing from isolated, or purely guerrilla operations, to what Mao Tse-tung refers to as a "war of movement." With government forces typically spread throughout the rural setting in a defensive posture, the insurgent forces are able to occupy and move freely among the villages, their direct line of support and communication with the political subversive element. All insurgent forces, spearheaded by guerrilla operations which then take on a conventional military restructuring, unite and concentrate the entire effort on one or a series of government targets. The shock effect, combined with thorough planning and military competence, is expected to send government forces reeling in a continuous state of defense, retreat, and then surrender. Unlike primary insurgency, a secondary strategy looks for the set-piece engagement with government forces, believing that a decisive, more conventional blow can achieve the desired success in a shorter period of time.[39] However, this transition into secondary insurgency is not an easy or readily apparent move for the subversive strategist. Pinpointing the exact moment at which a subversive movement should progress into a secondary phase is perhaps the most difficult part of the transition. Choosing the wrong moment or being poorly prepared could bring disaster. In Chapter 3 the concept of *equilibrium* will be discussed, specifically how it relates to choosing the most effective moment for transition to secondary insurgency.

There are two specific reasons why an insurgent leadership would choose the secondary strategy. First, there may seem to be no other option to the insurgents, thus it would be a last-gasp effort to perhaps ignite the passions of the people to rise and overthrow the government. But this would be premature revolution, and few insurgencies, if any, win by this method.[40] It is probably safe to say that complete revolution is not what the subversives planned for in the beginning, and failing to realize this limitation so late in the game is why disaster looms. Because there is nowhere else to go—government forces having grown stronger and the insurgency weaker—the inevitable turn is toward desperate strategy. This is a key example of how insurgencies literally self-destruct.

The other reason for choosing this secondary strategy is that it represents the next step in the evolution of the insurgent movement. The idea is that the insurgency grows stronger while its opponents grow weaker. Insurgent leaders find that their military units are in a position to level a decisive blow to government forces, and, with the popular base of support behind them, proceed quickly in that direction. Mao even warned of something called "guerrillaism," an overlong attachment to irregular methods. Successful insurgent leaders realize that undue delay in making that decisive blow can exhaust the popular base of support, therefore extending, unnecessarily, the guerrilla phase. But the opposite error seems historically more common, "as guerrillas succumb to the lure of uniforms, of heavy weapons, of being able to sleep at night, and of conventional, orderly battle."[41]

The transition from an irregular to a regular method of fighting is extremely complicated for the insurgent leadership to make happen in a short period of time. This is one reason why insurgents must take great care in walking that fine line between "guerrillaism" and moving too quickly. But complications are lessened and time is shortened for the insurgents when guerrilla operations can be incorporated into an existing conventional force allied to their cause. This means that the involvement of a foreign military can have the effect of stabilizing a situation which may be out of the insurgents' control or turn the tide toward a favorable insurgent outcome. In relationship to our working definition, it is also why an insurgency can evolve into, or develop from, a larger conventional struggle. Such a struggle may or may not be part of the insurgent cause. Under such circumstances, the insurgent is often caught up in fighting a war it does not want. This is represented in the Conflict Model where insurgencies may coexist with wars of foreign intervention (see Figure 1.2).

INSURGENCY VERSUS COUNTERINSURGENCY

If it were always true that any government with the best intentions of the people in mind was sure to triumph over an insurgent movement, there would be no need to understand the differences between insurgency and countering insurgency. However, as Thompson points out, there are real problems with the very use of the term *counterinsurgency*.

> Anyone having any responsibility for dealing with an insurgent movement must know his enemy and what that enemy is attempting to do at all stages. This does not mean that those responsible should be solely concerned with countering the enemy's moves. I dislike for this reason the very term "counter-insurgency." It implies that the insurgents have the initiative, and that it is the government's role merely to react and counter that initiative.[42]

During the subversive phase, signs of an insurgency are not always recognizable to a government, and when problems become evident, the people may be slow to arouse, and government forces may react inappropriately. In this instance, the government runs the risk of either acting too soon—appearing repressive because the subversion is little recognized—or acting too late. Although much evidence about the subversion is apparent in a late reaction, the government is already in the second phase, or open insurgency of guerrilla war. The trick for any government, then, is to recognize an insurgency during the subversive phase, which will require the least of the military solutions.

In keeping with Thompson's spirit about "counter-insurgency," this study then recognizes that the best counter to any insurgency can only be another insurgency. Because the idea of countering anything conjures up reactionary views, it is best to dispense with the confusion of the term *counterinsurgency* altogether. For a government to maintain authority and thwart an insurgency, that government cannot be countering anything; rather, it must initiate nearly all the political and military moves during the confrontation. The government must be prepared to make the initial moves at a moment's notice. A shrewd, offensive posture must be attained or maintained at all times for the government authority to assume victory. Thus, for a government to stay in power and succeed against a subversive insurgency, it must actually wage a better insurgency than the political subversives themselves. Indeed, a government must possess the "long-term aim" or face the consequences of adopting "short-term ad hoc measures merely as reactions to insurgent initiative or with the limited aim of attempting to defeat the insurgents militarily in the guerrilla phase."[43]

Thompson relates five basic principles from which all government measures must evolve:

1. The government must have a clear political aim: to establish and maintain a free, independent and united country which is politically and economically stable and viable.
2. The government must function in accordance with the law.
3. The government must have an overall plan.
4. The government must give priority to defeating the political subversion, not the guerrillas.
5. In the guerrilla phase of an insurgency, a government must secure its base areas first.[44]

There exists no better set of commandments for a government faced with waging an insurgency. As well, the same commandments could be intended for the subversive insurgents. Simply replace *government* with the term *subversive* and one has the same equation: (1) The subversives must have a clear political aim; (2) The subversives must function in accordance with the law (at least according to Mao); (3) The subversives must have an overall plan; (4) The subversives must give priority to defeating the government, not its army; and, (5) the subversives must secure their base areas first.

What exists in the end is nothing more than tried-and-true military theory maintaining the best intentions of Jomini and Clausewitz. Who can get there first with the most? Who has the best intelligence gathering apparatus? Who has the better strategy, resources, and manpower? Who has the support of the people? There should be no question that a government with the proper intent and motivation can swing public support away from any subversive organization. The following chapter will illustrate two key examples of how governments have succeeded along these lines. The will to maintain authority, and presumably law and order, as well as superior technology, are usually on the side of the government. When this is the case, there is no acceptable reason for achieving anything short of victory.

The strategic "imbalance of force" between the government and the subversives must be exploited by the government. Weaponry, aircraft, and a navy are all assets that subversives have trouble acquiring.[45] A government usually has a variety of light and heavy weapons at its disposal, an extensive transportation system, an assortment of aircraft and ships patrolling vigilantly, fuel, food, medicines, and some sort of industry that it controls. In addition, a government usually has ties with other nations that readily support its cause. Despite all this capability, a government still faces the one risk of relying too heavily on massive response—too much, too often. An insurgent strategy instead calls for just enough, at just the right time, in just the right place. One is challenged to envision a better concept of balance of force.

There are several strategic considerations for a government regarding balance of force during an insurgency. These include insurgent organization and size, the potential base for popular support, and logistic difficulties. It is likely that all of these elements will be directly affected by the terrain and the dispersement of the population. It is typical that the more rural and dense the terrain, the more sheltered the insurgent forces are. In a successful phase two, sheltering must then take shape outside the urban center. This will in turn aid the insurgents in their quest for a protracted struggle.

In speaking about open insurgency, or phase two of an insurgency, Thompson discusses three specific geographical areas in which insurgent activity takes place. There are first the populated areas within major cities and towns under government control where terrorist activity is the most prevalent. Then there are the rural populated areas where control is disputed between the government and the insurgents and where the guerrilla insurgent forces extend their operations. Finally, there are the more remote, "deep jungle" bases of the insurgent guerrillas, less populated terrain which is also usually difficult to traverse. It is here that the guerrillas place their logistical bases, where they rest, rearm, and plan future operations.[46] In military terms, it is in these base areas where the insurgent guerrillas are most vulnerable to government attack. Terrorist actions, while feared among the general populace, are easily recognized in the urban areas. What is usually the most difficult for government forces to quell are the combined subversive, terrorist, and guerrilla operations that are within that middle geographic area of the rural populated setting.

The great tactical error governments can make is assigning priority to these geographic areas. Often, the government concentrates on the outside and works in, instead of working from the inside out. Remote guerrilla base areas on the outside are not the source of the insurgent problem and therefore should not be the prime consideration for government forces in the beginning of an insurgency. Because the political subversion provides the impetus, it is the subversives that must be stopped. The population within the cities is perhaps the last element to support an insurgency, which is the very reason that the insurgents choose to surround the cities by infiltrating the villages.

It is the middle geographic area, the rural population, where the subversives launch their strongest opposition to the government.[47] The formation of a fair and resourceful constabulary must be the first order of business for any government combating an insurgent movement. The subversion must be stopped at the outset by extending the intelligence gathering arm of the government. Thompson sees this as a "thoroughly methodical approach," one which may appear slow in the beginning but encourages a "steam-roller outlook which provides the people with faith in ultimate victory. By preparing for a long haul, the government may achieve victory quicker than expected. By seeking quick military victories in insurgent controlled areas, it will certainly get a long haul for which neither it nor the people may be prepared."[48]

At the beginning of an insurgency, and at some time before the subversive element chooses to instigate a second phase of operations, the military—most likely of some regular, conventional structure—must be restructured almost wholesale. While some conventional force structure must remain in place to thwart a possible secondary insurgency, substantial training must be done to establish small-unit irregulars that can carry on guerrilla tactics themselves. With a broader range of technical advantages, the government "guerrillas" can presumably be provided with stronger intelligence information than the subversives, better weapons, equipment, supplies, food, pay, and medical treatment, all of which should provide a great morale boost. With air and naval assets, the government units should also have better combat support, and, perhaps the most important element of all, far better mobility.[49] Thompson states:

> The requirement is for a small, elite, highly disciplined, lightly equipped and aggressive army, with a supporting air force and navy of sufficient

capability to make the army highly mobile, so that it can fulfill its proper military role in support of the civil government and in accordance with the five basic principles.[50]

If a government is aware enough and moves in a positive direction early, it can take the necessary political and military steps to wage a better insurgency than the subversives themselves. However, the strategic and tactical means at hand must not first be put toward the military solution. For a government countering an insurgency, it is the political infrastructure of the insurgents that must be defeated, first and last. Such a strategy is so critical, Thompson cautions, that "even if an armed insurgency is defeated, the political and subversive struggle will go on and can still win."[51] Such a possibility can only be of nightmare proportions for a legitimate government that has expended its resources in an unwise, frivolous manner, extolling little virtue in its understanding of insurgency. Such a nightmare could easily extend to regional alliances, disturb the process of nation-building, and adversely affect desired regional security. This is as much a concern now as it was at the end of the Second World War.

NOTES

1. Stephan Lee Bowman, "The United States Army and Counterinsurgency Warfare: The Making of Doctrine, 1946–1964" (M.A. thesis, Duke University, 1981), 3–4. Also see John M. Gates, "Indians and Insurrectos: The U.S. Army's Experience with Insurgency," *Parameters* 13 (March 1983): 59–68.

2. Pike, "Conduct of the Vietnam War," 114. In contemporary criticism about the military's LIC doctrine, Col. Summers states that the army is today void of "a clear and precise definition of low-intensity conflict." He states that the military is in "big trouble" over its apparent confusion n defining LIC. See Harry G. Summers, Jr., "A War Is a War Is a War Is a War," in *Low-Intensity Conflict: The Pattern of Warfare in the Modern World*, ed. Loren B. Thompson (Lexington, Mass.: Lexington Books, 1989), 32.

3. *Oxford English Dictionary*, 2d ed., s.v. "insurgency."

4. Jack C. Plano et al., *Political Science Dictionary* (Hinsdale, Ill.: The Dryden Press, 1973), 197.

5. Roger Scruton, *A Dictionary of Political Thought* (New York: Harper & Row Publishers, 1982), 226.

6. Regarding the confusion of these and other terms used to denote "internal political revolution," see Sarkesian's excellent introduction to the work: Sam C. Sarkesian, ed., *Revolutionary Guerrilla Warfare* (Chicago: Precedent Publishing,

1975), 1–25.

7. U.S., D.A., Special Warfare School, *Counterinsurgency Planning Guide*, USASWS Special Text 31–176 (Fort Bragg, N.C.: USASWS, 1963). For a detailed reference listing of recommended supplemental publications for the time period, see pp. 182–90.

8. David Galula, *Counter-Insurgency Warfare: Theory and Practice* (New York: Frederick A. Praeger, 1964), 4–5.

9. Ibid.

10. Julian Paget, *Counter-Insurgency Operations: Techniques of Guerrilla Warfare* (New York: Walker and Company, 1967), 14–15.

11. Andrew M. Scott et al., *Insurgency* (Chapel Hill, N.C.: The University of North Carolina Press, 1970), 5.

12. Ibid., 10.

13. Ibid., 3–13 and passim.

14. Frank Kitson, *Low-Intensity Operations: Subversion, Insurgency, Peace-Keeping* (Harrisburg, Pa.: Stackpole Books, 1971), 95.

15. Roger Hilsman provides a succinct recollection of his own personal experience in forming limited strategic concepts during this period of "atomic age" thinking, particularly about Europe when related to the problem of NATO strategy. See Roger Hilsman, *American Guerrilla: My War behind Japanese Lines* (New York: Brassey's, Inc., 1990), 257–59. For further development of "limited war" strategies beyond nuclear deterrence during this early period, see the classic works by Robert E. Osgood, *Limited War: The Challenge to American Strategy* (Chicago: The University of Chicago Press, 1957); also, Osgood's follow-on, *Limited War Revisited* (Boulder, Colo.: Westview Press, 1979); Henry A. Kissinger, *Nuclear Weapons and Foreign Policy* (New York: Harper & Bros., 1957); "Limited War: The Prospects and Possibilities," *Army Information Digest* 13 (June 1958), 6–20; Morton H. Halperin, *Limited War: An Essay on the Development of the Theory and An Annotated Bibliography* (Cambridge, Mass.: Center for International Affairs, Harvard University, 1962)

16. Sun Tzu, *The Art of War*, trans. and with an introduction by Samuel B. Griffith (London: Oxford University Press, 1963).

17. Douglas Pike, *Viet Cong* (Cambridge, Mass.: M.I.T. Press, 1966), 32–33.

18. Sam C. Sarkesian, "American Policy on Revolution and Counterrevolution: A Review of the Themes in the Literature," *Conflict* 5 (summer 1984): 140.

19. Ibid., 33.

20. See for example, Otto Heilbrunn, *Partisan Warfare* (New York: Frederick A. Praeger, 1963); J. C. Murray, "The Anti-Bandit War," in *The Guerrilla and How to Fight Him*, ed. T. N. Greene (New York: Frederick A. Praeger, 1962), 65–111; Chalmers Johnson, *Revolutionary Change* (Boston: Little, Brown and Company, 1966), e.g., 88–118; Sigmund Neumann, "The International Civil War," in *Why Revolution? Theories and Analysis*, ed. Clifford T. Paynton and Robert Blackey (Cambridge, Mass.: Schenkman Publishing Co., Inc., 1971),

110–23.

21. Johnson, *Revolutionary Change*, 160.

22. Sarkesian, *Revolutionary Guerrilla Warfare*, 7.

23. W. W. Rostow, "Guerrilla Warfare in Underdeveloped Areas," in Greene, *The Guerrilla and How to Fight Him*, 60.

24. Robert Thompson, *Defeating Communist Insurgency* (New York: Frederick A. Praeger, 1966), 49.

25. From a purely strategic viewpoint, attention should be drawn to a more recent identification of four fundamental types of insurgency design: Leninist, Maoist, Cuban, and urban terrorist; see O'Neill, "Insurgent Strategies," 172. Although O'Neill's four insurgent strategies tend to maintain "communist revolutionary" overtones and would most likely place Thompson's views in the Maoist category, it is the belief here that much of Thompson's reasoning actually transcends all four categories. In essence, if O'Neill views insurgency as a top-down phenomenon, then Thompson sees it as a more bottom-up arrangement, meaning that the grass roots of tactical design actually dictates the overall direction of insurgent strategy—that is, if it is to succeed. For other top-down approaches, see Scott et al., *Insurgency*; John S. Pustay, *Counterinsurgency Warfare* (New York: The Free Press, 1965); John J. McCuen, *The Art of Counter-Revolutionary Warfare* (Harrisburg, Pa.: Stackpole Books, 1966). Also, one should compare with the classic work by Robert Taber, *The War of the Flea: A Study of Guerrilla Warfare Theory and Practice* (New York: Lyle Stuart, 1965). For further treatment during this early period, see Col. Ephraim M. Hampton, "Unlimited Confusion over Limited War," *Air University Quarterly* 9 (spring 1957): 28–47; Edward F. Downey, Jr., "Theory of Guerrilla Warfare," *Military Review* (May 1959): 45–55; Lt. Col. Donald V. Rattan, "Antiguerrilla Operations: A Case Study from History," *Military Review* (May 1960): 23–27; Maj. Thoung Htaik, "Encirclement Methods in Antiguerrilla Warfare," *Military Review* (June 1961): 90–95.

26. Robert Thompson, *No Exit from Vietnam* (New York: David McKay Company, Inc., 1969), 46–47. Also see, Thompson, *Defeating Communist Insurgency*, 28–29.

27. While there are several good works that recognize the unique strategic qualities of insurgency war, one might specifically refer to Liddell Hart, *Strategy*, 361–70; see also Mao Tse-tung on types of war, in *Mao Tse-tung on Revolution and War*, ed. and with an introduction and notes by M. Rajai (New York: Doubleday & Company, Inc., 1969), 232–37. For the first real post-Vietnam era criticism written by a U.S. military officer and scholar recognizing *insurgency* as a clear reason for the American defeat, see Cincinnatus, *Self-Destruction: The Disintegration and Decay of the United States Army During the Vietnam Era* (New York: W. W. Norton & Company, 1981).

28. Thompson, *Defeating Communist Insurgency*, 25–26.

29. Thompson states that the insurgents do not want to capture and hold the

cities, which would in effect mean the take over of the government. The cities remain a useful source of support, and the insurgents cannot be involved with the administrative problems posed by such a move. See ibid., 42.

30. For clear definitions of the terms *internal rebellion* and *coup d'etat*, see Johnson, *Revolutionary Change*, 135–43, 150–53. Although Johnson refers to these terms within the framework of "varieties" and "strategies" of revolution, the intended definition is compatible with our purpose. Also see John Shy and Thomas W. Collier, "Revolutionary War," in Paret, *Makers of Modern Strategy*, 818–19.

31. The use of the term "jungle" does not indicate that there is a unique quality between the concepts of *urban* and *rural* insurgency. There is but one kind of strategic insurgency, and it can be applied throughout a variety of settings, the urban setting being one of them. The term "jungle" is therefore used here as a common term, representing the development of bases outside the realm of urban logistical support.

32. Thompson, *Defeating Communist Insurgency*, 38.

33. See Thompson's discussion on morale of the civilian populace and how the insurgents use selective terrorism to further weaken support for the government. Also, note how insurgent cells increase the flow of recruits to guerrilla units. Ibid., 38–39.

34. In keeping with Mao's three phases of revolutionary guerrilla war, several sources authored during the 1960s attempt to distinguish between similar patterns in order to establish counterguerrilla theory on a strategic level. Because the definition of insurgency war given in this study does not confuse insurgent strategy with guerrilla tactics, the two phases of insurgency are believed to be more specific in their meaning and to lessen the cloud over what otherwise is tactical terminology. See Mao Tse-tung, *On Guerrilla War*, see also U.S., D.A., Special Warfare School, *Counterinsurgency Planning Guide*, 14 and passim; Paget, *Counter-Insurgency Operation*, 30–39.

35. Thompson, *Defeating Communist Insurgency*, 42.

36. This is an advantage over the Maoist concept which necessitates a third phase in its "revolutionary guerrilla warfare" scheme, a phase that maintains the vision of attaining conventional war; cf., U.S., D.A. *FM 100-20 Field Service Regulations, Counterinsurgency* (Washington, D.C.: GPO, 1964), which provides an official explanation of insurgency war based solely on Mao's three-phased principles. Also, see a later interpretation in USAICS, *USAICS Handbook on Urban Terrorism*, 409–12.

37. Primary and secondary insurgency as represented here differs greatly from Mao Tse-tung's concepts of "primary" and "supplementary" guerrilla war. Speaking directly about China's war of resistance against the Japanese, Mao indicates three stages: mobile warfare, guerrilla warfare, and mobile warfare again. His essential concern during the fighting of the Japanese army was to field a Chinese army that was strongest in tactical mobility. This meant that guerrilla operations, while significant for short-term, tactical expectations, would play a

decreasing role in the overall strategy of resistance. For a concise reading on these points by Mao, see *Mao Tse-tung on Revolution and War*, 288–90.

38. Thompson, *Defeating Communist Insurgency*, 43; cf. Paget, *Counter-Insurgency Operations*, 30–37, viz., "phases."

39. Thompson, *Defeating Communist Insurgency*, 42–43. For a discussion on the "regularization" of guerrilla forces during secondary insurgency, including some of the potential disasters facing such a move, see Peter Paret and John W. Shy, *Guerrillas in the 1960s* (New York: Frederick A. Praeger, 1962), 36–37.

40. Again the distinction is made between what the objective of insurgency is as opposed to that of revolution. See Thompson, *Defeating Communist Insurgency*, 49 and passim.

41. Paret and Shy, *Guerrillas in the 1960s*, 35.

42. Thompson, *Defeating Communist Insurgency*, 50.

43. Ibid., 52.

44. Ibid., 50–58; cf., Paget, *Counter-Insurgency Operations*, 156–57.

45. Thompson discusses several aspects of naval and air force assets in an insurgency. See, *Defeating Communist Insurgency*, 106–8.

46. Ibid., 104–5.

47. Thompson details the balance of force and basic operational concepts among insurgent forces in the rural populated areas. It is not the purpose of this study to establish new operational concepts of insurgent tactics; thus, I will leave those concepts established by Thompson (and others) for the reader to investigate. Ibid., 103–7, 111–20.

48. Ibid., 58.

49. In relation to helicopter and inland water mobility, see ibid., 106–8. Also see Paget, *Counter-Insurgency Operations*, 162–67.

50. Thompson, *Defeating Communist Insurgency*, 62.

51. Ibid., 47. Thompson completes the statement by relating such an outcome to the insurgency in Algeria. For a clear picture of the Algerian insurgency, see Peter Paret, *French Revolutionary Warfare from Indochina to Algeria: The Analysis of a Political and Military Doctrine* (New York: Frederick A. Praeger, 1964).

CHAPTER 2

An Analysis of Two Postwar Asian Insurgencies

At the end of the Second World War, both the United States and Great Britain found themselves immersed in tensions throughout Asia. Always related to the overt actions of cold war politics, both nations also found themselves involved in suppressing separate insurgencies as part of extending their individual foreign policy objectives. The United States was caught in the middle of helping to establish a friendly government in the Philippines, one sympathetic to U.S. security concerns after 1946. Even with the eventual loss of the naval facilities at Subic Bay and the volcanic destruction of Clark Air Force Base, the Philippines remain critical to U.S. global security interests.

Great Britain, in its own right, was attempting to quell a rebellion turned insurgency over its holdings on the Malayan peninsula. Partly due to U.S. pressure seeking a colonial-free postwar world, and due in large part to the faltering British economy, an initial step to make a clean but gradual break from its colonial holdings was in process. These affairs are important to this study for three critical reasons: First, they represent a wide variety of nationalist problems needing resolution after the Second World War and illustrate the kind of warfare both allies believed lay ahead for them in attempting to thwart the increasing tide of communism in a Third World wrought with cold war tensions. Second, they are the earliest of the large, modern insurgencies that took place in Asia in the post-1945 period and provided successful examples that would have direct impact on the conduct of American political and military operations in Vietnam. And, third, these events bring forth a new cast of characters who would have direct influence over American policies on insurgency warfare to be formulated and implemented in the future.

THE PHILIPPINES, 1946–1953

American involvement in the Philippines after 1945 took on an almost historical quality. Not only had the United States been involved in trade with the Filipinos for almost a century, it had been militarily involved in the region for nearly fifty years. The desire to maintain certain strategic control and security in the Philippine region seemed to be uncontestable, even natural, to many Americans by the time General Douglas MacArthur and the U.S. Sixth Army returned in October 1944. But the Philippines were in a desperate situation economically and politically following Japanese occupation, and the United States had pledged to grant them independence a year after the war ended. Thus, when the repatriated Philippine President Sergio Osmena asked President Harry S. Truman for economic help in 1945, he did not have to wait long.

While economic and financial needs were paramount, the weak political infrastructure in devastated Manila could not be ignored. Here, successive Philippine governments had wrestled with the problem of eliminating the most volatile of the competing political factions. The Hukbo ng Bayan Laban Sa Hapon, or Hukbalahap, a contraction meaning People's Anti-Japanese Army, was indeed the most serious threat to a stable Filipino government sympathetic to U.S. interests. The Huks, as they were commonly called, controlled a large part of the rice and cane growing areas of central Luzon. They carried out political and military operations throughout the archipelago, eventually bringing nearly 150,000 Filipinos in this region under their control. From the development of sound military training and operational experience in fighting the Japanese, the Huks were able to hone guerrilla war techniques. As a military arm of the Communist Party in the Philippines, however, Huk ambitions always exceeded mere anti-Japanese activities.

In spite of their initial base of support as a subversive organization, the Huks did not attempt an immediate overthrow of the government following the Japanese surrender. Claiming to want political solutions, rebel Huk leader Luis Taruc won a seat in the new Manila congress, elected in April 1946.[1] Disruptive as they were, their tenure was short lived, and the Huks were eventually disqualified from holding their congressional seat on the valid grounds that they used terrorist methods to persuade voters during the campaign. Representing more than a simple band of rebel thugs, this Huk organization, under the military leadership of Taruc, had developed into a competent insurgent political and military organization. Although inclusion appeared attractive in the beginning, the Huks decided that their strength and growing numbers warranted procession down a noninclusive track, a track that appeared to capture the common passions of the Philippine people. The bitter circumstances surrounding this newly established phase one insurgency ran deep. As Asprey states:

> Taruc and his associates represented a distinct challenge to the hegemony exercised by immensely powerful landowners and industrialists spawned during four decades of American overlordship. This group, which included substantial American interests, had usurped the old landowning role of the Church, which had made itself hated by peasants.[2]

With farmers only owning 10 percent of the land they tilled and paying to the government some 50 percent of its cash crop, a small plot of farmland was never destined to pay for itself. Farmers and their families were in a perpetual state of financial hardship, and in some cases, starvation. But this financial system was over four centuries old. It explained generations of "poverty punctuated by uprisings, and, in 1946, [it] explained a Communist popularity that a reactionary government was too greedy and frightened to admit or accept."[3] Communist Huks preyed upon the fragile nature of this peasantry, who themselves probably believed less in the virtues of communism than in the fight against a perverted democracy. Discarding any future intentions of provoking change through legislation, Taruc and his followers fled to the hills to provoke change through open revolt.[4]

The prospect of just such an eventuality had not gone unrecognized by Taruc and the Huks, nor was it a surprise to government officials. Taruc had already been arrested, released, rearrested, and released again by the Philippine government for inciting rebellion even before he was elected to office. That Taruc and many of his followers were prepared to go beyond peaceful reform and would now attempt the violent overthrow of the government was quite evident. Due to sound organization and thorough planning after the war with the Japanese, it was also quite possible that they might succeed.

Although the communist character of the Huks was not clear on the surface to some, roots ran extensively through the political organization. Huk legend speaks of a political and military training school established as early as 1942 on the slopes of Mount Arayat, a peak which looms above Huklandia, the nickname for the Huk controlled area in central Luzon. Here a competent Chinese officer corps helped to train personnel in guerrilla tactics and politically indoctrinate the future communist leaders of the Philippines. Although somewhat suspicious, the Armed Forces of the Philippine (AFP) handbook records that a "colonel," a member of the Red Chinese Eighth Route Army, instructed Huks in the art of guerrilla warfare. Works about guerrilla warfare by Mao Tse-tung and Chu-teh were used as fundamental textbooks. Even Edgar Snow's *Red Star over China* was said to have provided inspirational reading.[5]

A village network of Communist Party leaders was established called the Barrio United Defense Corps (BUDC). These farmer-by-day, guerrilla-by-night peasants would take on anti-Japanese operations based out of their own villages. The network helped provide the necessary intelligence information for exposing various targets of opportunity, assisting and providing reinforcements when needed, and simply helping to dominate the local citizenry. But a growing mistrust of the Huks came out of this period, particularly after many villagers witnessed murders, vendetta killings against other Huks, and the brutal techniques often used by Huk policing units. While there was a menacing side to the Huks, there was also the side that protected and nurtured the poor and established hope through sound organization. Still, the power over life and death in the barrio remained in the hands of the BUDC.[6]

With this vast infrastructure in place, it did not take Taruc and his followers long to begin operations against government forces. The period between 1946 and 1950 proved nearly disastrous for the struggling Filipino government. After elections in 1946 brought Manuel Roxas to the presidency, the government pledged to end the Huk insurgency within sixty days. This only led to a greater fiasco put on by the Philippine government and further angered the peasantry of central Luzon, where the Huks already enjoyed their largest support. Incidents such as off-handed killings by government troops and the shelling of barrios only fueled antigovernment sentiment.[7] Soldiers were placed in towns, and garrisons were established in villages and hamlets. Checkpoints were often used by the soldiers patrolling them as a way to line their pockets with "incentive monies" from villagers simply wishing to pass through. If a villager was too poor to make payment, the usual beatings ensued. Rampant abuse was permeating the otherwise confused intentions of the Roxas government. This "mailed fist" approach was widely viewed as inappropriate, reversing the trends that the United States had hoped from afar would take place.

However, two events occurred during the Roxas administration that particularly favored U.S. interests. One was the Military Base Agreement signed in March 1947. This effectively established an American military presence in the Philippines at both Subic Naval Station and Clark Air Field, a presence which would continue for nearly forty-five years. Most important, however, and particularly significant as related to the government conflict with the Huks, was Roxas's signing of the Military Assistance Pact with the United States which created the Joint United States Military Advisory Group (JUSMAG). Now the United States would be able to intervene directly by modernizing the Filipino military, teaching them current strategy and tactical concepts, and providing welcome supplies and equipment to beleaguered government forces.

When Roxas suddenly died in June 1948, his successor, Elpidio Quirino, offered the Huks "accommodation rather than confrontation." An attempt was made to appease the Huks through an amnesty program that brought Luis Taruc back to Manila. Taruc made several public appearances, collected back pay as a duly elected official, and then returned to the hills. He accused the government of wrong-doing and declared that the Huks would not surrender until reforms were attained.[8]

The promising overtures of compromise came to no avail. In 1950, Quirino maintained his political power in what seemed to many Filipinos to be a fixed election. The outrage that ignited in Manila did nothing to mend existing discontent throughout the barrios. Taruc and the Huks felt more convinced daily that victory lay around the corner.

Fortunately for the future of the Philippines, a thoughtful, honest, and charismatic leader emerged in 1950 and took the political scene in Manila by storm. This was the dynamic Ramon Magsaysay, whom Quirino appointed as Minister of National Defense. The forty-three-year-old congressman from Zambalas possessed a guerrilla background but had no formal military training. What he did have was the ability to attract "bright, young technocrats to his service and [inspire] the loyalty of his men."[9] Above all else, what Magsaysay had was a plan, the first part of which necessitated a trip to the United States to ask for more money. What he got when he arrived in Washington, D.C., was not the check for which he had hoped, but rather an introduction to a man that would eventually bring the most decisive changes to postwar politics in the Philippines yet seen, as well as an end to the Huk insurgency.

When Edward Lansdale was a lieutenant colonel, he was one of those officers that believed that a transfer from the army to the air force meant more "cutting edge" assignments for the future. But after his transfer in 1948, Lansdale was bored with his work. He was stationed in Denver, Colorado, as a teacher at Lowry Air Force Base and was quite unsettled with his situation.

Lansdale yearned for a more active life. After all, he had just returned from the Philippines where he had finished the war as public information officer for Armed Forces Western Pacific (later changed to the Philippines/Ryukyus Command). During the period following the Japanese surrender, Lansdale had made repeated trips into Huklandia in an attempt to uncover the true essence of the guerrilla movement. What fascinated him was the overwhelming support given to the Huks from the many barrios dotting the central Luzon plain. Villager support appeared resolute. Lansdale was not opposed to mixing in with the Huks to satisfy his curiosity further. On several occasions he could be witnessed camping on a Huk trail, often to the surprise of the guerrilla patrol that stumbled upon him. After the offer of cigarettes and a smile, there were brief opportunities to stop and speak to Huk patrol leaders about their philosophies, problems, and even tactics. Notes that Lansdale made after such meetings would prove invaluable to his future mission.[10]

During his early tenure, as his biographer Cecil B. Currey states, Lansdale also learned to walk the "labyrinthine corridors of Philippine politics." His acquaintance with political leaders from Manila, as well as newspapermen, journalists, and businessmen from the region, taught Lansdale what he considered to be the most important lessons of the time: that U.S. policy needed to take a close look at what it was attempting to accomplish in the Philippines and recognize the Filipino people as possessing ideals similar to those that once moved Americans toward independence. He believed that Filipinos and Americans shared the same ethics, principles, and dreams for democracy.[11]

His efforts paid off in that Filipinos gave Lansdale their lifelong admiration and friendship. What is more, they gave Lansdale an incurable desire to return one day and help the cause against Huk insurgency, which he wholly believed to be a misguided communist affair. That the Huks appeared to be gaining a stranglehold on the government by the late 1940s possessed Lansdale's thoughts almost daily.

Lansdale came to occupy a position as an intelligence analyst in Washington by 1949, where he was involved in the rather grey area of psychological warfare, or PSYWAR. His area of specialization was intended to be Eastern Europe, but out of habit, many discourses that he presented to senior military leaders at the Pentagon illustrated circumstances in the Philippines. By 1950, Lansdale was involved directly in preparing recommendations for the Philippine government when a friend and Filipino advisor, Major Mamerto Montemayor, introduced Lansdale to the Philippine defense minister. Magsaysay and Lansdale quickly became close friends, forming a relationship that would endure through the difficult times that lay ahead.

When Montemayor told Lansdale that Magsaysay had good ideas about changing the government's approach in dealing with the Huks, Lansdale's interest was piqued. Not only did the two discuss problems which beset the Quirino government, as well as problems with Filipino military strategy and its general officer corps, but they also found that they concurred on nearly every policy issue.[12] By the end of Magsaysay's visit to Washington, the two men had convinced policymakers that they understood the key to stabilizing the ongoing and problematic Filipino situation, and that there was little time left. The Huk insurgency was about to reach its largest gains in terrorist activity, guerrilla force numbers, and sympathetic support of the population. Shortly after Magsaysay left for home, Lansdale was packing his own bags for an extended tour in the Philippines.

When Lansdale arrived in Manila in early September 1950, he quickly took up his position with the Office of Policy Coordination (OPC) under the JUSMAG command. After some maneuvering, he managed to be essentially left alone, or at least to his own devices, and was able to report directly to JUSMAG command. Because the U.S. Central Intelligence Agency (CIA) would not absorb OPC into its ranks until the late 1950s, Lansdale had no direct affiliation with the intelligence community outside of his military links. In fact, as a means to extend his cover through OPC, Lansdale had his title changed in Washington from intelligence officer to psychological warfare officer.

His official mission was a difficult one. In just three months time, Lansdale was expected to protect American interests in the Philippines and consolidate a power base for Ramon Magsaysay. In addition, he was to provide counsel and support for the new defense minister, encourage positive change in the Philippine military, and help the government make progress in its war with the Huks, specifically by way of devising political reform that would be appealing to the people and feasible in the given time frame.[13]

The complete success of this mission brought about the demise of a serious Huk threat to the government's authority, the holding of "free" elections, and the cementing of U.S.-Philippine relations. While the end result is easy to see, what is important to this study is the path that was followed to reach such a positive outcome, or more specifically, the way in which an insurgent movement with the apparent upper hand was eventually derailed.

Success did not come easy, nor as quickly as some in Washington had hoped. But by 1953, the Huk rebellion was thwarted, Filipino corruption curtailed, and free elections held. The Huks exist to this day as guerrilla fighters, but the power base they enjoyed in the late 1940s exists no more. How did Lansdale and Magsaysay achieve this? While observers try to give credit to one man or the other, it is difficult not to view Lansdale as the true mastermind behind the success in the Philippines. Some state that Lansdale went on to groom Magsaysay for the presidency, a literal kingmaker. Still others state simply that Magsaysay was Lansdale's personal creation.[14] Perhaps a more accurate summation might be that neither had the power to change circumstances without the other. Magsaysay came along at an opportune moment in Philippine politics and at a time when Lansdale was able to advise him. Lansdale was quick to note that he intended only a background role for himself, and it was the Philippine people who should receive the credit. Much truth was perceived by Lansdale. While he possessed the concepts for success, it took the Filipinos to realize and implement those concepts. For Lansdale to see his ideas come to fruition, he knew that Ramon Magsaysay, and those following him, would have to supply the necessary leadership.

Magsaysay's talent therefore lay in an ability to understand the primary mission, the provision of effective government. Although the principal difficulties stemmed from the single popular grievance of land reform, Lansdale had always maintained that such problems were politically solvable. Heavy-handed authority and militarism was not the way to bring about a peaceful and equitable solution. Magsaysay could ensure that the government's actions were clearly defined within the parameters of furthering the primary mission: that government respect the wishes of the governed. He could also see to it that the government earnestly sought an effective, timely conclusion to the internal social strife, as well as the political turmoil, something which only discouraged democratic growth. "The blunt fact is," state two veterans of the Philippine insurgency, "that because it failed to do these things, the government of the Philippines from 1946 to 1950 failed to suppress the Huk movement."[15] Hardened discontent had led to the employment of force in order to effect a satisfactory peace. Clausewitz was correct when he implied that war is the final means by which to reach a political decision. And that war had still to be won.

Lansdale's ideas for defeating the Huk guerrillas stemmed first from the need to effectively organize. Not only was he a brilliant and imaginative man, but he was a theorist as well, and "steeped himself in the doctrines of warfare from Sun Tzu to Vo Nguyen Giap."[16] Lansdale was also a student of Mao Tse-tung's writings. He well understood Mao's three general rules: All actions are subject to command, do not steal from the people, and be neither selfish nor unjust. Mao expanded on these rules with eight remarks:

> Replace the door when you leave the house. (A frequent custom among Chinese in the countryside was to remove the doors of a house to use as a bed.) Roll up the bedding on which you slept. Be courteous. Be honest in your transactions. Return what you borrow. Replace what you break. Do not bathe in the presence of women. Do not without authority search the pocketbooks of those you arrest.[17]

These were indeed virtues on which the Filipino troops and constabulary during the preceding four years had fallen miserably short. It was also something about which Lansdale did not have to convince Magsaysay. Not long after the two men reestablished their connection in Manila, positive actions were being implemented. Magsaysay was noted for leaving in the middle of the night from his quarters, often with Lansdale at his shoulder, to spring any number of visits on an unsuspecting army field headquarters. Officers were typically not quite certain who Magsaysay was until Lansdale, usually in uniform himself, entered and explained the official nature of their visit. After the formality of salutes were exchanged, Magsaysay began tearing into file drawers, checking balance sheets, duty rosters, and whatever else came to mind. Discovering inefficiency usually did not take long, and once a thorough berating had been handed out, the commanders were given notice that no more would be tolerated. Magsaysay came from honest stock and expected the same honesty from fellow Filipinos—especially those charged with leadership in a military already in bad straits with the people. An immediate relief of command was also not beyond Magsaysay. Needless to say, Magsaysay's tactics were creating positive changes in the way officers were treating their responsibilities.[18]

One particular problem Magsaysay tackled was the continual promotion of officers who did nothing but run a desk in the safety of the rear area. There were certainly competent officers performing in necessary rear-area jobs, but Magsaysay uncovered a majority of officers who had accepted these positions as a way to get ahead. To Magsaysay, the way to get ahead in the Philippine army of 1950 was to kill Huks! And as far as he was concerned, little of that was being accomplished.

At one point, while reviewing a promotion roster, he asked about the first officer on the list and how many Huks he had killed. The answer was none. While board members extolled the virtues of the officer's noncombat performance, "Magsaysay tossed the recommendation back, refusing to consider him for promotion at [that] time. The remaining recommendations were reviewed in the same manner. All were turned down."[19] If an officer needed any clarification on how one was to be promoted under the current regime, he need only check the statistics regarding Huk battle casualties to see under who's sector of control the most kills were recorded. During the nine-month period from April to December 1950, AFP reports indicated that more than twelve hundred Huks had been killed, nearly two thousand for the entire year. By 1951, Huks were being killed at the astounding rate of forty to fifty a week.[20]

Lansdale and Magsaysay spent many hours conversing on such tactics. Killing for the sake of killing was not the purpose. In fact, it might likely be interpreted that body count was the essential ingredient to success. This posed obvious dangers, the least of which was the prospect of unconfirmed or inflated field reports. Magsaysay himself preferred, and eventually supported, a massive placement of Huk guerrillas on combined citizenry farms, giving each Huk family land to cultivate. Although such opportunities were not offered in central Luzon, the prospect of owning land by merely surrendering to the authorities seemed preferable to death. Magsaysay convinced the government of the viability of the plan by holding true to his word, making the appeal more attractive than fighting for disillusioned Huks. But before such promising avenues could be traveled, government units needed to become a force to be reckoned with for the Huk guerrillas, and a force to be trusted and relied upon for the tenant farmers. Otherwise, no Filipino was going to take the government seriously.

One critical change that Magsaysay saw to was the suspension of the writ of habeas corpus, a law which did more to protect the Huks than it did to guarantee justice. Under the old system, it was not uncommon for a suspect Huk guerrilla to be detained only to be released within a seventy-two-hour period if definite evidence on the charges could not be produced. This meant that the most carefully laid plans by the constabulary to capture Huk guerrillas were generally a waste of time, not to mention demoralizing. With the change, Huks that were captured remained captured, and were treated like the outlaws that they were. Magsaysay was pulling the government into accepting the principle of all out war, which was, he believed, the only way the government could save itself and his country from communist rule.

The Philippine army and constabulary forces were now being reworked by efficient officers into competent fighting units. One particular change for the army was the establishment of the Battalion Combat Team (BCT), a more lightly armed force that proved its efficiency in the jungles, where previous conventional units could not effectively work. Huk guerrillas found themselves being chased, cornered, and ambushed all over what was once friendly Huklandia. Though not all BCT operations were a success, the advent of such a diverse and aggressive force, one that could quickly react to sound battlefield intelligence, eventually devastated Huk guerrilla operations.[21]

Great reward also came from the way food and supplies were being denied to the guerrillas. Routes that were at one time unchallenged by government forces became critical ambush points to trap unsuspecting Huks. The sources for these Huk supplies, predominantly sympathizers in the larger towns and villages, were uncovered and broken up.

While all of these factors at one time or another were addressed or even suggested by Lansdale, perhaps his most important contribution lay within the field he embraced so wholeheartedly—psychological warfare, a discipline in which he believed his own country sadly lacked any great competency. Moreover, Lansdale possessed what was probably the perfect background to engage in a psychological warfare campaign against the Huks. Before he entered active service with the government in 1941, he ran a lucrative advertising firm in California.[22] Perhaps it is true, that the two professions, advertising and psychological warfare, do share common ground. Lansdale spent much of his time thinking up ways to implement PSYWAR and intelligence operations, and encouraged Magsaysay to create a PSYWAR division as part of his own personal staff. Thus was born the Civil Affairs Office (CAO), for which Lansdale envisioned two distinct missions: the performance of psychological combat operations, and an improvement in the attitude and behavior of troops toward civilians—"those masses whose loyalty is the imperative stake in a people's war as waged by the Communists."[23] Thus, CAO set out to make the soldiers behave as the "brothers and protectors of the people." Lansdale reflected that one of the main problems was getting troop commanders in the field to view such actions as greater than mere "politics," something outside the military realm. "If a commander were to practice civic action honestly and thoroughly," Lansdale guaranteed, "it would increase his unit's raw take of tactical intelligence by 100 percent in a week. It often took less time than that."[24]

The combat operations side of the house was where the real imagination of Lansdale took over. If one expected his PSYWAR proposals to consist of leaflets and broadcasts appealing to the enemy to surrender, as such things traditionally were, then one seriously underestimated Lansdale's view of PSYWAR as an art. Though certain proposals never made it off the drawing board, and others did not quite accomplish what was intended, most of the ideas worked splendidly. Some of these ideas deserve explanation.

One such operation included the direct work of the famed 7th BCT, under the steadfast Colonel Napoleon Valeriano. In 1947, Valeriano established a unit of soldiers who were pulled out of the conventional army and trained in unconventional methods. Although not too novel an idea on the surface, what this so-called Force X did was to pose as Huk guerrilla bands, with the entire purpose of drawing unsuspecting Huks into firefights and ambushes in which they would be at certain disadvantage. In 1950, as part of the CAO's PSYWAR program, Valeriano and the 7th BCT were called on again to form Charlie Company out of Force X veterans who volunteered. Taking the Force X principle one step further (perhaps two steps), Lansdale helped to create a unit whose sole purpose was the gathering of intelligence information. This represented serious danger for Charlie Company soldiers, as they were to eat, sleep, and breath among the Huks in the jungle while sending regular intelligence reports out to nearby BCT couriers. The success of Charlie Company was part of the reason why the Huks were being chased, cornered, and ambushed with such effectiveness by BCT units.[25]

One psychological warfare operation which Lansdale conceived had, as his biographer states, "a touch of the macabre." The story is well recounted by Lansdale himself, and crosses the border of PSYWAR into the realm of terrorism. In one particular area, Huk raids were becoming a regular occurrence, and BCT efforts to station more troops in the troubled areas were not working. The Huks felt so secure in certain towns that they openly took over after sunset. The night belonged to the enemy, so Lansdale went to work.

Stage one: He ordered PSYWAR teams to spread rumors, presumably believable, throughout public places in villages and towns, about an *asuang*, literally translated, a vampire. The stories were told in disjointed pieces and were based on the reputed soothsaying of a noted local prophet. In short, they predicted that men with evil in their hearts would be preyed upon by vampires.[26]

Stage two: They hunted for victims. PSYWAR ambush teams waited along a trail for a Huk patrol to make its way by. Letting the patrol pass, they silently snatched the last man,

... their move unseen in the dark night. They punctured his neck with two holes, vampire-fashion, held the body up by the heels, drained it of blood, and put the corpse back on the trail. When the Huks returned to look for the missing man and found their bloodless comrade, every member of the patrol believed that the "asuang" had got him and that one of them would be next if they remained.[27]

As the story goes, the patrol became so terrified that they cautiously but quickly made their way back to base camp, packed all their belongings, and abandoned their entire operation before dawn.[28]

Lansdale was shrewd enough to use local customs and superstitions to effect very real battle losses on the enemy. In these and other ways, CAO and its collection of PSYWAR teams built an impressive record of successful operations against the Huks. But in the end, it was the sum total of events that Lansdale was aiming for. Each isolated event was unimportant by itself. What mattered was the collective toll that his intelligence gathering BCT units, along with his PSYWAR infiltration teams, could level on the large population of Huk guerrilla bands. Lansdale's "total force" concept would eventually pay dividends.

Due in part to Huk miscalculation, but in much larger part to the intelligence-gathering system Lansdale had devised, the roof came crashing down on the Huk *intelligencia*. One early October morning in 1950, a Military Intelligence Service (MIS) team, waving search warrants, stormed a house in the suburbs of Manila. The raid accomplished nothing less than the capturing of the Huk politburo secretly meeting in what was thought to be a communist safe house. MIS teams were trained to carry out just such an operation and did so with perfection. Weapons, radios, code books, and the like were taken with the booty. Captured documents revealed that the Huks believed they were capable of somehow seizing power from the government relatively soon. Magsaysay and his people could never have been more grateful, for the MIS action paralyzed Huk political planning. While some of the communist infrastructure remained in the hills, the Huks could never replace what they lost on that morning.[29]

As a result, Huk guerrillas began acting in less consort after the politburo capture. Reckless and less organized terrorist actions were taking place more frequently. The result was that peasant allies were turning into government informants. Eventually, key Huk leaders remaining at large would either surrender or be hunted down and liquidated. Using the working model of insurgency from Chapter 1 as an overlay, one can see that the Huks never made it successfully out of phase one, at least not far enough to settle securely in phase two of their insurgency. In the end, Huk political organization lacked dominant and imaginative control over its terrorist and guerrilla arm, never acquired sufficient economic support to sustain its indigenous threat, and could not ultimately sway enough of the population to support its cause. With pressure from a decisive and unyielding government insurgent force, the Huks were clearly forced to make desperate moves at a time they could ill afford to do so. The critical lesson is that subversive organizations must be discovered during phase one of their insurgency, and pushed by the government insurgent apparatus into a defensive posture, one where the subversive organization is forced into countering government momentum. Under such circumstances, it might even be said that the Magsaysay government successfully usurped the insurgents' own agenda on land reform. When this was done the subversive insurgent force had little credibility with the people. Consequently, the legitimate Filipino government further "legitimized" itself by ridding the people of a potentially dangerous subversive group that appeared to be fighting only for its own self-aggrandizement.

Before Lansdale left the Philippines in 1953, Magsaysay gained the presidency. It was the crowning achievement for two men who had worked so diligently to restore the integrity of a people and its national sovereignty. Though some terrorist activity persists today at extremely low levels, the challenge of the Huk insurgency, vintage 1950, exists no more.

THE MALAYAN EMERGENCY, 1948–1960

Differences, as well as similarities, between the insurgency in the Philippines and the circumstances in Malaya are plentiful. The time period, postwar tensions, desires for national sovereignty, the challenge in political leadership, and the potential communist threat are all familiar ingredients. But while the conflict in the Philippines remained essentially an indigenous insurgency, a struggle between two separate internal political factions, the Malayan threat existed between two non-indigenous political factions—the British colonial rulers on the one hand and a Chinese population base linked to mainland China on the other. The opportunity for the Malayan Chinese to join the Malayan Communist Party (MCP), as well as their desire to separate themselves from the already diverse population mix, placed their interests and those of communist China in direct conflict with British designs for national unification and eventual independence for the Malayan people.

As with the Filipino Huks, the MCP was able to build a strong political base during Japanese occupation. The Malayan People's Anti-Japanese Army (MPAJA) was formed by Malayan Communist leaders in February 1942, and with British consent and support, it developed a guerrilla force to continue the struggle. The British were well aware of the MPAJA and its roots within the Malayan Communist Party, as well as its ultimate designs to manage a controlling political interest in Malaya after the war. But because the British also knew that the MCP was the only organization in Malaya capable of conducting guerrilla operations against the Japanese, they took a "calculated risk and supported the [MPAJA] with supplies, training, and direction."[30]

Subsequently, the MPAJA was reinforced in December 1943 when British Special Operations Executive (SOE) landed an advance element of Force 136, a special combat intelligence team that trained specifically for just such a guerrilla mission. But with the end of war in sight, the MPAJA increasingly turned its attention toward the task of planning the eventual seizure of power. The only action which curtailed that early attempt was the establishment of an effective British military administration immediately following the Japanese surrender.[31] When the war ended however, some four thousand of the original ten thousand MPAJA guerrillas remained in hiding. The coming struggle was readily apparent.

Three major ethnic groups exist on the peninsula: Malays, Chinese, and Indians. Immediate postwar attempts by the British to unify some 5.5 million people with such ethnic diversity, fell well short of the mark. The Union of Malaya, the first British plan, only created more problems for an already stumbling colonial bureaucracy. A political hiatus was thus caused by misguided planning, which suited the intentions of Malayan Communist leaders who were looking for time to develop further political support. This support came with the formation of the Min Yuen, a civilian-controlled organization which augmented the party hierarchy and broadened the support for the guerrillas in the field.

In early 1947, Ch'en P'ing replaced the ousted Loi Tak, an exposed British double agent, as the MCP secretary general. Loi Tak had suddenly disappeared, taking MCP funds with him, as well as a vast knowledge of the MCP infrastructure.[32] Things were not all going the way of the Malayan Communists following the war, and this grand disaster did everything to slow them down. Nearly a year later the Communists were still engaged in solving their internal problems, and in some quarters the Loi Tak affair was believed to hold the potential disintegration of the party.[33] Ch'en P'ing eventually rebounded from the loss, consolidated the party under the vast operations of the Chinese Central Committee, and was ready to begin a communist takeover of the government. This took place not more than three weeks after the issuing of the Loi Tak paper, which called for the greater scrutiny of future party leaders. Although the British government had received much information from Loi Tak, they failed to react quickly when he defected and therefore missed a chance to arrest several of the top party leaders before they too went into hiding to avoid capture.[34]

A major part of the MCP guerrilla force were the Min Yuen fighters, which effectively represented much of what Filipino Huks (the BUDC) were to their own brand of insurgency—the farmer-by-day, guerrilla-by-night communist soldier. In addition, there was the so-called Blood and Steel Corps, Ch'en P'ing's personal band of terrorists. This primitive organization was responsible for a growing number of strikes, bombings, extortions, robberies, sabotage operations, and murders by early 1949, but they were spread too thin and terrorist activity dropped sharply by the summer.[35]

While both the Min Yuen and the terrorists operated in the hills and in the jungle, it was the terrorists who proved most effective in the inner cities. In late 1949, Ch'en P'ing shifted many of his terrorist units from the rural arena in order to consolidate a ring of terror along the fringe of the jungle. The intent was to form communist "liberated areas." Now in phase one, terrorist activity quickly increased. Although Chinese Kuomintang leaders were the original targets of terrorist bombings and murder, uncooperative Malayans also found themselves on the wrong list. During all of 1949, some 723 people were killed, of which 494 were civilians. MCP hit-squads stepped up their activity the following year, committing some 534 acts by May alone.[36] The initiation of such widespread terrorist acts led quickly to an erosion of whatever base of support the Communist Malays had hoped for. A better understanding of why the MCP insurgency failed rests with this inability to follow perhaps the clearest of all Maoist principles, the winning over of the "hearts and minds" of the people.

In his superb analysis of the Malayan communist movement during this period, Lucian Pye indicates several reasons for the "cool reception" given the MCP by many Malays. The Malays were much more secure with social and cultural development than were the Chinese of the peninsula. Malayans were always able to turn to the country's industry, while maintaining closer ties with their traditional communities. They generally had cordial relations with the British, who were considered protectors and advisors. Thus, Malays "have been able to recognize the authority and the sternness of the British as those of a teacher and not a political foe."[37] The appeal of communism was therefore minimal among Malayans from the outset, and the hatred by the MCP of those Malays noncompliant with their own party doctrine increased.

Going further, Pye states that the "MCP was too foreign in nature to [even] offer a sense of security," especially to those Malays who showed the slightest bit of wavering. It also lacked the advantage of representing well-known institutions in the homeland. What the Communists did was to concentrate on infiltrating the leadership of existing groups, exploiting those concerns as if they were their own until their particular agenda became dominant.[38] With a few select killings here and there, the time frame for achieving that agenda seemed to shrink.

In direct relation to this Communist desire to do away with noncompliant Malays, especially those who stood intentionally in the way of MCP prerogatives, was a peculiar desire to keep Malays out of the political picture altogether. Though MCP objectives still centered upon ruling the country, its immediate purposes were served by "maximizing all desires for neutrality and non-involvement among the population. Only in very selective situations did the party require positive cooperation."[39] Participation in any form of political activity was made to seem excessively perilous. Terrorism as a tool encouraged precisely this outcome. "Thus the Emergency progressively took the form of a political struggle in which the MCP desperately sought to create a political vacuum among the Malayan Chinese."[40] Thus, the "hearts and minds" approach was not dropped in the eyes of the MCP, merely reestablished among a selective group.

Because the MCP was placing a greater reliance on terrorism as the approved method for achieving its political objectives, guerrilla units were placed under the auspices of the Malayan Races' Liberation Army (MRLA). The objective then became for the MCP to use its two elements, terrorism and the MRLA, to divide British troops in the field and the constabulary forces in the cities. The MCP was betting on certain limitations which they felt were inherent to British forces in Malaya. One was the fact that Britain, having other global commitments due to cold war tensions, would be forced to place a cap on the number of reinforcements they could send to the peninsula.

Another limitation had to do with the fact that the British were pledged to protect the Malayan population from harm. Since the MCP was directly targeting certain elements of the population through a seemingly unrestrained terrorist campaign, the British were believed to be in a no-win situation. Early on in the emergency, both limitations restricted the government's field forces from concentrating on guerrilla activities. But as police, guard, and special constabulary units were expanded, the army was released from its policing activities.[41]

To the MCP leadership, this strategy stemmed from their own interpretation of Maoist doctrine. And because of this interpretation, Gene Z. Hanrahan points out, they had no intention of relegating themselves to guerrilla warfare only. The terrorist actions were perceived as a means to effectively wage total war against the economy of a superior force, a force which the MCP believed was unwilling to suffer the kind of damage and humiliation it was felt could be leveled against it.[42] When terrorists perceived their actions as successful, the operational use of terrorism increased. This MCP model for an insurgent strategy of terror, which appeared to succeed in the early stages, from 1948 to 1950, began turning sour for the Communists by 1950, when the British introduced new emergency military measures. From 1952 to 1954 these measures bred success and the military defeat of the insurgents. After a brief foray at the bargaining table, Ch'en P'ing was turned away by a government that needed no compromise and demanded total surrender. It took five more years to complete the mopping up operations of the Communists. However, as in the Philippines, communist insurgent activities remain today at a low rumble, bombing and murder a favorite tool.

In looking at the outcome of the Malayan Emergency over a twelve-year period, one wonders whether the Communist defeat was attributable more to government success or to the failure of Malayan Communist strategy? Pye again provides the most in-depth account of Communist strategic imperfections. He cites three specific reasons for MCP failure. First, the MRLA faced tremendous logistical problems which impacted on their ability to organize large enough forces that could, at the very least, fight British troops to a stalemate. The Min Yuen also hampered MRLA organization and reduced its maneuverability in the field. Thus, by 1950, MCP security forces rather than MRLA units were engaged in the bulk of military field ambushes.[43]

Second, Pye finds that Maoist theory did more harm than good by misleading the MCP leadership at the outset. The writings of Mao Tse-tung indicate that the rural population will provide the base support for furthering guerrilla war. While in the overall revolution this strategy may need to be followed, the prospect for success in the Malayan jungles was doomed from the start. Not only is 75 percent of the terrain uninhabitable, the further the MRLA or Min Yuen receded into the deep jungle to avoid army capture, the further they ran from attainable food supplies and munitions. Since this was the very reason for establishing base camps, as Mao stated, the strategy executed by the MCP contained inherent faults which finally became irreversible.[44]

Third, the MCP was never able to solve communication problems. Crude methods of communication, which included couriers and prearranged jungle meetings, further crippled guerrilla strategy and meant that separate MRLA units could never coordinate and maneuver in a fluid manner under a centralized command. This in turn fed the demise of guerrilla operations and boosted indiscriminate terrorism.[45]

As inept as MCP actions may have been, the potential for ineptitude was equally great for a government which initially believed that it was on the defensive, and needed merely to react to insurgent tendencies. The MCP maintained the notion that terrorism alone was the primary impetus of their overall strategy. They believed the British did not possess the will to stay the course under such terrorist pressures. It is likely that most nations do not have the mettle to stay such a course, particularly when that course may be ill defined, the time frame for success unknown, and the cost too great in resources and manpower. Thus the MCP pushed hostilities in that direction for the express purpose of achieving British withdrawal.

Pye concluded that the primary reason why the MRLA did not succeed against British forces was because it could not raise an army of its own that was competent and large enough to defeat the conventional British military force.[46] However, this conclusion does not fit with the principal objective of the MCP, which was British withdrawal, not the defeat of the British military in the field. It may be difficult to understand, but the one is not equivalent to the other. It was highly possible for the Malayan Communists to have succeeded in obtaining British withdrawal, given their original strategy and the likely British reaction. But the British, much to their credit, changed their strategic philosophy from one which created reactive defenses, to one which created offensive opportunities within an insurgency framework. The outcome saw the Malayan Communists logistically too weak to then sustain a protracted struggle. All that was needed was the proper implementation.

To redefine its problem, the British Malayan government brought in the necessary planners and developed a clear course of action. The important aspect of revised British planning, much like that of Lansdale's and Magsaysay's in the Philippines, was that it was not based on futile, "counterinsurgent-type" objectives. As a result, the British were able to exploit obvious MCP inadequacies quicker and with greater precision. What the British Malayan government achieved was nothing short of stealing the initiative away from the Malayan Communists during the transition from phase one to phase two of their insurgency.

During the height of the emergency, from 1950 to 1952, the British employed a strategy which consisted of three key factors: an increase in able intelligence gathering and psychological warfare operations; small unit force structures that emphasized mobility and concentrated on specific targets; and the initiation of a "new village" program which would effectively remove the rural population base from Communist control. The first two elements, which Lansdale knew to be critical in seeking victory over the Huks, were perfected and employed by the British with clear intent. Intelligence operations became more compartmentalized, and thus, developed into a more focused government apparatus. An example of this is the development of Special Branch, an intelligence group which courted MCP suspects, encouraging surrender in exchange for amnesty. These so-called "surrendered enemy prisoners," were interrogated thoroughly, yielding much significant information about MCP planning and MRLA activities, and providing an opportunity to dispense government misinformation.[47] This misinformation campaign helped to strengthen psychological warfare operations in a way that effectively spread government propaganda into the rural areas.

The use of light military units was also something that aided the government. Much like the battalion combat teams utilized in the Philippines, British small-unit engagements were centered on closing with the enemy and destroying both him and his potential to exist. This strategy finally led to the implementation of a plan devised by a young Special Branch officer, Captain H. S. Latimer.[48] Conducted in two phases, Latimer's plan called for operations that first made a thorough reconnaissance of enemy guerrilla activities and base camps, and recorded MRLA movements and habits. Along with a thorough topographical study came an intense personality profile of MRLA leaders and supporters. Second, a curfew and a supply denial campaign were initiated with the main purpose of keeping the guerrillas from stores of food and supplies. A follow-on tactic was to bait the guerrillas into other areas which were misrepresented by Special Branch agents to be "safe areas" where food and supplies could be found. Unknowingly, the guerrillas would walk into "killing grounds," designated ambush and capture points. Because the plan eventually worked so well, guerrillas began surrendering in wholesale lots by 1954.

Third was the concept of the "new village," unique to British planning and based upon earlier British operations during the Boer War. Now centered on a scheme by General Sir Harold Briggs, the new operational chief in April 1950, it addressed the continuing problem of winning the population over to the government so as to deny the guerrillas necessary bases of support. Because the guerrillas controlled large segments of the Chinese squatter population, constabulary and security forces had a difficult time moving about existing villages and gathering intelligence information. Conversely, the guerrillas had no difficulty learning new information about government forces and intentions.[49]

Like earlier segregation schemes, the Briggs Plan was an ingenious resettlement operation, designed to move some five hundred thousand people into four hundred newly constructed villages, maintained and guarded heavily by the government. In effect, this is what would later be referred to in Vietnam as the strategic hamlet. As such, the "new villages" of the Briggs Plan allowed the successful implementation of Latimer's food denial program, a selective pacification strategy used against the MRLA. How much the MRLA was forced to channel their own supply routes to avoid government security forces was in direct relation to the number of new villages established and the number of people removed from rural areas. By 1954, the new village program reached its height when a large free zone, or "white area," was established, allowing inhabitants to go about their lives without the "irritations and hindrances of food controls, curfews, police identity checks or searches."[50] Its success allowed the proliferation of "white areas" to continue and bolstered confidence among the population when a new constitution was formed and free elections established in 1955. Eventually, "after 1959," Pye states, "it was the Security Forces rather than the MRLA who were laying most of the ambushes."[51]

Therefore, one can see that the three elements of British strategy were indeed three sequential steps, each following on the success of the previous element. The food-denial and search-and-destroy operations were successful because the new village resettlement plan effectively removed the population base of support from the guerrillas. This in turn was possible only after a thorough improvement of intelligence gathering techniques and psychological warfare operations. Because of such sweeping successes on the part of the British Malayan government, one can more easily recognize that it was the Malayan Communists who were eventually reacting to a British Malayan government offensive. The problems experienced by the MCP as outlined by Pye only sharpened in the face of certain defeat after 1954. As an insurgent movement reaches a declining state, desperate acts become even more desperate.

Several fine military and political minds surfaced for the British during this period. Officers like Briggs and Latimer helped to set the correct operational tone, while General Sir Gerald Templer, who arrived in early 1952 in the role of high commissioner, provided the necessary political outlook. But none who were involved understood the trappings of insurgency warfare better than Sir Robert Thompson. During the Second World War, Wing Commander "Bobbie" Thompson as he was affectionately known to his then boss, and commander of the famed Bush Warfare School, Brigadier Michael Calvert, made the best of an opportunity to learn the crucial techniques of guerrilla warfare—how guerrilla units interfaced with conventional force units, how they operated effectively in dense jungle terrain, and how they wielded their truly destructive capabilities on larger regular forces—this from one of the modern masters of guerrilla strategy, General Orde Wingate. Thompson and Calvert were two of a select handful of British officers who worked closely with Wingate during those early days of the Burma campaign, playing a key role in planning and carrying out operations for what would become some of he most intense and exhausting guerrilla fighting of the war. Becoming a veteran of both Chindit campaigns against the Japanese, Thompson was asked to apply his expertise after the war to the situation in Malaya, a land he was quite familiar with since joining the Malayan Civil Service in 1938.

Serving in Malaya as a civilian for the better part of a decade, the nature of his "special" assignments often making him appear a shadowy and elusive character, Thompson at first helped direct operational matters against the MCP. He soon moved to develop sound intelligence-gathering measures and combined them effectively with small combat teams in fighting the guerrillas of the Min Yuen. Finally, in 1957, he became secretary of defense for Malaya and coordinated the mop-up period to 1960. While Thompson spent time in later years deflecting attention from himself, giving credit to others for much of what he himself accomplished, his legacy of written works and future counsel to U.S. presidents remains as testimony to his strong convictions and experience in dealing with subversive insurgencies. Unfortunately, Thompson's nearly twenty-seven years of service in Southeast Asia has largely been ignored by historians.

Given the very nature of the established colonial government and the diversity of the Malayan population, Thompson never had the free rein that Lansdale experienced in the Philippines. However, Thompson's reasoning and knowledge about communist insurgencies and the success he helped to attain in Malaya won the admiration of several foreign governments. Consequently, Thompson would have a future role as head of the British mission to Saigon in the early 1960s, advising the South Vietnamese government as well as the American military assistance command. It would prove to be a far less rewarding assignment than anticipated, one fraught with jealousy, antagonism, and grave danger. And then there was the enemy.

NOTES

1. For a decidedly one-sided, but nevertheless compelling account of Huk actions and attempts at taking control after the Second World War, see Luis Taruc, *He Who Rides the Tiger* (New York: Frederick A. Praeger, 1967).

2. Asprey, *War in the Shadows*, 2:747.

3. Ibid, 748.

4. In a Rand Corporation memorandum from the late 1960s, Edward Mitchell produces a concise econometric study of the Huk rebellion, concluding that there is no one particular social group (at least in the Philippines) that is more susceptible than any other to joining a communist revolutionary organization, i.e., the Huks. Mitchell's quantitative approach was intended to illustrate how a pure economic definition of an insurgency could determine the socio-economic groups targeted by an insurgent faction. See Edward J. Mitchell, *The Huk Rebellion in the Philippines: An Econometric Study* (Santa Monica, Calif.: The Rand Corporation, 1969). Problems surfaced with Mitchell's design, and several analysts at The Rand Corporation took exception when the model was transposed to explain intelligence-gathering difficulties in Vietnam, especially after the Tet Offensive of 1968 surprised many counterinsurgency experts. For a critical, and somewhat modified approach, see Harvey Averch and John Koehler, *The Huk Rebellion in the Philippines: Quantitative Approaches* (Santa Monica, Calif.: The Rand Corporation, 1970). For a thorough analysis of lessons from the Huk rebellion, particularly those lessons based on ideas about government land-reform policies, see Uldarico S. Baclagon, *Lessons from the Huk Campaign in the Philippines* (Manila: M. Colcol & Co., 1960).

5. Eduardo Lachica, *Huk: Philippine Agrarian Society in Revolt* (Manila: Solidaridad Publishing House, 1971), 109. Lachica notes that the AFP handbook neglects to state how Chinese army officers were able to cross the South China Sea then infiltrate a Japanese-occupied country, something Lachica believes to be an improbable feat.

6. Ibid., 110.

7. Ibid., 121.

8. Ibid., 122.

9. Ibid., 130.

10. Edward Geary Lansdale, *In the Midst of Wars: An American Mission to Southeast Asia* (New York: Harper & Row, 1972), 9–12.

11. Cecil B. Currey, "Edward G. Lansdale: LIC and the Ugly American," *Military Review* 68 (May 1988): 46.

12. Cecil B. Currey, *Edward Lansdale: The Unquiet American* (Boston: Houghton Mifflin Company, 1988), 70.

13. Currey, *Edward Lansdale*, 79–80.

14. For discussion on this argument concerning the merits of Magsaysay, see Currey, *Edward Lansdale*, 89–90. For further treatment, representing Magsaysay in more individualist terms, see Nick Cullather, "America's Boy? Ramon Magsaysay and the Illusion of Influence," *Pacific Historical Review* (August 1993): 305–38.

15. Col. Napoleon D. Valeriano and Lt. Col. Charles T. R. Bohannan, *Counter Guerrilla Operations: The Philippine Experience* (New York: Frederick A. Praeger, 1962), 95.

16. Currey, "Edward G. Lansdale," 48. The study of eastern military philosophy was not made popular until Samuel Griffith published his seminal translation of Sun Tzu's *The Art of War*. Since Griffith did not accomplish this until the early 1960s, one sees just how far ahead Lansdale was from the pack of post-1945 strategists.

17. Asprey, *War in the Shadows*, 2:359–60. From Mao Tse-tung, *On Guerrilla Warfare*. For Lansdale's version of the Mao analogy about the people being the water and the guerrillas being the fish, see Currey, "Edward G. Lansdale," 51: "The people are like the water and the army is like the fish. How can it be difficult for the fish to survive when there is water?"

18. See Lansdale, *In the Midst of Wars*, 38–43, for specific anecdotes about Magsaysay's "surprise inspections."

19. Ibid., 45.

20. Lachica, *Huk*, 131.

21. For details on BCT operations from two colonels that participated in their development, see Valeriano and Bohannan, *Counter Guerrilla Operations*, 112–41.

22. Currey, *Edward Lansdale*, 68.

23. Lansdale, *In the Midst of Wars*, 70.

24. Ibid., 71.

25. Regarding Force X operations, see Valeriano and Bohannan, *Counter Guerrilla Operations*, 144–56. In reference to "Charlie Company," see Lansdale, *In the Midst of Wars*, 88.

26. Currey, *Edward Lansdale*, 102.

27. Lansdale, *In the Midst of Wars*, 72–73.

28. Currey, *Edward Lansdale*, 103.

29. Ibid., 62–64.

30. Sam C. Sarkesian, "The Malayan Emergency: The Roots of Insurgency," in his *Revolutionary Guerrilla Warfare*, 382. Also, see Sarkesian's more recent

treatment and comparative analysis of Vietnam and Malaya, in *Unconventional Conflicts in a New Security Era: Lessons from Malaya and Vietnam* (Westport, Conn.: Greenwood Press, 1993). For a good overview of the British experience with counterinsurgency operations, particularly as they culminate in Malaya, see Thomas R. Mockaitis, *British Counterinsurgency, 1919–60* (London: The Macmillan Press, Ltd., 1990).

31. Paget, *Counter-Insurgency Operations*, 44.

32. For a thorough explanation of the Loi Tak affair and its impact on the Malayan communists, see one of the more complete accounts in Anthony Short, *The Communist Insurrection In Malaya: 1948–1960* (New York: Crane Russak & Company, Inc., 1975), 38–43. Also see the name "Lai Teck" in Lucian W. Pye, *Guerrilla Communism in Malaya: Its Social and Political Meaning* (Princeton, N.J.: Princeton University Press, 1956), 83–86; and Asprey, *War in the Shadows*, 2:782.

33. Short, *Communist Insurrection in Malaya*, 42–43.

34. Loi Tak, upon his moment of defection, did, however, provide information that led to the capture of several supply and ammunition caches, much to the surprise of unsuspecting MCP officials. Nevertheless, the disappearance of Loi Tak from British hands is still a mystery. It is likely that he either remained in hiding to eventually lead other communist leagues or was hunted down and executed by a "killer squad" from China some years later. See Short, *Communist Insurrection in Malaya*, 40–41.

35. Asprey, *War in the Shadows*, 2:784. For statistics related to similar guerrilla activities in the early 1950s, see Gene Z. Hanrahan, *The Communist Struggle in Malaya* (New York: Institute for Pacific Relations, 1954), 68–69.

36. Asprey, *War in the Shadows*, 2:786.

37. Pye, *Guerrilla Communism in Malaya*, 50.

38. Ibid., 55.

39. Ibid., 103

40. Ibid. Pye states that the government's role was far more difficult in that it encouraged the Chinese to establish a free country that embraced democracy. This was of particular advantage to the MCP during the beginning of the struggle. For an example of how terrorist activities were unleashed by the MCP, see Short, *Communist Insurrection in Malaya*, 151–52.

41. Pye, *Guerrilla Communism in Malaya*, 97.

42. Hanrahan, *The Communist Struggle in Malaya*, 63–64. Hanrahan provides a good detailed analysis of how MCP officials integrated Maoist doctrine into the insurgency during this early period.

43. Pye, *Guerrilla Communism in Malaya*, 98.

44. Ibid., 99.

45. Ibid.

46. Ibid., 97. Pye further states that, ". . . this failure of the MCP is significant as a demonstration that guerrilla warfare cannot achieve victories of an enemy vastly superior by conventional military standards. Although the Security

Forces in Malaya have had a difficult and thankless task in fighting the Communists, they have proved that superior technology and resources provide the same advantages in irregular as in regular warfare" (Ibid., 95). To this statement, Asprey reacts, "nothing could be further from the mark" Yet, such beliefs are acceptable today within U.S. military circles. Such assumptions completely contradict lessons offered in other insurgencies and guerrilla actions globally, especially in the Philippines and Malaya. Asprey continues: "In Malaya, superior technology and resources played a shadow second to human performance in a war that blended civil and military factors to an almost inexplicable degree. . . . [Nothing] approached the importance of the individual working among the people, his determination and brain his best weapons." Asprey, *War in the Shadows*, 2:793.

47. For a detailed account on the effectiveness of the SEP campaign by Special Branch, see Col. Richard L. Clutterbuck, "The SEP—Guerrilla Intelligence Source," *Military Review* 42 (October 1962): 13–21.

48. For a detailed description of the Latimer Report, see Richard Clutterbuck, *Conflict and Violence in Singapore and Malaysia, 1945–1983* (Boulder, Colo.: Westview Press, 1985), 217–19.

49. Asprey, *War in the Shadows*, 2:788.

50. Quoted in Larry E. Cable, *Conflict and Myths: The Development of American Counterinsurgency Doctrine and the Vietnam War* (New York: New York University Press, 1986), 88.

51. Pye, *Guerrilla Communism in Malaya*, 98.

CHAPTER 3

The First Vietnamese Insurgency, 1945–1954

A true paradox, and, indeed, one of the more significant events relevant to the fate of American relations with Vietnam, occurred late on an April evening in 1945. At a Kunming airfield in southern China, an American C-47 landed carrying advisors from the Office of Strategic Services (OSS) who were on a mission directly initiated by President Franklin D. Roosevelt. This mission was supervised from Washington by the director of the OSS, William Donovan, and, for all intents and purposes, headed in-theater by a U.S. army captain (promotable), Archimedes L. A. Patti. Patti, in a few months time, would attempt to secure peaceable relations between Vietnam and the United States in an effort to fulfill Roosevelt's ardent desire to stem the tide of postwar European colonialism throughout Asia. The French were determined to maintain control over Indochina, and Roosevelt was, in Winston Churchill's words, more outspoken against such an arrangement after the war than about any other colonial matter.[1] The OSS mission not only produced positive relations with the Vietnamese, but helped to establish a provisional government in Hanoi that considered the United States to be its chief ally in the summer of 1945.

The paradox is really tragic double irony in that Patti and his entire OSS mission arrived in Kunming on the evening of 13 April, the very day that President Roosevelt died in Warm Springs, Georgia. The objectives of this OSS mission were apparently unknown, or at least unattended to, for a number of weeks by the most senior advisors in the new presidential administration. What seemed insignificant at first might have turned out to be one of the great opportunities in American relations with Southeast Asia, and an opportunity to take a firm stand in the direction of anti-colonialism. The initial purpose for this OSS mission was now lost with the death of Roosevelt, and so too was the rationality for any potential anti-colonialist stance by the United States. With Truman's attention focused on ending the war, events in Indochina were perceived as being a cumbersome sideshow, even a hindrance to what was believed to be the more pressing issues of maintaining a balance of power in Europe after the defeat of Germany, and seeing to the stabilization of the Asian mainland after the surrender of Japan. But nothing was as simple as the Truman administration might have hoped, and the OSS mission would be the first of many casualties in the coming American political effort in Vietnam.[2]

BACKGROUND TO INSURGENCY

After arriving in April 1945, Patti had met with a little-known Vietnamese nationalist by the name of Ho Chi Minh, who was a proven leader in war-torn Indochina fighting to oust the Japanese. He had been identified some time before by American intelligence and military leaders as the best man to establish an independent Vietnamese government.[3] Although Ho and his organization were openly known to be communists, possessing a widely regarded checkered past, they had worked hard during the Japanese occupation to provide the Allies with intelligence information, as well as to return downed Allied pilots through Japanese lines. Patti believed that Ho's ties were realistically defined within the concept of Vietnamese nationalism, more so than the communist ideology of the International Cominform.[4] When Patti left Washington, his intentions were to seek out Ho Chi Minh and the other Viet Minh political leaders at the earliest possible moment and to define their capabilities.

Patti carefully examined the Viet Minh movement in the north and rapidly surmised that it was "real, dynamic, and bound to succeed." In his reports to higher officials in both China and in Washington, Patti stated that the popular endorsement enjoyed by the Viet Minh was based upon specific political objectives and good organization. He saw the Viet Minh as a movement not to be narrowly viewed as a group of "communist expatriates aided and abetted by Moscow, Yenan, and Chungking," but as a people who thoroughly despised the French colonialist and who would do nearly anything to attain independence.[5] Patti concluded that,

... the independence movement was only a medium for the first cause—
the instinct for survival. If national independence could assure a
Vietnamese of survival, he saw the Viet Minh as the answer. It mattered
not to him whether the medium was democratic, socialistic, or
communistic. The question was to be free from want, to enjoy the fruits of
one's labor, and to exist unmolested.[6]

Patti's mission received little sympathy from the new presidential
administration. Friendly interaction with known communist leaders was
something Truman believed most Americans would not tolerate.
Moreover, in a postwar Europe, with cold war tensions mounting,
Truman did not have the desire to force instability among the allies to
satisfy Roosevelt's anticolonial passions.[7] Beyond the rancorous political
tone, Truman was also concerned about Charles de Gaulle's statements
protesting any U.S. interference in the affairs of France, including his
complaints about an "anti-French" attitude in Indochina being promoted
by U.S. officials. Truman became a much more willing listener to de
Gaulle than Roosevelt had ever been. Indeed, the world situation after
1945 appeared less stable to the United States if wartime Allied unity
became jeopardized, something that seemed probable if the French were
provoked over the question of Indochina, and certain if the British were
provoked over their holdings in India and Hong Kong. Because
Roosevelt included his vice-president in little foreign policy
decisionmaking, Truman was left to walk the tightrope of postwar affairs
void of any real experience. If any charge can be leveled against the
Truman administration in those last days of the Second World War, it is
certainly that Truman himself was unable to finesse his opponents in a
manner that would help to carry forth the vision of a postwar world left
behind by Roosevelt.[8] If any man was unprepared for Roosevelt's death,
it was Harry Truman. But this is really more a criticism of Roosevelt
than it is of Truman.

Roosevelt had maintained staunch beliefs about postwar global
security arrangements and accepted Indochina as a key to maintaining
that security, not only for friendly nations throughout Southeast Asia, but
for the entire Western Hemisphere. It was believed that colonialist
tensions in the region would not allow the United States to effectively
maintain peace in its design for postwar global stability, perhaps the most
important objective in Roosevelt's agenda leading up to the Yalta
conference in February 1945. Roosevelt believed, as had many, that
America had spent enough in blood and treasure to now take the lead in
international policy matters. Such matters clearly advocated an end to the

influx of European colonial states, particularly in Asia. In the search for global stability, Indochina was desired as a "strategic base" from which both the United Nations and the United States could better maintain the postwar peace.[9]

Working from this philosophical directive, and after months of preparation, Patti was not about to change his intention to establish a working relationship with the Viet Minh. Furthermore, the Viet Minh leadership believed the sincerity of the U.S. mission in Hanoi to be a preamble to open relations and recognition of a sovereign Vietnamese state. That this "new" Vietnamese state should somehow remain within the sphere of French control was inconceivable to the Viet Minh leadership. Patti believed that what he and the other OSS advisors were doing was crucial to postwar relations, and he made friends among the Vietnamese quickly. Viet Minh leaders "succeeded in establishing close, if not deeply sincere, bonds with the United States representatives in Hanoi."[10]

It still conjures ghostly images to think of that sultry September day in Hanoi when the American national anthem rang out while Vietnamese stood saluting the Stars and Stripes flying along-side the Viet Minh flag, and Ho Chi Minh read familiar quotes from the American Declaration of Independence. To commemorate Vietnamese independence, Patti and the American advisors were invited to a short ceremony in honor of the occasion as personal guests of Ho.[11] It was 2 September 1945 and war with Japan was over. Rapidly the French, as well as the British, were working hard to reestablish their prewar Asian empires.

Such a notion of independence was a long way to come in just four months time for the Vietnamese, particularly after some eighty years of stiff colonial rule by the French. Patti knew it and so did Ho. But the relationship enjoyed by both men in fostering what the Vietnamese hoped would be a nationalist partnership was coming to an end. As early as May 1945, the entire OSS mission to Hanoi was in question, as was Roosevelt's earlier anti-colonialist designs in the region. With a potential invasion of Japan looming after the defeat of Germany, Truman was not ready to throw off potential military assistance from France, or Great Britain. In a lengthy cable, General [later Ambassador] Patrick Hurley voiced concern to President Truman over the American delegation at the United Nations conference in San Francisco which "seemed to support the theory of imperial control of colonies and dependent nations by the separate or combined imperialist nations and not a United Nations trusteeship."[12] The acceptance of trusteeship was central to the anticolonialist cause, if only that it provided a vehicle to project U.S. power in what was perceived by Roosevelt to be America's primary role in global security after war ended. If Hurley's concerns proved to be true, it would seem to undermine the entire American intelligence mission in Indochina.

In late May the White House sent the State Department a reply that focused on the British reoccupying Hong Kong and the French reinstating themselves in Indochina: "The President has asked me [Hurley] to say that there has been no basic change in [U.S.] policy."[13] In other words, the idea of trusteeship was fading fast. Patti writes:

Sometime in mid-June [Col. Richard] Heppner [Chief of OSS, China] was given the opportunity to see the full text of the message and was authorized to divulge pertinent passages to selected members of his staff. . . . To Heppner and me it was obvious that the Truman administration had capitulated to de Gaulle's insistence that Indochina could be placed in trusteeship only with the consent of France.[14]

The results of this communiqué proved to be the noose that would strangle the whole OSS postwar mission to Indochina.

By the end of September, Patti had received the change of orders which reflected Truman's intentions about policy for the region. Patti and other OSS team members had already become less favored in Hanoi after a U.S. State Department cable reached the Viet Minh on 25 October, which stated blandly: "The United States will respect French sovereignty in Indochina."[15] The end of October saw the evacuation of the OSS mission from Indochina, and soon after, intelligence operations in China would "die a quick death, unnoticed by the American public, who were to [later] pay dearly for the omission."[16]

Such was Patti's evaluation of the events America found itself a part of at the end of the Second World War. Roosevelt's Indochina gambit had failed. From this point on, U.S. policy appears to be extremely consistent with the public record, that is, encouraging a resolution through French channels. It would appear that the United States missed at least a partial opportunity to help stabilize the region, even to win the hearts and minds of a people little before noticed by American foreign policymakers. Although it would not be the last opportunity, the Patti OSS mission may very well have been the first, and perhaps best chance at securing some kind of peaceable resolution in Vietnam politics.[17] However, it would have meant siding with the Viet Minh, the only faction in Vietnam at the end of the war that showed any real viability at being able to govern. As time went on, the United States would attempt recognition of a host of different Vietnamese governments and political personalities, none of which possessed the quality of leadership that stabilized the Viet Minh.

Circumstances remained volatile during this evanescent period in Vietnam politics. Throughout the remainder of 1945, and most of the following year, the Viet Minh spent time consolidating their insurgent political apparatus. Although Ho Chi Minh was president of a new provisional government, planning by Viet Minh leadership continued along the lines of a phase one insurgency. It was known that the French had pledged themselves to consolidate power in Indochina. This included an Indochinese Federation to be made from the countries of Cochin China, Annam, Tonkin, Cambodia, and Laos. The Viet Minh were viewed merely as an inconvenient and dangerous roadblock to French interests. It got to a point where Ho believed it was realistic to expect military opposition from the French sooner than later. After a series of attempts to establish a compromise between the Viet Minh and the French fell through, shooting began in late 1946.

Progressively, the international situation changed to such a degree that the French presence in Indochina became appealing to the United States, which found itself "hard-pressed to provide economic and particularly military resources necessary to fight a world-wide cold war."[18] Nearly five years would pass before Ho Chi Minh would completely turn his back on the United States. "Relations" continued between the United States and Hanoi until as late as 1948.[19] But, with Mao's victory over Chiang Kai-shek in 1949, and the outbreak of the Korean conflict in June 1950, France and the United States eventually found themselves "vilified equally" by the Viet Minh.[20]

PHASES OF VIET MINH INSURGENCY

For the Viet Minh, the official date of commencement for the War of Resistance was 19 December 1946. The sudden attack upon French forces was quickly realized by Viet Minh leaders to be ill advised. The strength and quality of the Viet Minh forces was revealed to be lacking the decisive combat edge and physical character necessary to dispel French control, let alone wage a competent phase two insurgency. General Vo Nguyen Giap possessed an "over anxious" tactical character as well, and this fiasco was case in point. The Viet Minh had barely arrived at phase one of their insurgent movement when Giap took it upon himself to initiate conventional fighting against well defended French positions. Strategically, this was not guerrilla or mobile warfare as promulgated by Mao Tse-tung, but positional warfare, the very thing Mao cautioned against. In discussing these three types of war—positional, mobile, and guerrilla—Mao stated:

> . . . the pivotal strategy must be mobile warfare. Positional warfare is also necessary, but strategically it is auxiliary and secondary.
> . . . So long as we lack a large army or reserves of ammunition, and so long as there is a single Red Army force to do the fighting in each base area, positional warfare is generally useless to us. For us, positional warfare is generally inapplicable in attack as well as in defense.[21]

By the spring of 1947, the Viet Minh had retreated in desperation to the mountainous areas surrounding Hanoi. In March, Ho Chi Minh asked that negotiations with the French be reopened, but was rebuffed as the French simply replied with terms for an armistice. When Ho flatly refused these terms, French offensive operations were launched in turn with tremendous ferocity. So devastating were these initial French attacks that by October they barely missed destroying Giap's forces and capturing Ho Chi Minh himself.[22]

These vastly complicated military operations, known as "Lea," were designed exclusively to destroy the enemy's battle force or capture the insurgent leadership. Bernard Fall states accurately that

> As yet unacquainted with the principles of revolutionary war, the French were thus unaware that capture of the enemy's leadership might be only a temporary blow, not necessarily knocking the enemy out of the fight. The Dutch, for example, captured Sukarno and his staff without altering the fate of their war with the Indonesians; and the capture of several senior Algerian leaders (notably Ben Bella) by the French in 1956 in no way altered the outcome of the Algerian War. . . . "Lea" failed . . . leaving much of Viet-Nam's countryside open to Communist infiltration.[23]

The French were successful in their initial efforts to chase the Viet Minh from Hanoi. But this led to a belief that the war against the Viet Minh was purely a military struggle, one that only necessitated a military solution. Consequently, by the close of 1947, the French were less willing to listen at the political bargaining table, and the French Expeditionary Force to Indochina increased troop numbers significantly. As the year went on, the French forces filled out with units of Algerians, Moroccans, Tunisians, Senegalese, and French Foreign Legion troops, bringing the total of in-country forces under French control to over one hundred thousand. To further complicate and blur their vision to the real fight against the political subversives who were now struggling in phase one, the French also brought in large numbers of tanks, armored personnel carriers, heavy artillery, aircraft, and coastal gunboats.[24]

Impressive as this show of force may have been, the intent seemed to be more of a bluff. When the rainy season ended in October, the French launched no significant offensive operations against the Viet Minh until 1948. Giap concluded from this that the French were accepting a defensive posture and had reduced their goals for success in the region. The French launched small search and destroy operations, but the results were far from conclusive. It is questionable whether French units actually identified any Viet Minh base camps at all, something that should be the priority of any early government military action against an insurgency. It appeared that the French were more concerned with posing a military threat in the hope that it would be a deterrent to actual bloodshed and lead to a peaceful resolution on their terms.[25] Giap surmised correctly when he later judged that the chance for French success had slipped dramatically after 1947.

All indications to the French were that their efforts were paying off. This despite the fact that Operation Lea had failed and that the Viet Minh were gaining greater control of the countryside. Asprey states that "perhaps French commanders would have admitted some concern had the Viet Minh fielded its own army. Lacking direct confrontation, [they] spoke in terms of mopping-up operations. They failed to realize either that the Viet Minh were building a regular army behind a screen of guerrilla operations, or that the Viet Minh were simultaneously mobilizing large parts of the population to fight a war beyond the limits of their comprehension."[26]

Now committed to insurgency against the French, Viet Minh leaders consolidated their resources and prepared for a protracted struggle. Although the Viet Minh launched limited guerrilla operations against the French from 1946 to 1949, most operations were terrorist in nature, intended to sidetrack the French.[27] This first phase of the insurgency effort was used by Ho and Giap to build forces, to indoctrinate their soldiers, and to cultivate leadership. The greatest error would be an attempt to prematurely move into phase two, risking everything on an enemy that had already assumed the defensive. While French capabilities could not be underestimated, the Viet Minh could not afford to overestimate their own abilities again.[28] There was a need to go back to basics.

In Mao Tse-tung's four golden rules we find the following wisdom advanced:

1.   When the enemy advances—we retreat.
2.   When the enemy halts—we harass.
3.   When the enemy avoids battle—we attack.
4.   When the enemy retreats—we follow.

Edgar O'Ballance astutely compares these four principles with seven principles formulated by Giap during this period of rethinking. This was Giap's way of translating Maoist doctrine into a tactical hierarchy for fixing Viet Minh problems, and are indicative of the real difficulties they were having in understanding Maoist doctrine. As a way to help develop a clear line of communication between his officers and men, particularly in gaining a clearer understanding of the commanders' battlefield intent, Giap advanced his own principles: (1) good intelligence gathering; (2) surprise and deception; (3) aggressive will to fight on; (4) resolute attitude; (5) secrecy; (6) speed and swiftness; (7) aim of perfection.[29]

Problems had been encountered regarding the recruitment and indoctrination of leaders. Many officers were weeded out and good replacements found, replacements who would follow directives from above. Also, in December 1949, Mao Tse-tung, in firm control north of the Indochina border, sent a political-military mission to assist Ho. This was a most welcomed and timely visit. Ho himself returned the visit in April of the following year to ask for material assistance. Material aid was promised and delivered that same year.[30]

It became apparent that the Viet Minh were now gradually moving from phase one into phase two. Along with an increase in military activity against the French, the Viet Minh began taking French prisoners, whether from guerrilla or terrorist engagements. Though it is not unusual for subversive insurgents to take prisoners, the vast numbers taken by the Viet Minh proved to be unmatched by other subversive groups, including the MCP and the Huks. Between the years 1945 and 1950, the Viet Minh captured some two thousand French prisoners. During the fight at Cao Bang Ridge in October 1950, a French disaster of great proportion, another six thousand French prisoners were taken. The curious aspect to this is that the Viet Minh never built or maintained prisoner of war camps until the number of French prisoners rose to almost ten thousand. Prisoners were usually kept in tow behind Viet Minh headquarter units; when they moved, the prisoners moved.[31] It is astounding that a single insurgent group to which the French gave so little credit could not only take large numbers of prisoners, but could also build the needed POW facilities to keep them in.

Giap saw the winter of 1949 to 1950 as a period of visible progress for the Viet Minh. "The rate of preparation increased, offensive actions became more frequent and daring, and small units were developing into larger line units."[32] Because Giap believed that the Viet Minh were already in Mao's second stage (our phase two), his intentions were to begin emphasizing regular force operations and lessen guerrilla activity. There were several reasons that appeared to justify Giap's beliefs. By early 1950 the size of the Viet Minh regular forces was approaching that of the French Expeditionary Force, which was now clearly on the defensive. Moreover, captured French prisoners reported declining morale among the ranks of otherwise noted elite French units. The arrival of Red Chinese troops at the border in late 1949 portended outside aid. As well, French delays over Vietnamese independence angered a growing majority of the Vietnamese people.[33]

Militarily and morally supported, Giap announced in February 1950 that the period of guerrilla warfare was over and the final stage, which he called "the general counteroffensive," was about to begin. Most observers agree that Giap was premature and that he might have said that, while guerrilla warfare would become less important, they would not abandon it altogether. In fact, Giap was again proving overanxious in his estimation of the situation, counting on what he thought the Viet Minh were capable of doing versus what they were actually able to do.[34] O'Ballance explains, "Giap did not understand the theory of the progressions of guerrilla warfare as well as Mao Tse-tung, although he was very realistic. His terms and expressions were at times loose and a little blurred. Giap was always the opportunist, always a trifle eager and always a little headstrong. Ho Chi Minh, more cautious and patient, complemented him perfectly."[35]

But Giap's first assaults of 1950 came early and came swiftly. In northeastern Tonkin a string of French fortifications were easily overrun by Viet Minh forces made up of five regular-force regiments aided entirely by the guerrilla actions of regional units, who provided delaying and ambush operations against French retreat. Ensuing campaigns against Lao Kai, Dong Khe, and Cao Bang Ridge lasted throughout the summer and into October. Throughout those difficult months, Viet Minh guerrillas interdicted French supply columns while regular-force units were moved in from outlying training areas to take up the fight. It looked as if Giap had indeed calculated correctly as they moved from primary into secondary insurgency without problems.

At the start of Giap's offensive in 1950, French commanders erred in two ways. First, they were still reluctant to believe that Giap possessed the Chinese aid necessary to fight lengthy campaigns. In fact, Chinese advisors had already reported with aid in hand some weeks before operations began. Second, Giap had always kept his main force out of the way of battle, and the French believed he would continue to do so.[36] With over sixty battalions of Viet Minh regular troops at his disposal, Giap operated with the confidence of a general no longer embroiled in an insurgency. This is easy to understand since he never fought with less than a three-to-one advantage. At Cao Bang Ridge alone he possessed an advantage of eight-to-one. However, Viet Minh efforts would soon bog down again.

During the following year Viet Minh fortunes were reversed. Defeats at Vinh Yen, Mao Khe, and the Day River severely shocked Giap. Circumstances became so desperate that Ho Chi Minh had trouble retaining his position until a scapegoat, by the name of Nguyen Binh was found. As leader of the regional forces, Nguyen Binh had provided perhaps the best possible diversionary tactics in the raids and ambushes through which he had led his guerrilla units, buying much-needed time for Giap to withdraw his regular forces when it became necessary to do so. It is hard to believe that any one officer, other than Giap, could be blamed for the over aggressive policies of 1951, particularly someone like Nguyen Binh who had performed so well, though in a much lesser role. Never able to clear himself, Nguyen Binh was killed in an engagement with French troops after being recalled to Viet Bac.[37]

With the crisis over, Ho Chi Minh concentrated upon strengthening his political hold once again. As for Giap, any hopes he harbored of reinvigorating a conventional-force offensive would have to wait. As in 1946, Giap's overanxiousness had cost the Viet Minh dearly. Although 1950 had begun with such promise and optimism, success was not to be. The Viet Minh were forced into rebuilding the following year. In 1946 Giap had tried to move too quickly from phase one into phase two of the insurgency. In 1950, after succeeding in reaching phase two, Giap had tried to move prematurely from primary to secondary insurgency, into what Mao represented as "mobile warfare." Without sufficient strength, equipment, or reserves, the Viet Minh had been unable to carry the assault to the capital city. The thought of reverting back to guerrilla warfare was something Giap approached with despair. But, in fact, he had never actually left phase two, and that phase of guerrilla operations was what the Viet Minh needed to spend time perfecting.

Taking a long look at their previous campaigns and comparing old notes on guerrilla tactics with a closer scrutiny of Maoist doctrine, Giap

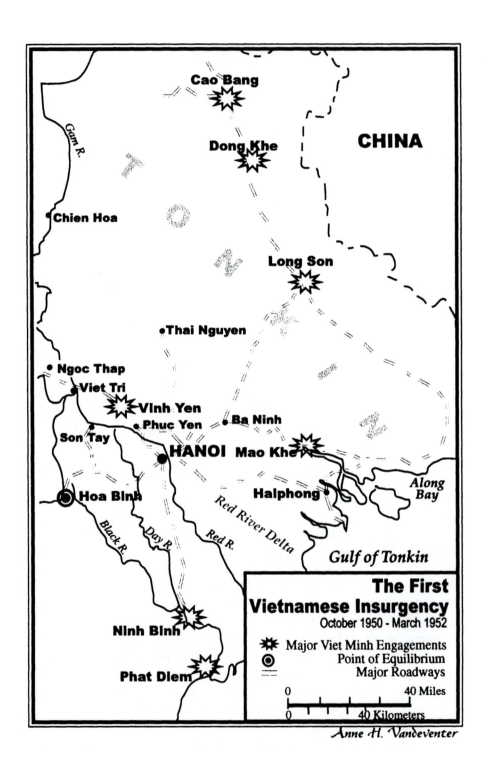

CHINA

Cao Bang

Dong Khe

Chien Hoa

T O N K I N

Long Son

•Thai Nguyen

• Ngoc Thap

•Viet Tri

Vinh Yen

• Phuc Yen

• Ba Ninh

Son Tay

HANOI

Mao Khe

Along
Bay

Hoa Binh

Haiphong

Red River Delta

Black R.

Day R.

Red R.

Gulf of Tonkin

Ninh Binh

Phat Diem

**The First
Vietnamese Insurgency**

October 1950 - March 1952

✹ Major Viet Minh Engagements
◎ Point of Equilibrium
--- Major Roadways

0   40 Miles

0   40 Kilometers

Anne H. Vandeventer

Gam R.

hoped to consolidate his forces along a more solid foundation. Perhaps the biggest change in Giap's thinking was that the regional troops would now bear the brunt of the fighting and would continue to do so until he was absolutely certain that his regular forces could engage the French in effective "mobile warfare."[38] As reflected upon by Mao, this meant that guerrilla operations from phase two would need to exact a greater toll on French forces than Giap had originally intended. He hammered lesson after lesson home to his regular officers and his lowliest part-time guerrilla commanders alike. One must believe that he did much soul searching, for he blundered twice. A third blunder might bring an end to the Viet Minh altogether.

Throughout much of the political apparatus and structure of subversive organizations, selective acts of terrorism and intelligence-gathering operations during the guerrilla phase remain consistent with previous examples (see Chapter 2). The one factor that sets the Viet Minh apart from other insurgents is their ability to move into a secondary insurgency when it became necessary to do so. This ability is not found in either of the subversive failures in Malaya or the Philippines. For the Viet Minh, it was translated into Mao's principles on a "war of movement." Giap knew, after the military blunders in 1946 and again in 1951, that thorough preparation was necessary if viable regular-army units were to be employed in fighting the French. Giap had believed that, by the end of 1950, with a substantial increase in recruits, competent training, and expertly led regular forces of their own, the Viet Minh would be able to target the French regular forces. But timing was everything, and Giap had suffered two separate reverses.

The fact that Giap and the Viet Minh were able to rebound so effectively is owed to the stagnation of French forces in the north. The French defensive posture continued, allowing Giap to steal away and reconsolidate again. Though the Viet Minh were not as vulnerable as they had been after the 1946 failure, they were confused and distraught. A government force with half as much initiative as the French, and with at least some rudimentary understanding about insurgency war, could have systematically destroyed Giap's guerrilla units in phase two. Fortunately for Giap, the French solution was simply one of conventional military posturing.

Giap, through later writings, attempted to justify his "premature" decisions in 1946 and 1950 by referring to his own "precepts of revolutionary warfare." He indicated that,

. . . the general law of a long revolutionary war is usually to go through

three stages: defensive, equilibrium and offensive. . . . Following the
failure of the enemy offensive at Viet Bac, equilibrium gradually came into
being. We decided to launch an extensive guerrilla war. From 1950
onward, campaigns of local counter-offensives were successively opened
and we won the initiative on the northern battlefield.[39]

Reference made by Giap to his three precepts of revolutionary
war—defensive, equilibrium, and offensive—directly correspond to
Mao's precepts on guerrilla war: strategic defensive, strategic offensive,
and development into mobile war.[40] Neither of these theories accurately
relates to our definition of insurgency war, nor do they precisely indicate
what was accurately happening with the Viet Minh. However, both
theories maintain the general theme, and indeed help to clarify the timing
for transition from primary to secondary insurgency. As we have already
discussed, Mao's idea of "mobile warfare" (or a "war of movement")
most closely represents our movement from primary to secondary
insurgency. Giap's interpretation of this transition to mobile warfare, as
compared to Mao's, is crucial:

Guerrilla warfare gradually developed to mobile warfare—a form of
fighting in which principles of regular warfare gradually appear and
increasingly develop but still bear a guerrilla character. Mobile warfare is
the fighting way of concentrated troops, of the regular army in which
relatively big forces are regrouped and operating on a relatively vast
battlefield, attacking the enemy manpower, advancing very deeply then
withdrawing very swiftly, possessing to the extreme, dynamism, initiative,
mobility and rapidity of decision in face of new situations.[41]

The moment at which this transitional aspect occurs is perhaps best
represented in Giap's stage of "equilibrium," the idea being that
equilibrium must be achieved before transition to secondary insurgency
(Mao's "war of movement") is possible. When Giap announced in late
1950 that the great Viet Minh "counteroffensive" was about to begin,
then promptly failed against French defenses that next year, it is possible
to accept that his failure was one of misjudging the exact moment of
equilibrium.[42]

Equilibrium should not be seen as a precise moment during the
insurgency, but rather as a series of events that lead up to an apparent
change, or switch, in overall momentum. In specific relation to this point,
Michael Elliot-Bateman explains, in his superb analysis of Maoist theory
and practice, that a "point of balance" was reached by the French and the
Viet Minh somewhere between November 1951 and February 1952.[43]

The French, unable, or unwilling, to hold onto their defensive position at Hoa Binh after a lengthy struggle with the Viet Minh, managed to pull out and avert defeat at the last moment. The Viet Minh, who were unwilling to occupy Hoa Binh during this period, also abandoned their efforts along the Black River in southern Tonkin at the last moment, in favor of not providing the French with any fixed target or fortification to counterattack. The added bonus for the Viet Minh was that this battle, a fight Bernard Fall called "the meat-grinder," caused the French to begin receding from the Red River delta.[44] Because both opposing forces might also be seen as having maneuvered into a stalemate with one another, leaving nothing to be gained by continuing siege or defense, Giap's "balance point" with French forces was achieved.[45] When a state of equilibrium is reached by both sides, the subversives must act quickly in order to escalate the conflict by unleashing the final and decisive strategy of secondary insurgency. As explained in the first chapter, guerrilla operations take on a lesser role, while the regular forces are mobilized in such a way as to take on the primary military role. As in the example of Hoa Binh, large maneuver forces may be employed to accomplish that task.

Since our definition of insurgency accepts that the subversive organization must already be in a state of political, economic, and military balance in order to successfully conduct primary insurgency during phase two, the move to secondary insurgency must occur as a result of opposing force capabilities and inabilities. This is a key difference between Mao's precepts on "mobile warfare" and our explanation of insurgency. It is not necessary for secondary insurgency to take place unless the circumstances for subversive victory dictate such a move and the balance of force between the subversive insurgents and their opposition allow it to happen. It is clear that in the case of Malaya and the Philippines, government opposition to the subversive insurgency would not allow a successful move out of primary insurgency to occur. Although it may not always assure subversive victory, if secondary insurgency is an objective and is at some point attained by the subversives, it will prove tremendously difficult, if not wholly impossible, for the opposing forces to reacquire the initiative. This is particularly true when that opposing force is non-indigenous to the population base.

For the Viet Minh, the move into secondary insurgency after Hoa Binh brought them exponentially closer to the revolution that they sought. Failure on two successive occasions had not been met with decisive, or even competent French countermoves, but rather the establishment of fixed fortifications begging to be overrun by even the lightest of Viet Minh guerrilla units. Consequently, from the moment equilibrium was reached, the Viet Minh moved in for the final chapter of the removal of the French colonial regime. In borrowing from one group of authors, we find that "when the insurgents become strong enough to engage counterinsurgent troops on a large scale, . . . the insurgency has been transformed into essentially a civil war (or, in the case of insurgency against a colonial power or an invading army, a quasi-conventional war against a foreign power)."[46] However, it is clear that, in order for the Viet Minh to achieve revolution, they needed to establish something more conclusive than subversive brute force. They needed to become the national cause.

As established in Chapter 1, a successful insurgency does not typically represent a national cause, where, in fact, revolution must if it is to succeed. As well, the hierarchy of a subversive movement alone is not enough to establish and carry forth a successful revolution. The support of an even broader majority of the people is necessary for the insurgency to transform itself into revolution or civil war. Ho Chi Minh appears to have understood early on that national revolution is impossible without identifying, or at least seeming to identify, an accepted national agenda.[47] Thus, even though secondary insurgency was achieved, and perhaps would be able to be maintained for an indefinite course, for the Viet Minh to evolve from insurgency into a national, or anticolonial revolution, they would need to have broader appeal.

Only after insurgency war was well under way did the vision of revolution come into clear perspective for the Viet Minh—its formal purpose, timeline for accomplishment, and the mechanisms to be implemented. When the notion of U.S. support evaporated in 1945, and war with France over political sovereignty appeared immanent, insurgency became the natural vehicle to achieve revolution. In 1951, after consolidating the major communist and nationalist movements in the north, Ho Chi Minh changed the official party name to the Viet Nam Dang Lao Dong Party (Vietnam Workers' Party). The somewhat isolated personality of the Viet Minh was broadened for greater public appeal. The hope was to reel in a larger cross section of the population.[48] The year 1951 also saw active support from the communist Chinese who had already succeeded at their own revolutionary/civil movement. Estimates of popular support, both internally and externally, increased after Viet Minh competency was exemplified throughout phase two of the insurgency, and Chinese support became visible. Thus, broader public appeal for the Viet Minh cause came about due to positive internal, as well as external political changes.

Militarily, the Viet Minh were succeeding against a European power. After reconsolidation and a return to guerrilla warfare in 1951, the Viet Minh retained their chance to achieve equilibrium and therefore transition into secondary insurgency. The successful move into secondary insurgency after the Hoa Binh stalemate, coupled with continued French military errors, brought a sense of realization to the Vietnamese citizenry that perhaps revolution and an independent Vietnamese state was not impossible. By the end of 1953 there can be little doubt that the French were being defied by something larger than a small subversive group. Indeed, the Viet Minh were becoming the national cause.

NOTES

1. Robert Dallek, *Franklin D. Roosevelt and American Foreign Policy, 1932–1945* (London: Oxford University Press, 1979), 461.

2. Archimedes L. A. Patti, *Why Vietnam? Prelude to America's Albatross* (Berkeley, Calif.: University of California Press, 1980), 61.

3. The first formal findings on Ho Chi Minh in U.S. intelligence files exist in OSS/State Department Intelligence and Research Reports, Postwar Japan, Korea, and Southeast Asia, *Biographical Information on Prominent Nationalist Leaders in French Indochina*, Indochina, no. 11 (25 October 1945): 1–99 (Washington, D.C.: University Publications of America, 1977, text-fiche), 15–16. The biographical passage is slanted heavily toward Ho's "communist" sympathies and mentions little about nationalist ties or early desires to ally with the United States.

4. Ho Chi Minh was first pressed into service for the Allied cause in 1943 after extensive negotiations between the OSS and the Chinese. Ho had been a "guest" of Marshal Chang Fa-kwei at the Tienpao prison since early 1942 for conduct against the Chinese government. For details on Ho's early collaboration with the OSS and his nationalist relationship with the United States, see Patti, *Why Vietnam?* 49–58.

5. Along these same lines other sources echo similar arguments: ". . . the U.S. failed to recognize in Ho Chi Minh a potential Asian 'Tito.' This view holds that Ho has always been more concerned with Vietnam's independence and sovereign viability than with following the interests and dictates of Moscow and Peking. With U.S. support . . . Ho would have adopted some form of neutrality in the East-West conflict and maintained the DRV as a neutral and durable bulwark against Chinese expansion southward. Thus, if it were not for 'U.S. communist blinders,' Ho would have served the larger purposes of American policy in Asia."

In *The Pentagon Papers: The Defense Department History of United State Decisionmaking on Vietnam*, Senator Gravel ed., (Boston: Beacon Press, 1971), 1:47–48.

6. Patti, *Why Vietnam?* 131–32.

7. This argument is not a new one. The French journalist Bernard Fall first discusses the Truman reversal of Roosevelt's "anti-colonialist" intentions in his 1967 book *Last Reflections on a War*. Here, Fall categorizes six periods of American-Vietnamese relations: "(1) Anti-Vichy, 1940–1945; (2) Pro–Viet Minh, 1945–1946; (3) Non-involvement, 1946–June 1950; (4) Pro-French, 1950–July 1954; (5) Non-military involvement, 1954–November 1961; (6) Direct and full involvement, 1961–." According to Fall: "Whether this was due to a deliberate policy in Washington or, conversely, to an absence of policy, is not quite clear. . . . The United States, preoccupied in Europe, ceased to be a diplomatic factor in Indochina until the outbreak of the Korean War." Quoted in *The Pentagon Papers*, Gravel ed., 1:1. Also see Bernard B. Fall, *The Two Viet-Nams: A Political and Military Analysis* (New York: Frederick A. Praeger, 1963), 49–54.

8. Jean Lacouture states: "At the end of 1949, impelled chiefly by the need to preserve France's loyalty within the framework of the Atlantic Pact, Secretary of State Dean Acheson persuaded President Truman to turn his back even more fully on the Rooseveltian tradition in Indochina by backing the French war effort there." See Jean Lacouture, *Ho Chi Minh: A Political Biography*, trans. Peter Wiles, trans. ed. Jane Clark Seitz (New York: Random House, 1968), 273. As a follow-on, see Acheson's views spelled out in Memorandum for the President from the Department of State (2 February 1950), in *The Pentagon Papers*, Gravel ed., 1:64–65.

9. Dallek, *Franklin D. Roosevelt*, 461–63 and passim. The author provides insightful accounts of the situation between Roosevelt and de Gaulle at the end of the war and illuminates intentions on the part of the United States toward Indochina during the postwar years.

10. Lacouture, *Ho Chi Minh*, 115.

11. Ibid. For an intriguing account of the events from Patti's perspective, see Patti, *Why Vietnam?* 223–24. Ho Chi Minh was fascinated with American culture, and moreover, with America's tradition of "anti-colonialism." Ho believed Abraham Lincoln to be the complete "antiracist," which to Ho implied anti-colonialist. Lacouture writes: "One result of his brief American experience was a deep absorption of Lincoln's speeches and writings. Even before the proclamation of independence in 1945, [Ho's] work as a journalist and polemicist was faintly inspired by Lincoln's ideas." See Lacouture's discussion about Ho's "Lincolnisms," 263–65.

12. Ibid. For an excellent summary of Roosevelt's concept of trusteeship as it pertained to Indochina, see *The Pentagon Papers*, Gravel ed., 1:9–15; also see Dallek, *Franklin D. Roosevelt*, 536–37 and passim; David G Marr, *Vietnam 1945: The Quest for Power* (Berkeley, Calif.: University of California Press, 1995), passim. Overall, for one of the finest narratives of this period, see William J.

Duiker, *The Communist Road to Power in Vietnam* (Boulder, Colo.: Westview Press, 1996), passim.

13. See partial reprint of Hurley cable in Patti, *Why Vietnam?* 119–20.

14. Ibid., 120.

15. Lacouture, *Ho Chi Minh*, 271–72.

16. Patti, *Why Vietnam?* 364.

17. Lacouture states: "One may doubt whether without [the OSS mission] the Viet Minh would have emerged so strongly and so quickly or whether the confidence of the new leaders would have been so complete." In *Ho Chi Minh*, 269.

18. Asprey, *War in the Shadows*, 2:692.

19. One striking note about U.S.–Viet Minh options comes from a cablegram by an American diplomat in Hanoi, identified as Landon, to the State Department, entitled, "Report on Ho's Appeals to U.S. in '46 to Support Independence," in Neil Sheehan et al., *The Pentagon Papers: As Published by the New York Times* (New York: Bantam Books, Inc., 1971), 26.

20. Lacouture, *Ho Chi Minh*, 273.

21. *Mao Tse-tung on Revolution and War*, 287, 291.

22. Edgar O'Ballance, *The Indo-China War, 1945–1954: A Study in Guerrilla Warfare* (London: Faber and Faber, 1964), 85; George K. Tanham, *Communist Revolutionary Warfare: From the Vietminh to the Viet Cong* (Santa Monica, Calif.: The Rand Corporation, 1961), 9.

23. Fall, *The Two Viet-Nams*, 107–8. Fall's Indonesian and Algerian examples are well taken and show the reverse side to government successes against the Huks in the Philippines. As the reader will recall from Chapter 2, the capture of the major Huk leadership in Manila proved a decisive blow to the progress of the insurgency and specifically thwarted an attempt to capture the legitimate Philippine government.

24. O'Ballance, *Indo-China War*, 87.

25. "The French military, . . . confident of their armor and mechanized equipment, which had just helped defeat the Wehrmacht in Europe, also felt that a military solution could still provide a cure-all for the hopelessly tangled political situation." In Fall, *The Two Viet-Nams*, 75. The French never understood the subtlety of the subversive insurgent organization the Viet Minh had assembled.

26. Asprey, *War in the Shadows*, 2:693.

27. "It was only when the guerrillas were in overwhelming strength that they would ambush or attack French patrols or convoys. They seldom, in 1948, assaulted French defensive posts, as losses of December 1946 were still fresh in mind." In O'Ballance, *Indo-China War*, 91.

28. In accordance with Maoist principles, Giap believed in 1947 that the Viet Minh were in stage two of a three-stage protracted war. However, this second stage, the guerrilla-war phase, would actually not begin in earnest until 1950.

29. O'Ballance, *Indo-China War*, 147–50; cf., *Mao Tse-tung on Revolution and War*, 293–312.

30. For treatment of Chinese support and influence of the Viet Minh during these crucial early years, see Qiang Zhai, "Transplanting the Chinese Model: Chinese Military Advisors and the First Vietnam War, 1950–1954," *The Journal of Military History* 57 (October 1993): 689–715.

31. O'Ballance, *Indo-China War*, 116n.

32. Tanham, *Communist Revolutionary Warfare*, 19. To further explore Giap's dilemma during this troubling period, see the truly marvelous work by Cecil B. Currey, *Victory at any Cost: The Genius of Viet Nam's Gen. Vo Nguyen Giap* (New York: Brassey's (US) Inc., 1997), 156–70 and passim.

33. Ibid., 20.

34. "Most observers would place the beginning of phase two in 1949, as the French retained the initiative during 1947–49 and the first Vietminh attacks of a formal nature did not occur until 1949." Ibid., 17n.

35. O'Ballance, *Indo-China War*, 106.

36. Ibid., 109–11.

37. Thompson, *Defeating Communist Insurgency*, 141–42.

38. Ibid., 146–38.

39. Vo Nguyen Giap, *People's War, People's Army*, foreword by Roger Hilsman, profile of Giap by Bernard B. Fall (New York: Frederick A. Praeger, 1962), 101.

40. *Mao Tse-tung on Revolution and War*, 308–14.

41. Giap, *People's War*, 106.

42. See Thompson on equilibrium, in *No Exit From Vietnam*, 52–54.

43. Michael Elliot-Bateman, *Defeat in the East: The Mark of Mao Tse-tung on War* (London: Oxford University Press, 1967), 111. A common use for the term "equilibrium" can be found in Duiker, *The Communist Road to Power in Vietnam*, 141–43. It should be noted that Duiker's use of the term has nothing to do with our use of the term in understanding insurgency.

44. Detailed summaries of Hoa Binh and ensuing battles are provided in several of the sources already cited throughout this chapter. Still, the most complete account of these campaigns can be found in Bernard Fall's *Street without Joy: Indochina at War, 1946–1954* (Harrisburg, Pa.: Stackpole Company, 1961).

45. Duiker, *The Communist Road to Power in Vietnam*, 153–60. Elliot-Bateman provides a broader interpretation of Giap's equilibrium in *Defeat in the East*, 109. Specifically, he represents *equilibrium* as the precise moment when the subversive movement is "organizationally, politically, economically, and militarily established."

46. Scott et al., *Insurgency*, 112. After further investigation and reading, their term *quasi-conventional war* is accepted here as best referring to the Jominian concept of revolutionary/civil conflict.

47. In a report made to the Communist International in July 1939, one Nguyen Ai Quoc (Ho Chi Minh) stated that "the Party must strive to organize a broad Democratic National Front," one that claims democratic rights, "freedom of

organization, freedom of press and freedom of speech." See, Ho Chi Minh, *Ho Chi Minh on Revolution: Selected Writings, 1920–1966*, ed. Bernard B. Fall (New York: Frederick A. Praeger, 1967), 131–32.

48. This is not to say that because the Viet Minh talked of nationalist goals all Vietnamese understood or accepted their intentions. It was common for the Viet Minh to infiltrate nationalist organizations, particularly those in the south, and politically realign them to fit the overall Viet Minh scheme advocated by Hanoi. It was done in this manner because the Viet Minh subversives were so often successful at acquiring already established nationalist sponsors and converting them to the Viet Minh way in a relatively short period of time. Douglas Pike eloquently calls this the "time-tested Ho Chi Minh technique of destroying an organization by joining it." The Viet Minh did not merge, but swallowed their opposition whole. *Viet Cong*, 27.

CHAPTER 4

Seeds of American Commitment

Although the United States harbored an increasing concern over events in Indochina, postwar policy continued to regard the conflict as primarily a French matter. It is evident from the record that the United States expected few positive results from backing France's designs in the region and consistently deplored the prospect of a protracted war. However, the United States was stuck in quicksand over its views about Ho Chi Minh. The thought of supporting an avowed communist leader was unthinkable given the circumstances that the West faced in Europe. What is more, the events in China of 1948 and 1949 brought the United States to a heightened awareness, even a sense of urgency, over its policy of containment on the Asian mainland.

With the advent of the North Atlantic Treaty Organization (NATO), a search for similar security arrangements in Asia was instigated. Through a string of events in 1949, the Truman Doctrine took on an entirely new look in arenas where European colonialism was being dismantled. Well before President Dwight D. Eisenhower would refer to "dominos" in his April 1954 press conference, the National Security Council (NSC) met with President Truman and formulated the domino concept. NSC 48 (*U.S. Policy Toward Asia*) was drafted in June 1949 establishing the idea that if Indochina were "lost," the whole of Asia would be in jeopardy.[1] In October 1949, the United States passed the Mutual Defense Assistance Program (MDAP), through which U.S. arms, military assistance, and training would be provided to allied governments globally. In December 1949, the NSC met with President Truman again to discuss and approve measures that would lay down the "guidelines" for accepted American policy in the future with regards to Asia. The meeting brought forth the following:

> The United States should continue to use its influence in Asia toward resolving the colonial-nationalist conflict in such a way as to satisfy the fundamental demands of the nationalist movement while at the same time minimizing the strain on the colonial powers who are our Western allies. Particular attention should be given to the problem of French Indo-China and action should be taken to bring home to the French the urgency of removing the barriers to the obtaining by Bao Dai or other non-Communist nationalist leaders of the support of a substantial proportion of the Vietnamese.
>
>   . . . Recognizing that the non-Communist governments of South Asia already constitute a bulwark against Communist expansion in Asia, the United States should exploit every opportunity to increase the present Western orientation of the area and to assist, within our capabilities, its governments in their efforts to meet the minimum aspirations of their people and to maintain internal security.[2]

Such were the intentions of American policymakers in the closing months of 1949. To block the further expansion of communism in Asia, the United States intended to provide collective security, if the Asians themselves were forthcoming with appropriate and trustworthy leadership that pledged to provide internal assistance, and to collaborate with the major European allies in cementing a positive, noncommunist outlook for Asian trade and foreign policy. This road appeared to be the most prudent, and perhaps best way of achieving success without getting directly bloodied. Within a year though, the entire picture would change.

When Kim Il-sung marched his army south across the thirty-eighth parallel in June 1950, the American decision to resist communist aggression in the overt manner it did sharpened the entire national outlook with respect to Southeast Asia. The Korean conflict not only tied American idealism to its struggle to achieve freedom and security in Korea, but focused attention on allied struggles for "freedom" elsewhere in Asia. The French struggle against the Viet Minh was now something that Americans could recognize as another critical opportunity to stop communist aggression throughout the world. U.S. containment policy took on a more integral position with regard to security interests in Southeast Asia, and, accordingly, the United States enlarged and intensified its programs for aid and military assistance to the region. In September 1950 the first echelon of U.S. advisors arrived in Vietnam as part of the newly formed Military Assistance Advisory Group (MAAG).

Within a month the contingent of officers and enlisted men grew to some 65 and were commanded by Brig. Gen. Francis G. Brink, an officer with extensive experience in the Philippines, Singapore, Burma, and China. Military aid shipments to Indochina, by 1951, acquired the highest priority, second in size only to that aid earmarked for Korea.[3]

Shortly before Chinese intervention on behalf of the North Koreans in late 1950, one of the first official "realizations" about the special type of conflict taking place in Southeast Asia made its appearance through NSC 90, *Collaboration with Friendly Governments on Operations against Guerrillas*. Here, in a forward-looking piece by Dean Rusk, is a prudent call for "cooperation" among allied security partners to combat the efforts of "guerrilla" armies throughout Southeast Asia. Not only are efforts in Indochina discussed with respect to the "lack of French understanding" about the problems posed by guerrilla operations, but also efforts taking place in nearby countries. This appears to be one of the first official positions attempting to explain the reason for continued French blundering. Rusk cites both the U.S. investment in the Philippines and the British involvement in Malaya as stopgaps to key insurgency efforts on the part of communist subversive organizations.[4] Although no specific theories are put forth about guerrilla warfare, or for that matter about insurgency, NSC 90 is a noteworthy document because it provides insight as to why the United States was so critical of the conduct of conventional military operations by the French. Essentially, by 1951, an official U.S. position was emerging which held that guerrilla warfare waged by the Viet Minh would be the cause of eventual French military downfall in Indochina.

American fears of being embroiled in an Asian land war were being realized in Korea. The potential for Chinese intervention in Indochina— similar to what had happened in Korea—came to dominate American strategic thinking after 1950. Such an intervention would not have been too surprising given the large numbers of Chinese troops positioned along the northern Vietnamese border and the Chinese aid and assistance provided to the Viet Minh by 1951. As the U.S.-led United Nations forces eventually struggled to a stalemate in Korea, the French situation in Indochina continued to deteriorate. But in spite of this deterioration, U.S. intelligence estimates from 1950 to 1954 reflect a lessening of fears about Chinese intervention and even about the loss of the region altogether.

In a position paper put out by the Central Intelligence Agency (CIA) in October 1950, it is flatly stated that "Communist domination of mainland Southeast Asia would not be critical to U.S. security interests . . . [which] meant that the loss of the   area to Communist domination would not have a decisively adverse effect on the capabilities of the U.S. to win a global war."[5] As true as this may have been, the only department to side with the CIA's estimate was the navy. Three separate enclosures from the Departments of State, Army, and the Air Force clearly refute the CIA position about the region's strategic worth. While the State Department wanted more study, and the army held to the strategic domino theory, the air force would only accept a statement which read completely opposite from the CIA's: "Communist domination of mainland Southeast Asia could be critical to United States security interests; it would have serious immediate and direct, as well as long-range, consequences."[6] The split between the military and intelligence communities on this point is important because it illustrates how the communities would later be split on the way to wage war once the United States firmly committed itself to the Saigon government.

Still, in February 1952, NSC 124 (*U.S. Objectives and Courses of Action with Respect to Communist Aggression*) was produced. It proposed courses of strategy in the event that a "resolute defense" of Indochina became necessary to thwart further communist aggression.[7] By June, U.S. policy strongly opposed French withdrawal primarily because of the possibility of a conflict between the United States and the Chinese, not the Viet Minh. If the United States were to get involved in a ground war in Indochina—one necessitated in screening a French withdrawal—it was believed that the Chinese would not hesitate to meet them there, with or without Viet Minh consent. Although it appeared that the United States was staking a claim to Indochina, it was really using the French to fight the ground campaign it did not want to engage in itself. In fact, NSC 124 made it clear that no matter how involved it got with the Chinese over Southeast Asia, the United States would not commit ground forces to Vietnam in support of the French. By then, the widely accepted official view was that Vietnam was to be "an example" of democracy making its Asian stand—a carefully crafted, but empty threat contained in the follow-on document NSC 124/2.[8]

One of the more revealing documents to be disseminated by the National Security Council, one that specifically provided "alternative" courses of action based upon the experience of fighting against the Chinese in Korea, was NSC 177 (*U.S. Policy and Courses of Action with Respect to Southeast Asia*). Two courses of action were put forth in this December 1953 position paper, one that favored strengthening current conventional forces in Indochina, and a second that favored "an aggressive military, political and psychological program, including covert operations, to eliminate organized Viet Minh forces by mid-1955."[9] The interesting aspect to this proposal is not so much the entertaining of a "counter-guerrilla" strategy to thwart the Viet Minh, but the time in which these NSC analysts believed it could be accomplished. It is representative of the kind of misjudgment U.S. policymakers were to commit in the future, an overestimation of U.S. capabilities and an oversimplification of the insurgency problem.

Nevertheless, if the French proved unable to provide a timely victory over the Viet Minh, or at least show that they could regain some control of the dismal situation, the United States was leaning toward the latter of the two strategies. There appeared much confidence among policymakers and analysts alike in 1953 that dealing with "guerrilla bands" would be a desireable scenario given the ongoing predicament in Korea.[10] They believed that somehow limited war begets limited war. Moreover, NSC proposals had been made back in July for the employment of "indigenous guerrilla and para-military forces capable of effective active defense against communist invasion and infiltration of Thailand."[11] Vietnam was a convenient buffer zone for the Thai border, and it seemed reasonable to make it the first line of defense, particularly if the French could not hold on. During that same year, in a national intelligence estimate, the CIA gave up any hope of a French victory over the Viet Minh, stating that the French position would continue to decline, even "during the period of writing" the estimate. The CIA believed, rather prophetically, that the French would suffer greatly at the hands of the Viet Minh sometime that following year.[12]

In March 1954, under the direct command of Vo Nguyen Giap, the Viet Minh began their assault upon the French stronghold at Dien Bien Phu. Part of a larger plan by the French to secure a base area in northwest Tonkin, it was an opportunity to force Giap's forces into disarray and cut his all-important supply lines through upper Laos. Since the Viet Minh were using this region to profit from the sale of opium by turning revenues into weapons purchases, the benefits of wresting control of this area seemed to outweigh the risks. The place chosen by the French to make that stand was Dien Bien Phu. The plan which carried the name of the French general who developed it, the plan which was so controversial, so managed by outside interests, so carefully watched by the international community, and so overwhelmingly endorsed in the end, failed miserably. General Henri Navarre believed that the Viet Minh would be able to get no more than sixty cannon to the outskirts of the French defensive perimeter he established, just in time to be blasted from their revetments by his own superior long range guns and air support.

The complicated story of Dien Bien Phu is well told elsewhere, often with great intensity and detail. Let us simply leave it that never have battlefield commanders so underestimated the capability of their enemy. With many more soldiers and four times as many field guns as expected, with technical sophistication not believed, the Viet Minh would assure the death of the Navarre Plan at Dien Bien Phu before it was ever initiated.

However, even with the destruction of French forces at Dien Bien Phu so complete and the United States so involved in supporting the French, there was no overt American military commitment. In fact, the decision had been reached by President Eisenhower in April that there would need to be three specific conditions met before he would endorse such U.S. intervention. The first, and most important condition was the formation of a "united coalition force" with active British support which would intervene militarily alongside the United States. The second condition was to have a "full political understanding" with France and other countries, while the third condition was to secure complete congressional approval "to commit belligerent acts" in Indochina.[13] Because both the British and the French opposed "united action" and neither Eisenhower nor Congress was prepared to move without a "Korea-like" alliance, there was to be no immediate, overt action. Therefore, as much as the United States planned for the contingency of French military demise, it possessed no immediate intentions to intervene.

It should also be noted that the French defeat at Dien Bien Phu did not destroy their military might in the region, nor did it cause them to quickly retreat en masse from Tonkin, let alone from Indochina. For the French, Dien Bien Phu represented the straw that broke the weakening back of the Laniel government in Paris. However, it would be several years before the entirety of the French military and political presence would make its way out of southern Vietnam.

As for the United States, the fall of Dien Bien Phu and the loss of Tonkin, the retreat of the French military in the face of superior Viet Minh forces, and most critically, the dangerous increase of communist control over the region, caused a rethinking of the domino theory. Up to that time this theory had been the centerpiece of American policy for Southeast Asia. But four days after the French surrender at Dien Bien Phu, Secretary of State John Foster Dulles observed in a press conference that "Southeast Asia could be secured even without perhaps Vietnam, Laos and Cambodia." Noting further that, although he would not want to underestimate the importance of these countries, he was not willing to concede that "if events that we could not control, and in which we do not anticipate, should lead to their being lost . . . we would consider the whole situation hopeless and we would give up in despair."[14]

As the domino theory was being adjusted to fit the changing circumstances in Southeast Asia, so too was the concept of "united action." Transformed into a "long-range collective defense alliance," its intention was to offset the loss of Tonkin. As the United States resigned itself to the political settlement at Geneva, it also redefined its objectives so as to prevent any further losses. Northern Vietnam had been conceded to the Ho Chi Minh government, but only so long as a partition was maintained along the seventeenth parallel to clearly define just who was in control, and where. Consequently, the long-feared loss of Tonkin was now perceived to be a less serious outcome of the whole affair. The United States was forced to accept intelligence estimates from 1950 to 1954 which no longer viewed the loss of a single region as something which would automatically lead to swift and complete communist takeover. Thus the establishment of the Southeast Asian Treaty Organization (SEATO) in 1954, sought by the United States in order to create an alliance among regional states so as to avoid any future falling dominos, was the quid pro quo for "united action."[15]

America was now caught up in Vietnamese politics in a far more intimate and confused way than it had ever intended. Since 1945, the U.S. had chosen to stay out of the Indochina problem, standing on the sidelines attempting to manipulate political participants as if they were mere pieces on a chessboard. Undeniably, the United States itself was, by 1954, one of the chess pieces. Moreover, the United States was being drawn into a role that it was neither equipped nor prepared to take on. Still considering itself to be an "advisor" to the chess game, it failed to realize just how critical its position was becoming. Indeed, the United States was already caught up in a second Vietnamese insurgency, presenting it with a kind of second opportunity to succeed where the French had failed. But it seemingly chose to ignore the importance of this situation and made no clear attempt to seize the initiative from the subversive element during the most crucial stage of the insurgency, a failure it had criticized the French for in 1951. As a result of U.S. miscalculation, both Vietnam and America would face hardships they had never imagined. The United States would end up spending a great deal in human and material resources, only to obtain valuable lessons it should have already learned. As for the subversive faction, its insurgency would eventually lead to civil war and the realization of a Vietnamese nation without compromise.

NOTES

1. "President Eisenhower's News Conference, April 7, 1954," *Public Papers of the Presidents of the United States: Dwight D. Eisenhower 1953–1960*, (Washington, D.C.: GPO), 382; also, National Security Council, *U.S. Policy Towards Asia*, NSC Doc. 48, 10 June 1949 (Washington, D.C.: University Publications of America, 1980, test-fiche), 65.

2. Excerpt provided in *The Pentagon Papers*, Gravel ed., 1:39–40. For complete text, see National Security Council, *The Position of the U.S. with Respect to Asia*, NSC Doc. 48/1, 23 December 1949 (Washington, D.C.: University Publications of America, 1980, text-fiche).

3. See "Impact of Start of Korean War," in *The Pentagon Papers*, Gravel ed., 1:83-85.

4. National Security Council, *Collaboration with Friendly Governments on Operations against Guerrillas*, NSC Doc. 90, 26 October 1950 (Washington, D.C.: University Publications of America, 1980, text-fiche), 4.

5. Central Intelligence Agency, CIA Research Reports: Vietnam and Southeast Asia, 1946–1976, *Consequences to the U.S. of Communist Domination of Mainland Southeast Asia*, 13 October 1950 (Frederick, Md.: University Publications of America, 1983, text-fiche), 1 and 2n.

6. Ibid., 13.

7. National Security Council, *U.S. Objectives and Courses of Action with Respect to Communist Aggression in Southeast Asia*, NSC Doc. 124, 13 February 1952 (Washington, D.C.: University Publications of America, 1980, text-fiche).

8. National Security Council, *U.S. Objectives and Courses of Action with Respect to Southeast Asia*, NSC Doc. 124/2, 25 June 1952 (Washington, D.C.: University Publications of America, 1980, text-fiche), 10.

9. National Security Council, *U.S. Policy and Courses of Action with Respect to Southeast Asia*, NSC Doc. 177, 30 December 1953 (Washington, D.C.: University Publications of America, 1980, text-fiche), 11.

10. National Security Council, *U.S. Policy and Courses of Action with Respect to Southeast Asia*, NSC Doc. 177, special annex, 31 December 1953 (Washington, D.C.: University Publications of America, 1980, text-fiche), enclosure A, 4.

11. National Security Council, Minutes of the Meetings of the National Security Council, with Special Advisory Reports, *U.S. Psychological Strategy with Respect to the Thai Peoples of Southeast Asia*, 2 July 1953 (Washington, D.C.: University Publications of America, 1977, text-fiche), 3–4.

12. Central Intelligence Agency, CIA Research Reports: Vietnam and Southeast Asia, 1946–1976, *Probable Developments in Indochina through mid-1954*, 4 June 1953 (Frederick, Md.: University Publications of America, 1983, text-fiche), 2–5.

13. See "U.S. Decision Not to Intervene Unilaterally," in *The Pentagon Papers*, Gravel ed., 1:100–01.

14. See "Reappraisal of Domino Theory After Dien Bien Phu," in Ibid., 106.
15. Ibid., 107.

CHAPTER 5

The Second Vietnamese Insurgency: Phase One

The impact that war in Korea had on American policymaking after 1950, particularly in relation to events in Southeast Asia, has not been underrepresented. This "Korea syndrome," which permeated American political and military thinking during the 1950s and 1960s, is accepted as the primary reason for the cloudiness of the early strategic planning efforts of the United States in Vietnam. In a more recent article, Robert Komer, the man who was at the helm of U.S. pacification endeavors in Vietnam after 1965, agrees that this Korea syndrome is primarily to blame for American policy blunders during this critical period. He goes further, asking the question: "Now why did a decade's worth of military advisors keep giving the wrong kind of advice to the Vietnamese and equip the Vietnamese for the wrong kind of war? Wrong tactics, wrong equipment, wrong everything else? It was because the only model we had to go on was Korea. And consequently we tried to do it on the Korean model."[1] This is a fairly typical complaint of those who criticize the early efforts of pacification in South Vietnam. The problem with this statement is not that it is inaccurate, but that its premise is incorrect.

Certainly Korea was not the only model. The French debacle with the Viet Minh was in the foreground for anyone and everyone to view. But obvious lessons were not obvious to U.S. leaders of the day. Perhaps it was because the outcome for the French was so negative, their policy intentions so suspect, and their strategy so endlessly debated by American military advisors that the French lessons proved unpalatable to American policymakers. In spite of the less than desired outcome in Korea, the United States did find solace regarding Indochina in 1954 at

Geneva. Not only did the accords eliminate the American dilemma of "trying to stop communism without serving colonialism," but they also salvaged half of Vietnam, which had not appeared to be possible at the outset of the conference. As Pike soundly evaluates, only the Viet Minh, the "winners" of the war against the French, lost at Geneva.[2]

With the French out, the United States found itself actively entertaining the "irregular war" proposals which had been put forth by the intelligence community a year before. But out of the Korea syndrome debate, a debate which hampered American political-military policy in South Vietnam for two decades, comes one more bit of irony. What the United States feared most might happen in Southeast Asia, a "Korea-styled" conventional war with Chinese intervention, would probably have been a more desirable and better understood course than the one it was about to embark upon.

From the outside it is difficult to identify the exact moment when any insurgency begins. Several different timeframes have been offered by various analysts regarding the beginning of the southern insurgency in Vietnam. These usually range from 1956, when the first recorded encounters with communist terrorist bands occurred, to 1961, when the United States finally established an "official plan" to counter the insurgency. These are acceptable timeframes if one is limiting the advent of insurgency in the south to direct communist intervention from the north. Consensus seems to be found in the period of 1956 to 1957, a period in which George Tanham believes terrorist activity began and when the [communist] insurgents were "making their presence known."[3] Identifying the precise moment when an insurgency begins is perhaps the single most critical stage for a government in making positive inroads toward countering a subversive threat. The one caveat to keep in mind is that by the time it is realized that an insurgency does exist it may be too late. Even when the subversive threat is identified during phase one, there is a high probability that its political organization has already existed for some time.

In July 1954, Ngo Dinh Diem, the third son of an aristocratic Catholic family, was appointed by Bao Dai to the premiership in Saigon. Bao Dai proved to be completely ineffectual as a ruler. Unable to satisfy the nationalistic desires of the people, he was also often inept when it came to matters of state. Because of this, his only prospect for remaining in power was to become a stooge for the French, something that must have caused him great pain, given his earlier, more noble anticolonialist roots.[4] When France was ousted from control in 1954 and the Viet Minh were expected to obtain control of the entire country, Bao Dai wanted out. Even after the Geneva Accords partitioned the country, Bao Dai saw no reason to stay against the wishes of the United States and was finally able to convince Diem to accept the position of premier.[5] Diem believed that he had support from the southern nationalists, and that he would have complete support from the United States.

U.S. policymakers did not have to prompt Diem on matters of internal security and the need to thwart further Viet Minh aggression. The accords allowed a period of time for free passage across the parallel to occur, and it was during this period that an estimated eight hundred thousand to one million people moved south, and an estimated thirty to one hundred thousand moved north.[6] Of those that moved north, many planned to return in order to fight the Diem government, planting several hundred weapons caches to redistribute upon their return. As well, many covert agents remained south to continue the recruiting, organization, and planning for the expected struggle.[7] Terrorist activity was already taking place, and with the capture of several agents and caches in 1954, the subversive quality of an organization bent on political control in the South was becoming apparent.[8] This alone is enough to view the subversive political threat as having its beginnings in early 1954.

As if the direct threat of invasion from the north was not enough, the southern political apparatus belonging to the Dai Viet (Greater Vietnam) organizations, as well as a variety of militant religious and cultural sects, began determined opposition to the Diem government. One of these sects, a secret society of gangsters known as the Binh Xuyen, actually controlled Saigon at the time that Diem first took over. Their control of the city, which had been sanctioned some years before by Bao Dai, who received compensation for his head turning, would cause enormous difficulties to the provoked and hard-driving Diem. Members of another sect, the Cao Dai, a religious group which would eventually become the largest political movement in Cochinchina, declared themselves loyal followers of Bao Dai, and immediate antagonists to Diem. With nearly twenty thousand armed personnel, the Cao Dai ruled the region northwest of Saigon. A third sect, the Hoa Hao, controlled much of the area southwest of Saigon and found themselves at odds with the other two groups. Fighting among these groups continued in tribal fashion until an alliance formed the United Front of Nationalist Forces.[9] In March 1955, fighting broke out in Saigon in an attempt to overthrow Diem. By May, Diem had put an end to the rebellion and regained much of the waning confidence of his American allies.

Although the immediate overt threat from these sects was nullified, much of their subversive political structure was left intact. Consequently, they became perfect targets for the Lao Dong (communists) during the mid-1950s.[10] Their established political apparatus and hatred of Diem made them ripe for infiltration by the north. Throughout the next five years, infiltration, reorientation, and insurgent activity occurred among these groups, initiated by communist subversives who were eventually able to unify the sects political cause of nationalism with the underlying message of the Lao Dong.[11] Drawing on years of Viet Minh experience, the Lao Dong appealed to the peasants, not as Marxist revolutionaries proposing drastic social upheaval, but as conservative nationalists compatible with the "village-centered" traditionalism of the farmer. They presented their movement as an alternative to the hated modernization programs of Diem.[12] In the area around Hue, Dai Viet organizations exhibited tremendous hostility toward the Diem government and would have been a more viable tool for the Lao Dong if internal jealousies had not eventually torn them apart. By the early 1960s the Dai Viet would again emerge to join the Lao Dong–inspired insurgency.[13]

By the end of 1954 the Diem government had begun a program of pacification in the southern countryside, not only to chase away the militant sects, but also to stem the growing tide of Lao Dong influence. The sects were never completely destroyed, and those who did not flee into Cambodia or Laos continued to fight and grow with the Lao Dong. Subversive propaganda efforts and terrorism increased throughout 1955, and by 1956 it should have been obvious that a subversive insurgency was firmly established in the south. Not only were there anti-Diem political organizations developing, but those that could be unified by northern agents had begun taking orders directly from Hanoi.[14]

Diem is blamed for mishandling government policy during this critical period, creating much disaffection among the South Vietnamese people. Pike aptly states that "the new government under Diem began in just about as total an organizational vacuum as is possible." Foreign to almost every aspect of southern politics, "Diem had no party faithful, no corps of loyal political cadres, no trusted organization. Until the army opted for him he had no means of enforcing a governmental order." The government of South Vietnam (GVN) was unable to cope with the subversive threat internally.

> Steeped as were all Vietnamese in the tradition of the clandestine organization, Diem knew well that the greatest threat to his government came not from men but from men in organizations. But countering the clandestine organization required abilities he did not have. The chief threat

was the remaining communist apparatus of the Viet Minh, not so much because of its ideology as because of its organizational building powers.[15]

Although the United States maintained great suspicion about Diem and his real abilities to solve the problems of instability in the south, a grudging faith in his independent control would go on until the coup of November 1963. A good portion of this faith had been restored when Diem won the presidential election of 1955. Although the elections were suspiciously run, Diem did win by an overwhelming majority. Premier Diem thus became President Diem in what might best be termed a "quasidemocratic" show of intent. It is apparent now that reliance on Diem to foster and execute U.S. policy was a mistake. This reliance has allowed many to conveniently blame Diem's inadequacies for what was really an American failure to accurately assess the southern insurgency in order to plan and engage the insurgents in a timely manner, even if it necessitated going beyond Diem's rule. Robert Thompson's view is accurate when he indicates that "the real problem with South Vietnam has been to have a Government at all, whether democratic or not. It does not matter to me very much what the political top is. If there is no machinery underneath it to carry out a single instruction of the government, a government is not going to get very far, whatever aims and high ideals it may have."[16]

President Eisenhower, in his first State of the Union message in 1953, characterized Indochina as part of a global communist plot of aggression.[17] With so much at stake in Vietnam during the 1950s—at least as far as U.S. policy perception would have it at the time—why did the U.S. government not take control of its own destiny in Vietnam then as it would later attempt to do in 1965 by escalating the conflict? The answer to this question resides somewhere between the ramifications of insurgency war and the old saying that governments and militaries typically prepare to fight the next war with strategies that won the previous war.

Eisenhower's views are mentioned above because they represent the American government of the 1950s, which was headed primarily by ex-career military personnel who knew how to win wars based upon the "conventional" school of thought. Because the military also possessed a mind-set forged during World War II, their mutual support made it nearly impossible for those who differed in their thinking to emerge within these institutions.[18] Thus, both the military and political communities during the 1950s maintained a climate that discouraged opposing views and awarded advancement to those who complied with the existing consensus.[19] Because of the "conventional" view maintained by the government hierarchy, even the task of identifying that an insurgent problem existed separately in South Vietnam after 1954 was made extremely difficult. As well, any real ability to combat an insurgency would have had to be written into U.S. military training and doctrine, but these had yet to reflect any real progress on the subject.[20] It was not enough to simply allude to the subject in the titles of army field manuals. Published in 1951, *FM 31-20 Operations Against Guerrilla Forces* discusses the guerrilla fighter merely as a conventional threat, and historical examples provided in the text give little help in understanding the situation in Indochina. In a 1953 edition, *FM 31-21 Guerrilla Warfare and Special Forces Operations*, "irregular war" operations are discussed in much the same way as they were discussed and conducted in Burma during World War II. These, as well as other manuals, were steps in the right direction, but they still emphasized the use of guerrilla fighters only in the capacity of enhancing the capability of a conventional army.[21] They explained traditional concepts, such as harassment behind enemy lines, rear-area security, airborne operations, and limited screening missions, as if they were somehow made different simply by tagging them with the term "guerrilla war." None addressed the strategic design of insurgency war.

In 1953, as a prelude to his assuming command of the Military Assistance Advisory Group, Indochina, Lt. Gen. John W. O'Daniel headed an advisory mission to Saigon. The O'Daniel mission, as instructed by the Joint Chiefs, was simple and had nothing to do with supporting the Vietnamese. He and his staff were to survey the French military requirements, provide support to the French high command, and reinforce the need for "aggressive implementation of military plans for successfully concluding the war in Indochina."[22] When O'Daniel arrived in Saigon on 20 June, he was to assist the French general Navarre in his new and aggressive plan to halt the Viet Minh at Dien Bien Phu, not help thwart an insurgency. Few military and political analysts understood the parameters of an insurgency war, let alone concepts such as *equilibrium*. That an eventual battle like Dien Bien Phu was inevitable after the battle at Hoa Binh was not conceivable in conventional military thinking. Thus, when O'Daniel arrived, his first inclination was to find ways for the French to win, decisively and quickly. Realistically though, the French military was about to lose its toehold in Indochina, a point made clear by nearly every U.S. intelligence estimate of the French situation. Nevertheless, O'Daniel supported the military solution sold by General

Navarre, and returned to Washington voicing total confidence that the outcome would be in favor of the French.[23]

The commander of MAAG during this period, Brig. Gen. Thomas J. H. Trapnell, did not share O'Daniel's optimism and sent one of his subordinates, Lt. Col. Robert C. Taber, to visit Dien Bien Phu. Taber concluded in his report that Navarre was actually conducting a "minimum casualty holding action in Indochina . . . with a view to eventual negotiations." As such, the French had manifested little progress in the fields of training and psychological warfare, exhibiting "staff thinking and procedure vintage 1935–39."[24] The report ended up on the desk of General Matthew B. Ridgway, and Trapnell was invited to submit his own appraisal of the situation as a follow-up. In the end, though both reports caused some stir in Washington, neither warning of impending French disaster resulted in much militarily.

With the MAAG commander's report reflecting views similar to those held in the separate field report from Taber—that the French were erring strategically in their outlook on the Viet Minh—one would conclude that a sense of alarm might have caused some rethinking of U.S. military policy toward Vietnam. However, during House and Senate testimony at about the time the French were being surrounded by the Viet Minh at Dien Bien Phu, UnderSecretary of State Walter Bedell Smith and Admiral Arthur M. Radford discounted any "alarmist interpretations of recent military operations" in Vietnam. Taber was finally summoned by the U.S. ambassador to Saigon, Donald Heath, and asked to stop sending messages that questioned the French ability to win the war. In response to the conflicting reports, Admiral Radford stated at a subsequent NSC meeting that "our attaches tend to become frustrated as a result of continuously being on the scene. They tend to look at the situation from strictly a service point of view."[25]

Discontent with French operations and a growing realization among several analysts that the United States was becoming embroiled in something that the believers in conventional methods could not fully appreciate had been building since the inception of the advisory group in Indochina, as early as 1950. There were, in fact, a number of American officials who had suggested that the best way for the French to meet the Viet Minh's unconventional threat was to wage unconventional warfare themselves. Just how this was to be accomplished, particularly on such a large scale, was something no one had really thought out. Nonetheless, suggestions on how to implement an "unconventional war strategy" had been voiced to an uninterested French general de Lattre by the CIA as early as 1951. Secretary of the Army Frank Pace, Jr., had suggested in

1952 that a joint operation involving U.S. agents and Vietnamese nationalists could be formed to assist the French in intelligence gathering and psychological warfare. Needless to say, the suggestion had not been well received by military planning staffs concerned over the numerous obstacles which existed.[26]

The segregation between the conventional thinking military and those that were pushing for other than conventional strategies seemed to begin in earnest during the early years of Eisenhower's presidency. The very nature of the Vietnamese struggle, and particularly the way in which the French had been defeated, brought the issue to the forefront. As one official source explains, the Eisenhower administration stopped "tinkering with strategy, training techniques, and manpower policies . . . [only to continue] on a far larger scale."[27] Although O'Daniel replaced Trapnell as head of MAAG in March 1954 specifically to see if he could fix the French problem at Dien Bien Phu, the sudden French disaster seemed to breath new life, and perhaps a renewed sense of urgency, into the unconventional school of thinking. As the debate continued another American officer was already on his way to Saigon.

Shortly after his return home from the Philippines in January 1954, and after taking part in the O'Daniel mission the previous summer, Edward Lansdale was told to pack his bags again, this time for a more extended stay in Vietnam. Lansdale arrived at Tan Son Nhut airport in Saigon in late May holding the nominal title of air attache to MAAG.[28] His real position was head of the Saigon Military Mission (SMM), a special CIA team which was separate from the CIA organization already working in-country. The purpose of the SMM was to circumvent the French and enter Vietnam quietly to assist the Vietnamese in preparing for unconventional warfare against the Viet Minh. As Lansdale later stated in his report regarding the covert mission, "the French were to be kept as friendly allies in the process, as far as possible." However, there were great differences in what had confronted Lansdale in the Philippines compared to what he was walking into in Vietnam. In the Philippines Lansdale had been supporting an indigenous government against an internal subversive threat. His first mission statement for Vietnam in 1954 was to work with the Vietnamese to pacify an insurgent threat against a colonial regime, something he probably had deep reservations about. But after the settlement at Geneva, his mission was broadened to encompass the undertaking of "para-military operations in Communist areas rather than to wage unconventional war."[29] Thus, the intent became to help insulate the Diem government and fight a "quasi-internal" insurgency threat waged by the Viet Minh.[30]

Lansdale's operation was conducted similarly to the one he had begun in the Philippines just four years before.[31] Two elements that had proved to be hallmarks of his success in the Philippines were to come together again in Vietnam. He hammered home repeatedly the need for both gathering meaningful intelligence on the enemy and for conducting a competent psychological warfare campaign. Within days of his arrival, Lansdale set up a "refresher course" in psychological warfare operations for Vietnamese officers. Identifying the insurgency threat in the south, Lansdale set out to implement his first programs even before Diem officially came into office.

The primary SMM team consisted eventually of about twenty hand-picked men, one of whom, Major Lucien Conein, arrived immediately on Lansdale's heels in July. Conein was a well known paramilitary specialist who had helped the French operate the maquis in Tonkin during 1945. Lansdale interestingly referred to him as the "one American guerrilla fighter who had not been a member of the Patti Mission."[32] As Lansdale well knew, creating unnecessary barriers by openly antagoniz-ing the French would help no one. Conein, as well as all the other SMM agents, were assigned to MAAG headquarters as a cover to their real CIA connection.

In July, Diem arrived on the scene only to witness a bleak picture of Vietnam from his Saigon ministry office window. With the countryside already in disunion, militant sects vying for power, and a nonexistent political organization, it is no wonder that Diem found Lansdale's open friendship comforting. Soon the two men were meeting on a daily basis to discuss matters of policy. As the French gradually receded militarily from the south, growing unrest mounted in the capital's surrounding provinces. It became obvious to Lansdale that the first order of business would be for Diem to stabilize the internal political atmosphere while he, himself, worked on calming the popular unrest. SMM operations were to be conducted both against the Viet Minh in the north and the militant sects in the south. The situation was so dismal that in September, highlevel Washington officials who visited Saigon privately indicated that "current estimates led [them] to the conclusion that Vietnam probably would have to be written off as a loss."[33]

But progress in the countryside, however slight, was being made. Lansdale believed that "winning the hearts and minds" of the people, no matter how trivial it may have sounded, was a most critical kind of PSYWAR in and of itself. Thus, volunteer medical teams of Free Asians were already being sent into depressed areas to provide the peasant population with much-needed care. Refugee programs were also set up to provide food and shelter for the influx of Vietnamese coming down from the north.[34] Because the migration was so great immediately following Geneva, it became a chore just to determine who was there to be friendly and who wanted to aid the subversive cause.[35]

If medical support and provisions of food were the brighter side of Lansdale's PSYWAR campaign, then the rumor campaign had to be the darker side. There were no rumors that could compete with the macabre "vampire stories" which Lansdale's PSYWAR teams had circulated in the Philippines. However, some sophisticated work was done to capitalize on Vietnamese superstitions. These operations were planned in the G-5 section, PSYWAR, headed by a Captain Pham Xuan Giai, a young, trustworthy Vietnamese officer with whom Lansdale worked closely. While Hanoi was still a viable target during the summer of 1954, SMM PSYWAR teams infiltrated north to plant everything from "fake" Communist manifestos to "soothsayer" almanacs, all composed by consummate artists in the Saigon G-5 section.

The manifestos were pretentious, though quite ingenious. Printed to look like an authentic announcement put out by the Lao Dong Party, these papers proclaimed, among other things, a seven-day holiday for all Hanoi residents—a celebration of "independence" from French authority that called for "dancing in the streets." The proclamation appeared to be so real that lower level cadre went from house to house to make sure that the turnout would be 100 percent. As the story goes, not even a last-minute Lao Dong radio broadcast could stop the event because residents believed it to be a French attempt at "counterpropaganda." In Lansdale's words, "a three-day work stoppage was a substantial achievement for a piece of paper."[36]

Lansdale seemed to be equally pleased with the almanac produced by the G-5 section, especially since it rapidly became a best-seller in the northern port city of Haiphong. The almanac predicted "troubled times" for the Communists during 1955. To Lansdale's own amazement, it did predict some actual happenings, such as splits in the politburo and the bloody suppression of farmers who opposed land-reform policies. Because the Vietnamese were so taken by the book, a large reprint order promptly sold out on the black market.[37] PSYWAR was now a proven art, and Lansdale's people were getting results. As the G-5 section continued work around the clock, the field agents were not to be outdone.

In response to known southern Viet Minh infiltration, as well as to heightened terrorist activity sponsored by the north, Lansdale established two paramilitary units. One unit was known as the Binh team, the other, formed later, was known as the Hao team. After being briefed by Major

Conein, the Binh team was the first to go into action. Binh was carefully inserted into North Vietnam in stages over a thirty day period, acting in the role of "normal" citizen as cover. They were secretly resupplied through Civil Air Transport (CAT), a Taiwan-based airline directed by General Claire Chennault, who smuggled supplies regularly into Haiphong. Those operations ceased when the city was finally closed to outside traffic in May 1955.

The Hao team was itself broken into two units so that it could operate on both sides of the Vietnamese border. While little is mentioned about southern-unit activities in Lansdale's report or in his memoirs, there is some information available on the northern unit. It apparently consisted of twenty-one agents recruited from the Saigon area and trained to carry out much of the same type of operation as the Binh team. After these teams were trained on Saipan and briefed by Major Fred Allen and his officers at a holding area at Clark Air Force Base in the Philippines, the northern Hao team was taken by the navy to Haiphong where they "gradually slipped ashore." Lansdale and the SMM had the entire operation in place before Haiphong came under Viet Minh control that May, and it appears that both the Binh and Hao teams conducted operations well into the next year.[38]

While these northern operations were being conducted, the political unrest in the south was reaching a severe boiling point for Diem.[39] The situation first exploded in March when Diem refused to grant governmental powers to the sects. When Hoa Hao and Cao Dai cabinet members resigned, the two sects formed the United Front of Nationalist Forces. It was a few days later that Binh Xuyen units attacked the presidential palace. Perhaps Diem did not realize how critical his situation was. Not only were the militant sects trying to sack him, but if it were not for the support of Lansdale, Washington was prepared to quickly replace him with a coalition government, though just how this was to come about was never really made clear.

Eisenhower had sent a trusted representative, retired General J. Lawton Collins, to Saigon some four months before. In a letter of instruction, Collins was given "broad authority to direct, utilize and control all agencies and resources of the U.S. government with respect to Vietnam."[40] Collins had consistently maintained dislike for Diem, and with the present uprising, it appeared to be a natural time to change the Saigon leadership. With Eisenhower's support, the change seemed complicated but inevitable.

Then, to the surprise of everyone, Diem called upon what loyalty was left in his army and crushed the Binh Xuyen. Within a month, both the Cao Dai and Hoa Hao sects were in full retreat from the capital. Although Lansdale does not explicitly take credit, it is obvious from the timetable laid down in his memoirs that, through his conversations with Diem just before the army's counterattack was made, he was able to light a passage for Diem to find a way out.[41] And what a way out! Not only were Collins's arguments against Diem rebuffed, but Diem suddenly became the strong leader America was looking for to carry on a "mutually" desirable Vietnamese policy. Judging by his large margin of victory in the presidential elections which quickly followed, it appeared that he also had a public mandate. Growing confidence among U.S. advisors was now being exhibited. That is, among all but Lansdale.

By late 1955, it appeared that Lansdale had developed a dark outlook for the American effort in Vietnam.[42] Lansdale, outside of the mainstream of military circles, retained no great ally in the American military mission to Saigon. Though his cover was with MAAG and his paycheck came from the air force, he worked for the CIA. There was no secret in this, but there must have been much resentment. With O'Daniel having no control over him, Lansdale often implemented programs that were quite alien to the MAAG officer's thinking, and therefore alien to any real supporters in Washington.

Problems likely became worse for Lansdale when O'Daniel's replacement arrived in Saigon on 15 November 1955. Lt. Gen. Samuel T. Williams, known affectionately as "Hanging Sam," was not the man to embrace the notion of irregular or paramilitary operations. Williams's background was as an armored commander, and when fighting alongside Patton in Europe he had exemplified the steadfast principles that saw the battlefield in terms of "putting steel on target." Even more recently, Williams had commanded the Twenty-fifth Infantry Division in Korea from 1952 to 1953. He distinguished himself in that conflict and solidified a reputation for being a "no-nonsense" leader of armies.[43] But along with this came the fixation that there was a need to prepare for the set-piece battle on the Asian mainland. All historical lessons about Vietnam aside, Williams believed that the threat of a Chinese invasion was a reality whose time had come. O'Daniel, too, had been convinced that a conventional military threat from the north was the primary element confronting the GVN, and he had quickly initiated a restructuring of GVN units to look like U.S. conventional forces, organizing them into division and corps levels.[44] Williams continued to prepare GVN forces along these lines, believing, perhaps more earnestly than O'Daniel, that the Viet Minh were preparing a large "Soviet-styled" invasion.[45] Although Lansdale spoke of Williams fondly as being almost "grandfather-like," there existed deep divisions between the two men on the conduct of future American policy and the formulation of a viable South Vietnamese army. Lansdale recorded some years later:

> [Williams] kept visualizing a surprise invasion by the Communist forces and had small confidence in my own prediction that the North Vietnamese would come south secretively, not in an overt invasion. . . . My own crystal-ball predictions were based on what I knew of the characters of Ho, Giap, and other North Vietnamese leaders. Despite the fluke of the vast open battle at Dien Bien Phu, I believed that they still thought in terms of guerrilla and clandestine operations. An open invasion would be looked upon by them as too unconventional and hazardous, when they had more proven means to use.[46]

Although there was much difference of opinion between the Joint Chiefs, the army, MAAG, and Pacific Command on just how to approach the threat from North Vietnam, the JCS did make it clear in September 1955 that the major threat to South Vietnam was from "subversion." In line with that thinking, CIA put out a report a month later stating that "should the Viet Minh initiate large-scale guerrilla operations supported by substantial infiltration from the north, the South Vietnamese government would be hard pressed. . . . If the operation were prolonged, the government probably could not survive without military assistance from outside."[47]

Williams's ideas on the subject of combating guerrilla forces were representative of the thinking armywide during the 1950s. Guerrillas were usually envisioned as troops that were part of regular army units, whose tactics of rear-area operations and screening missions were the highlights of their capability on the battlefield. Combating only guerrilla units was a special skill, relegated to special operation forces training. Little if any counterguerrilla training in the field was given to officers or enlisted personnel, the belief being that the four hours of classroom instruction already afforded soldiers was more than enough.[48] In other words, the army perceived no serious threat from even the largest of guerrilla forces, irregular tactics proving to be no discernable match for the already proven conventional philosophies of the Second World War and even Korea. With warnings of Jomini's "national wars" a shrouded, distant memory—if they were remembered at all—the United States chose to see the French experience of fighting the Viet Minh as an aberration.

Lansdale's change in vision had come about quickly. This was not like it had been in the Philippines, a situation which had occasioned far less attention from so many different U.S. government departments. Lansdale no longer believed that he could work out the ideas that had proved so successful in the past. He faced too many detractors, too much opposition, too little faith. Lansdale came to believe that many U.S. representatives, probably those in MAAG and other CIA personnel in Saigon, were directing South Vietnam on a sure course toward disaster. Rather than fight it, he simply wanted out.

After a short trip back to Washington in a vain attempt to convince policymakers that an ill wind lay ahead for Vietnam, Lansdale agreed to finish out his assignment through 1956. Upon returning to Saigon, his impressions became increasingly melancholy.[49] His fondest memories are from days spent relaxing on a quiet Vietnamese beach with the Diem family and friends close by. Lansdale tried to discuss with Diem future political and constitutional problems about the Saigon government. He found that discussions on Confucian principles were the most appropriate since these were principles that he believed formed "the true Vietnamese ethos upon which their government should be based."[50]

Lansdale would return to South Vietnam on two separate occasions, once as a government observer, another time as a civilian employee. His 1954 to 1955 mission had been first and foremost to install Diem as president. With that task completed by the end of 1955, the mission was effectively over. Generally, the Eisenhower administration did not believe that Lansdale's methods were appropriate given the circumstances of the overt military threat from the north, Chinese as well as Vietnamese. To be fair, as stated before, the insurgency in South Vietnam was not the insurgency which had faced the Philippines. This is not to imply that the U.S. government was clear on that point, but simply to question Lansdale's real opportunity for success in Saigon. Even if his ideas had been wholly adopted by the MAAG mission, it is questionable whether the subversive tide would have been stemmed given the momentum it already possessed. Due to the fact that so many government agencies were represented in South Vietnam, it is natural that the division between proponents of conventional and insurgency strategies became magnified during that period. The Kennedy administration would look more favorably on "perceived" insurgent war strategies, and Lansdale would again be asked to lend a hand. The problem was that by then the subversive insurgents had nearly succeeded, having reached the critical stages some years before. Such attempts to turn the clock back by instituting counterinsurgent methods so late in the game would only prove futile for South Vietnam.

NOTES

1. Komer, "Commentary," 124.

2. Pike, *Viet Cong*, 52. Pike proposes that Ho Chi Minh was actually "sold out" by a joint Sino-Soviet effort to get Ho to settle quickly with the understanding that the entire country would be his after the coming elections. "His willingness to accept partition after Dien Bien Phu proves, as nothing else can, his deep loyalty and fidelity to international communism." Of course, with no one else willing to give the Viet Minh aid, Ho would have been a fool to turn his back on his communist supporters.

3. Tanham, *Communist Revolutionary Warfare*, 119–21; also, see Fall, *The Two Viet-Nams*, 316.

4. Marr, *Vietnam 1945*, 439. A superb, much overdue study about this most critical period in twentieth century Vietnamese history.

5. Diem had already vacated a junior position in the Bao Dai government some twenty years before due to his distrust of Bao Dai and the role he played in the French scheme of control. Diem spent two years living in the United States before returning to South Vietnam to accept the position as premier from Bao Dai. For a concise discussion of the events that brought Diem to power, see Asprey, *War in the Shadows*, 2:826–27.

6. Pike, *Viet Cong*, 53n.

7. In an interview with Pike, Dr. Wesley Fishel of the Michigan State University advisory team, stated that in 1954 the Viet Minh left a network of about ten thousand agents in the south. Ibid., 75n.

8. A CIA report from four years earlier outlined the use of terrorism by southern subversive groups, indicating that the resistance was "largely successful in maintaining a facade of genuine nationalism; whether willing or not, four-fifths of the population of Vietnam profess adherence to Ho Chi Minh." Central Intelligence Agency, CIA Research Reports: Vietnam and Southeast Asia, 1946–1976, *Crisis in Indochina*, 10 February 1950 (Frederick, Md.: University publications of America, 1983, text-fiche), appendix A, 6. It is estimated that some sixty thousand men were serving in organized Viet Minh units in South Vietnam at the end of the Franco–Viet Minh conflict. *The Pentagon Papers*, Gravel ed., 1:328. Also, see Joseph J. Zasloff, "Origins of the Insurgency in South Vietnam, 1954–1960: The Role of the Southern Vietminh Cadres," RM 5163 (Santa Monica, Calif.: Rand Corporation, March 1967).

9. Ibid., 1:293–95; also, see Fall, *The Two Viet-Nams*, 245–46.

10. Tanham, *Communist Revolutionary Warfare*, 120.

11. Some have gone so far as to say that, with cadre meetings and limited terrorist acts beginning in 1954–55, "Diem inherited the insurgency with his accession to power." William A. Nighswonger, *Rural Pacification in Vietnam* (New York: Frederick A. Praeger, 1966), 34.

12. *The Pentagon Papers*, Gravel ed., 1:332. Also see the comprehensive section on socioeconomic conditions under Diem in Pike, *Viet Cong*, 61–68.

13. Pike, *Viet Cong*, 69.

14. Tanham, *Communist Revolutionary Warfare*, 120–21; also, see Fall, *The Two Viet-Nams*, 316–17.

15. Pike, *Viet Cong*, 58–59.

16. Clutterbuck, *Conflict and Violence*, 187.

17. *Public Papers of the Presidents: Eisenhower, 1953*, 16.

18. Traceable evidence of dissent within the military does exist within many of the military publications of the period. A survey of articles between 1954 and 1960 in the *Army Information Digest*, *Military Review*, *Combat Forces Journal* (predecessor of *Army*), *U.S. Naval Institute Proceedings*, and *Air University Quarterly Review* shows an increase in the interest on pieces dealing particularly with guerrilla war. For a concise review of themes related to the "guerrilla phenomenon" in military periodicals during the post-1945 period, see Bowman, "U.S. Army and Counterinsurgency Warfare," 53–63.

19. For a discourse about "policy convictions" within the Eisenhower and Kennedy administrations, see Roger Hilsman, *To Move a Nation: The Politics and Foreign Policy in the Administration of John F. Kennedy* (Garden City, N.Y.: Doubleday and Company, 1967), 10–20. It should be noted that General Maxwell Taylor resigned as army chief of staff in 1959 over a long running dispute over "mass retaliation" versus "limited war" policies. Problems at that high level were indicative of problems undulating at lower levels. See Taylor's own discussion of these events in *Swords and Plowshares* (New York: W. W. Norton & Co., 1972), 164–83 and passim.

20. For a detailed look into these early days of U.S. Army politics and "counterinsurgency doctrine," see the notable study by Andrew F. Krepinevich, Jr., *The Army and Vietnam* (Baltimore, Md.: The Johns Hopkins University Press, 1986), 38–42 and passim.

21. U.S., D.A., *FM 31-20 Operations against Guerrilla Forces* (Washington, D.C.: GPO, 1951); *FM 31-21 Guerrilla Warfare and Special Forces Operations*, 1953. The lack of change is also consistent in these follow-on manuals: U.S., D.A., *FM 31-21 Guerrilla Warfare*, 1955; *FM 31-21 Guerrilla Warfare and Special Forces Operations*, 1958; *FM 31-21 Guerrilla Warfare and Special Warfare Operations*, 1961; *FM 31-21A (SECRET) Guerrilla Warfare and Special Warfare Operations*, 1961. Also, see the U.S. Army's special studies series on Vietnam, specifically: Brig. Gen. James Lawton Collins, Jr., *The Development and Training of the South Vietnamese Army, 1950–1972* (Washington, D.C.: GPO, 1975); Col. Francis J. Kelly, *U.S. Army Special Forces: 1961–1971* (Washington, D.C.: GPO, 1973); Maj. Gen. William B. Fulton, *Riverine Operations: 1966–1969* (Washington, D.C.: GPO, 1973); Lt. Gen. John J. Tolson, *Airmobility, 1961–1971* (Washington, D.C.: GPO, 1973); Maj. Gen. Joseph A. McChristian, *The Role of Military Intelligence, 1965–1967* (Washington, D.C.: GPO, 1974).

22. Ronald H. Spector, *Advice and Support: The Early Years of the U.S. Army in Vietnam, 1941–1960* (Washington, D.C.: CMH, 1983), 174.

23. "Throughout O'Daniel's visit the service attaches and CIA

representatives attempted to correct what they believed to be the excessively favorable picture the French had been painting for his benefit." Ibid., 176. But in August, the JCS was willing to support the French program, and the State Department and NSC proposed a $400 million increase in aid to the French military effort.

24. Ibid., 187. It can be stated that General Brink, though an army officer of merit with an affinity for the region, suffered physically and mentally for several years. His suicide in July 1952 while on a visit to Washington, D.C. brought upon his replacement in Brig. Gen. Thomas H. Trapnell.

25. Ibid., 187–89.

26. Ibid., 164.

27. Ibid., 165.

28. Lansdale, *In the Midst of Wars*, 131. It should be noted that in his report to Washington in 1956, Lansdale states that he "officially" arrived in June.

29. "Lansdale Team's Report on Covert Saigon Mission in 1954 and 1955," in *The Pentagon Papers*, Gravel ed., 1:574.

30. The phrase "quasi-internal insurgency" is used to reflect the growing coordination of internal sect opposition and Lao Dong influence against Diem which had begun in 1954.

31. Much of the information about Lansdale's exploits comes firsthand, from Lansdale's own memoirs, and from a CIA field report he produced after returning to the United States in 1956. The report is partially reprinted in *The Pentagon Papers*, Gravel ed., vol. 1, and is the one referred to here.

32. Ibid., 575. Conein never was in agreement with French political interests in Indochina. For a view of Conein's early involvement in Vietnam see, Patti, *Why Vietnam?* 113, and passim.

33. *The Pentagon Papers*, Gravel ed., 1:577.

34. Ibid., 576.

35. Lansdale considered the greatest threat in early 1955 to be an organization of about one hundred Viet Minh cadre who infiltrated into the south with the intention of disrupting the communications and logistic lines of the National Army. Because the National Army represented the strongest organization in the country, the Viet Minh made it a priority target. See "Lansdale Team's Report," 581.

36. Lansdale, *In the Midst of Wars*, 225–26.

37. Ibid., 226–27. Also, see Currey's excellent recounting of the experiences of Lansdale's two SMM teams and their operations in North Vietnam, in *Edward Lansdale*, 147–85, and passim.

38. *The Pentagon Papers*, Gravel ed., 1:582–83. All expenses for the SMM, excluding officer pay and weapons costs, totaled a mere $228,000. The largest item paid out was listed as payment for operations, and included agent transportation, safe houses, and pay and expenses. In Sheehan et al., *The Pentagon Papers*, 16–19.

39. It is probable that much of Lansdale's knowledge of sect and Viet Minh

activities in the south, which actually proved to be quite substantial, was gained through southern Hao team efforts. One must consider Lansdale's views on how such intelligence-gathering operations should be carried out, particularly as seen in his Philippine operations cited in Chapter 2. See Lansdale, *In the Midst of Wars*, 71.

40. Spector, *Advice and Support*, 232.

41. Lansdale, *In the Midst of Wars*, 260–81.

42. Lansdale's outlook for South Vietnam was gloomy for many reasons, not the least of which was the fact that Diem could no longer give assurance that his forces would remain loyal to the cause. In Robert Buzzanco, "Prologue to Tragedy: U.S. Military Opposition to Intervention in Vietnam, 1950–1954," *Diplomatic History* 17 (Spring 1993): 218. It was not that Lansdale had not already known this, it was that Diem could not understand the gravity of this predicament.

43. From the early days of Williams's enlistment as a soldier in the Texas national guard (circa 1916) to his command of MAAG in Saigon, see Col. Harold J. "Jack" Meyer, *Hanging Sam: A Military Biography of General Samuel T. Williams, From Pancho Villa to Vietnam* (Denton, Tx.: University of North Texas Press, 1990).

44. Lansdale, *In the Midst of Wars*, 338. It should be noted that both Lansdale and Williams maintained a friendly correspondence with each other for some years after their "official" involvement with Vietnam ended. Both men of strong conviction, neither was persuaded by the other to change his views.

45. Spector, *Advice and Support*, 272–73.

46. Lansdale, *In the Midst of Wars*, 337.

47. Quoted from Spector, *Advice and Support*, 272.

48. Ibid., 273. Army field manuals were most representative of the military's belief in training and doctrine (see note 21 this chapter).

49. One of Lansdale's greatest problems with Diem came from the formation of the Can Lao Party, Diem's own political organization, which acted to crush all opposition to its platform. A platform of dictatorial rule was gradually instituted and aggressively maintained by Diem's Can Lao Party's officialdom. See Lansdale, *In the Midst of Wars*, 343–45.

50. Ibid., 363.

CHAPTER 6

The Second Vietnamese Insurgency: Phase Two

In November 1960, a South Vietnamese Army (ARVN) intelligence report indicated that over one hundred thousand known Vietnamese Communists were active in the south.[1] In December, the formation of the National Liberation Front (NLF) was announced, making it official that the Lao Dong had pulled the southern insurgents together into a cohesive political network, an organization for anti-Diem activity.[2] The formation of the NLF was no surprise to many of the intelligence analysts keeping tabs on the subversive movement. Since 1959, when the Lao Dong Central Committee had met in Hanoi to declare that the time had come to "smash" the GVN, there had been strong indications that they were providing increased direction in the south. The outcome, as illustrated by Pike, was that "through their efforts the insurgency, previously sporadic and patternless, began to take shape."[3]

This, however, raises several questions: Did armed violence before 1960 really just consist of a series of aimless guerrilla incidents? Was it possible for the subversive organizations to come together without the formation of the NLF? Was the Lao Dong humiliation at Geneva so complete that there existed a firm desire to unify all of Vietnam as quickly as possible? And, did this lead the Lao Dong to sponsor "revolutionary guerrilla war" in the south, taking advantage of the militant sect opposition to Diem? A general answer to these questions does not necessitate a focus on the NLF, nor does it mean having to grasp concepts of revolutionary guerrilla war as proposed by the Lao Dong.

That Communist organizational influence from the north existed

before and after 1954 in the south has been established. That this
extensive Lao Dong cadre in the south was attempting to infiltrate a
number of militant political organizations that were working to disrupt or
overthrow the Diem government has also been noted. What is imperative
to understand, however, is that the insurgency in the south was not a
growing communist revolutionary guerrilla war as some might suggest,
but remained an anti-Diem, anti-American insurgency in spite of Hanoi's
desire for a unified Vietnam. Originally comprising the fragmented
opposition of the various militant sects, including roaming Lao Dong
sympathizers, the southern insurgency more quickly unified itself and its
political-military goals than the timing of NLF formalization would
indicate. What the organization of the NLF did do was to provide a
much-needed centralization of subversive political planning and field
coordination, as well as confirm the prospect of transforming what was
already a "quasi-internal" insurgency to one that would become
primarily external. Support from North Vietnam would eventually keep
the southern elements from being utterly destroyed when the United
States escalated the war in the spring of 1965.[4] But neither the advent of
the NLF, nor the infiltration of Lao Dong cadre into the south, transformed the southern insurgency into revolution. In fact, in many respects,
early support from Hanoi can best be seen as providing little more than
foreign aid, "non-indigenous" support to an insurgency that remained
indigenous to the South.

The events that sent Secretary General Le Duan of the Lao Dong
Party to visit South Vietnam in the early winter of 1959 also signaled
that the southern subversives were graduating to phase two of their
insurgency, guerrilla warfare.[5] This is not to say that these operations
were being conducted on a scale comparable to those of the Viet Minh in
1949. But because the southern insurgents did begin supporting guerrilla
operations with terrorist actions, and that terrorism was not being
practiced alone as it had been up to 1957, the move into a second phase
can be readily perceived.[6] Selective terrorist acts continued with great
success, particularly in the rural setting, where GVN forces were the
weakest.[7] The intensity of guerrilla/terrorist operations increased in an
attempt to place great strain on the lines of communication in the
countryside. The Saigon newspaper *Thoi Luan* reported in December
1957:

> Today the menace is heavier than ever, with the terrorists no longer
> limiting themselves to the notables in charge of security. Everything suits
> them, village chiefs, chairmen of liaison committees, simple guards, even

former notables. . . . In certain areas, the village chiefs spend their nights in the security posts, while the inhabitants organize watches.[8]

As in almost any insurgent transition to guerrilla operations, there were heightened acts of terrorism that worked in conjunction with the guerrilla-launched operations.[9] During 1957, a hardened group of Lao Dong cadre formed a number of six-man killer squads with the express purpose of assassinating village and province officials. The southern rural districts were particularly hard hit because that was where the guerrilla units were establishing base camps. All terrorist opportunities were seized to keep GVN forces off balance, particularly in these critical areas. By the end of 1955, most American analysts believed that Diem's pacification programs in the rural districts were succeeding.[10] However, it would not take long for Diem's programs to run into trouble, a situation which roughly coincided with the departure of Lansdale. Between 1957 and 1960 there were an estimated two thousand kidnap- ings and some seventeen hundred assassinations, all carefully planned, organized, and carried out.[11]

At the beginning of 1956, the GVN attempted to extend its area of control throughout a war-torn countryside in order to achieve military stability.[12] But when Diem enacted his land-reform program, under Ordinance Fifty-Seven, which to some degree established the process of redistribution of French-owned land, he appeared almost oblivious to the real land-reform problems that were at the base of the subversive movement. Not only was Diem unable to find any equitable solution to the differences between the landlord and the tenant farmer, but any part of the program which did show promise was sabotaged by corrupt GVN officials. Diem's ability to control government projects fairly was diminishing at a rapid pace, and his insensitivity to the rural land problems that beset South Vietnam only added to his growing unpopu- larity.[13] Many disheartened peasants began viewing the elections of 1955 with greater suspicion.[14] Throughout the next ten years similar programs ensued, including the agroville, the land development center, the strategic hamlet, the New Life Hamlet program, and the revolutionary development program. Most of these programs were vague attempts to improve upon each previous failure.[15]

In response to these failures by the Diem regime, the sects looked increasingly toward the support of the South Vietnamese Communists, and in combination, these groups did exercise a low level of coordination of terrorist and guerrilla operations. Pike makes a great deal of sense when he states that the "guerrilla ambush might get the headlines, but it was the . . . [subversive] village agit-prop meeting that did the most to move the cause toward victory."[16] What these meetings accomplished was the coordination of guerrilla and terrorist manpower, which allowed for an increasing number of decisive military engagements with GVN forces to take place. Although most of these guerrilla operations consisted of hit-and-run ambush tactics, one must keep in mind that this is precisely the way even the largest of guerrilla operations starts out. Increases in the strength of the subversives, together with GVN force inadequacies, unquestionably brought the insurgency militarily into phase two. The desire and leadership to pursue these activities was there in the subversive organization even if the political timetable proved somewhat premature. This is one major reason why the NLF had such military success so soon after the official announcement of its existence in late 1960.[17]

In response to their collective activity in 1957, and as a derogatory propaganda ploy, the Diem government began identifying these Vietnamese Communist subversives as Viet Cong (VC). In July 1957, a Viet Cong–supported Hoa Hao battalion intentionally struck at an entire ARVN division, leaving the scene only after damage was inflicted. Later that same month, a Hoa Hao raid on the town of Chau Duc killed seventeen people. Clashes of this sort continued, including Binh Xuyen raids at Ha Tien and Binh Hoa. These were not terrorist targets or terrorist-type missions for the insurgents. They included large-strength guerrilla units attacking mostly larger-scale military targets. This point was made obvious by a Binh Xuyen battalion-size assault on the Minh Thanh rubber plantation during this same period. Not only did the assault impair production at the factory, but it caused the movement of two entire ARVN divisions into the area of operations as a defense measure.[18]

One of the largest Viet Cong guerrilla operations during this period came in August 1958. A Viet Cong force of nearly four hundred men, led by a known Binh Xuyen commander, attacked the Michelin rubber plantation just north of Saigon in a night assault that took the two hundred–man GVN security force completely by surprise. While several GVN casualties were sustained, the real story was the large number of weapons and ammunition captured by the VC.[19]

From 1957 to 1958, the number of guerrilla incidents rose country-wide. During the first month of 1957 alone, the GVN clashed with Viet Cong guerrillas in the Mekong Delta region no fewer than seven times. Later on that fall, the recorded number of terrorist acts—assassinations, murders, kidnapings, bombings, etc.—climbed to over one hundred in a single quarter.[20] It is difficult to establish an exact count of the actual number of guerrilla and terrorist operations during this early period.

Most operational accounts during this period come from the few after-action reports that were recorded. What is clear is that when Le Duan made his way back to Hanoi, his report on southern insurgent operations expressed a confidence that brought into question previous North Vietnamese misgivings about the resolve and strength of the South Vietnamese movement.[21] There can be little doubt that if Le Duan could not have provided hard evidence of South Vietnamese resolve upon his return, Hanoi's support would not have increased as soon as it did. Terrorist activity alone could not have made his point.

After the Viet Minh had obtained full control of the southern movement sometime toward the end of 1957, they consolidated the local guerrilla forces into two separate groups. The *village guerrilla* was an untrained, poorly equipped, but well-intentioned older peasant who was primarily concerned with local defense and logistic support. The *combat guerrilla* was a younger man who seemed to be a promising candidate for the regular-force units, once these regular units were up and running. They engaged in guerrilla operations outside the village confines and would eventually support the operations of regular-force units during the transition to secondary insurgency.[22]

The next level up from the guerrilla bands, or "popular forces" illustrated above, were the local forces, or regional troops. Organized in larger units than the village and combat guerrillas, these units emphasized larger tactical operations, carried modern weaponry and equipment, and acted as support forces for the regular units.[23] In the end, regular units were intended to bring final victory over the government, as provided in Mao Tse-tung's concept of mobile warfare, or a move from primary to secondary insurgency, if it becomes necessary and is a viable option. If this all seems reminiscent of Viet Minh force structure during the first Vietnamese insurgency, it is because the same organizational influence was eventually put to work in the south.[24]

Apparently the U.S. advisory mission did notice a definite increase in guerrilla activity after 1957. However, the MAAG commander showed little concern. General Williams believed that the Viet Cong posed a diversionary threat, with tactics that were intended to erode the conventional force structure the United States was attempting to build into the fledgling ARVN. Given the state of the South Vietnamese army in 1957, this is an understandable judgment. But the inability to recognize the insurgency for what it was, and the conviction that a conventional invasion from the north was inevitable, allowed the real war—an insurgency now well aged—to grow in intensity under their own feet. What is more, Williams convinced Diem that the Viet Cong only meant to disrupt the ARVN training program in the hope that the army would dispense with its centralized conventional program for the purpose of launching misguided counterguerrilla activities. In a letter of explanation to U.S. Ambassador Elbridge Durbrow, Williams indicated that the lack of sufficient Viet Cong strength—the fact that they did not possess a substantial popular base of support—was countered by a central government whose ability to deal with the subversive threat had gradually improved.[25] Of course, there was no real basis for this assumption since the ARVN forces had not been tested to any great degree, and the only proposed way of dealing with the Viet Cong threat was a conventional military posture.

Since North Vietnam did not represent the same strategic concerns as did North Korea, the question looms large as to why Williams and the MAAG mission were unwilling to even consider earlier warnings from the American intelligence community that a "guerrilla war" might indeed be the reason for French defeat in 1954. The way that the U.S. advisory mission was training ARVN troops and preparing ARVN officers to engage the "expected" large-scale invasion from the north only solidified the position of the Viet Cong, and insured that the ARVN and its American supporters would suffer the same consequences that the French did on their path to Hoa Binh, and their eventual fate at Dien Bien Phu.

Much of the trouble facing MAAG can be traced to a split in how the problem in South Vietnam was being approached. Inherent difficulty between the intelligence and military communities was amplified during the 1950s. As illustrated through a series of CIA and NSA documents from 1950 to 1959 (see Chapter 4), it is clear that the intelligence community believed that the French failed in their conduct of the war against the Viet Minh because of their inability to cope with "guerrilla warfare." The same community fostered the idea of forming large numbers of "anti-guerrilla" forces to help put a stop to the insurgency. Examples pertaining to both the Philippines and the British experience in Malaya were offered. However, when it came to convincing the military advisory mission in South Vietnam that similar circumstances were occurring again in 1957, the intelligence community proved inept at making its case. Both the military and the CIA were at cross-purposes, thrown together in circumstances that became highly volatile.

As a result of the National Security Act of 1947, the CIA gained responsibility for carrying out clandestine activities abroad, which included Vietnam. A fundamental dispute over the tactical relevance of this decision was constant. Ronald Spector states that "Army commanders in the Far East, at all levels, were unhappy with this state of affairs." With the differences in interpreting Vietnamese strategic thinking between the two organizations, "unhappiness" grew. MAAG complained that CIA was not providing the type of intelligence information it needed to better understand its enemy. Moreover, the kind of battlefield intelligence reports that the military is used to providing for itself was disallowed during these early periods, mainly because MAAG was considered to be supporting "clandestine" activities, and therefore reliant on CIA findings. While General Williams complained vigorously about the lack of quality tactical information provided on the North Vietnamese, it is doubtful that a separate MAAG intelligence service would have been more enlightened about the actual insurgency taking place.

Since Vietnamese partition in 1954, the fundamental CIA complaint was that it had been continually hampered in its clandestine activities in North Vietnam. Few "stay-behind" units in the north were able to function after the agreement at Geneva, and when the border closed permanently the CIA was ineffective at infiltrating northward any significant number of agents. Reasons for this occurring can be traced to the inefficient management of the intelligence-gathering infrastructure. Not only was agency infighting a big problem, but there existed a kind of typical bureaucratic hesitation in making important decisions quickly, especially when critical problems were becoming routine. Thus, U.S. intelligence operations in Vietnam, such as they were, began to lose credibility over their insurgency argument with MAAG commanders. A breakdown in the CIA's Saigon intelligence community was also perceived by others outside MAAG.

Initially, bureaucratic conundrums seemed to influence Edward Lansdale little. It is important to recall that during Lansdale's tenure in Saigon, he operated separately from the main CIA station in the south. This was not simply indicative of dual or separate missions, but of a split in CIA thinking over the conduct of clandestine operations throughout Vietnam. The split in CIA thinking about Vietnam occurred well before Lansdale arrived, and it is probable that Lansdale's superiors in Washington expected him to take matters into his own hands. At least that appears to be the way Lansdale viewed his own circumstances, and his actions indicated that, as long as the mission was accomplished, he did not care who in MAAG or CIA he antagonized. His flare for the creative and unusual, his independence and brashness, would eventually take a toll on the relationships he maintained throughout the government hierarchy back in Washington. In spite of his tremendous background in understanding insurgency warfare, Lansdale would soon begin to find himself sitting on the sidelines. Many political leaders began to believe his expertise was easily duplicable, and Lansdale, himself, expendable.

Regardless of his personality, the very presence of Lansdale in Vietnam was troubling, not only to MAAG and to the CIA station in Saigon, but to Diem's brother Ngo Dinh Nhu. Lansdale was well aware of Nhu's sinister influence over his older brother, and tried vainly to ease Diem away. But, Lansdale had other pressing aspects to engage his attention, the least of which was his special teams operations, both in the north and the south. As support for his programs started to dwindle, Lansdale began doubting his own earlier optimism for success of the mission. This must have been especially true after he realized, in late 1955, that he was only in South Vietnam to install Diem—really an insult after what he had accomplished in the Philippines just a few short years before. When he first left Vietnam at the end of 1956, Lansdale's programs were discontinued, not because they were ineffective, but because too few really understood what they were all about. From that point on, it is known that the CIA's failure to conduct clandestine operations in the north hindered the gathering of vital information about the southern insurgency, evidence of direct northern support that might have proved irrefutable to MAAG.[26] But, that Saigon operatives discontinued programs initiated by Lansdale out of what appears to be petty jealousy and personnel inadequacies, is inexcusable. This is especially true when such programs were proven to work as effective intelligence-gathering apparatus. These were programs that, even on the surface, appeared necessary in stimulating the minimum in reliable intelligence information. There would be those within the "Lansdale camp" who would attempt to make their presence known some years later. Even Lansdale would be asked to make several reappearances to Vietnam. However, by then, it was far too late to do any good against a southern insurgency well established. The intelligence community may have been working for a common cause, but it was not working toward common goals. And, to players who understood the game, it was becoming all too obvious.

Robert Thompson warned, in practical terms, against a split in intelligence operations when working in any given foreign mission. It is difficult to define separate responsibilities or simply to coordinate the activities of more than one intelligence-gathering organization. Moreover, rival organizations will tend to conceal information from each other in order to exploit it and obtain credit for themselves. Out of the suspicions and jealousies come spying activities launched against one another, with the primary purpose of making the other organization look bad.[27] Most likely, because of the manner in which Lansdale's organization was being run, both internally and from Washington, the kinds of problems mentioned by Thompson began happening in earnest around

1955. That these organizational problems could have ever been healed during the tenure of U.S. involvement in Vietnam is most unlikely. In fact, a good case could be made that this problem worsened after 1965, just when things were felt to be more in hand.

By mid-1959 General Williams had concluded that the CIA was unable to fulfill his requirements for intelligence gathering, and he proceeded to enlist the support of the South Vietnamese army to provide its own field intelligence.[28] In September the ARVN chief of staff, Le Van Ty, formally requested that training be given to the South Vietnamese army intelligence staff by U.S. advisors. Specifically, training was given on the collection of enemy intelligence and other clandestine activities. Finally, by October 1960, the CIA agreed to also help in the formation of an intelligence/counterintelligence team within the structure of the ARVN ranks. However, as Spector so accurately states, "this concession came far too late to aid General Williams or the advisory group on charting the course of the ballooning Viet Cong insurgency during the critical period from 1957 through 1959." Spector concludes that the available intelligence data throughout this critical period made it "easy to underestimate the strength of the insurgents and to dismiss the murders as isolated acts of terrorism or banditry."[29]

Several key reasons exist for the failure of the South Vietnamese government at this critical stage, and for the continued success of the subversive insurgent threat into phase two. It is questionable if any of the key players at MAAG understood the parameters of insurgency war, or for that matter, that an insurgency war was even taking place. Much of the initial blame has fallen upon Diem, his corrupt regime, his insensitivity and ineptitude at governing. Although Diem was an American creation, propped up daily by American money and propaganda, he continues to provide analysts today with a ready-made villain.

Though not as well represented, but equally villainous, was the failure of the intelligence community, a group which played a confused and inefficient role in being able to convince the MAAG command of the seriousness of the "guerrilla" threat. Even if intelligence gatherers were unable to recognize the basic parameters of insurgency warfare, this community needed to more vigorously and clearly express the dangers of pursuing conventional policies, particularly in light of the French experience against Vietnamese guerrilla units. Furthermore, when evidence needed to be provided on the cohesiveness of clandestine activities in the South, let alone subversive political development in and around Saigon, the intelligence community proved it was not up to the task.

There is no doubt, however, that the greatest amount of blame for the rapid deterioration of South Vietnam, and the inability on the part of the American advisory mission to stop that decline, must fall upon the U.S. military advisory group. It was unwilling, and probably unable, to perceive the real threat of the southern insurgency. General Williams possessed the qualities of a commander that had served his country well during World War II in the great land campaign of Western Europe. After commanding the U.S. Twenty-fifth Infantry Division in Korea from 1952 to 1953, Williams was further reinforced in his assumption that America's military structure need not adjust itself for success to be found in land campaigns throughout Asia. For Williams, and for those that placed him in command, the brewing trouble in South Vietnam represented nothing short of a preamble to a coming land war, one that had to be dealt with in appropriate American military fashion. This did not include mental flirtation with counterinsurgency theories. America's past successes and daunting superiority in military, political, and economic might left no room to doubt its global security prowess. All that remained was to apply itself vigorously to that "new" theater of operations.

American policymakers too were satisfied with their arrogance. Consequently, there was never any real attempt by the military hierarchy to see the equation in Vietnam as having anything other than a conventional military solution. The future pursuit of counterinsurgency theories during the Vietnam era was never taken seriously by the U.S. military, though passing lip service was given. In fact, most of the time spent on counterinsurgency planning dealt with how to avoid any real implementation of programs that would detract from the military's already proven conventional policies. It was believed that there was no problem in South Vietnam that could not be cured by a conventional military solution. The only trouble with this assumption was that there existed no conventional war for MAAG to prepare for, only the guise of one. What exactly was happening in South Vietnam was something Williams and the others in MAAG had no desire to uncover. For whatever reason, Williams was convinced to leave the solitude of his final years in Texas at Fort Sam Houston and venture to the MAAG command in Saigon. Williams was certainly not the first to be sucked into this abyss, and he would not be the last. Vietnam would prove a "quagmire" for many reputations, military and political.

In a larger sense, while the United States did end up holding excess French political baggage in the region by the mid-1950s, it was a voluntary burden which the United States had taken upon itself. Through a series of complex events dating back to 1945, the United States always represented the last bastion of support for a region which it considered to be part of a broader Communist plot for global domination. Yet, through three presidential administrations, Americans were consistently afflicted with guilt over Vietnam, and had to continually find renewed justification for a growing political and military presence. As one source asserts, "South Vietnam (unlike any of the other countries in Southeast Asia) was essentially the creation of the United States."[30]

The problem, of course, was that the U.S. advisory mission proved just as ineffective at combating the insurgent threat as U.S. policy had proved in helping to achieve an independent Vietnam at the end of the Second World War. An American legacy was begun in Vietnam early on, one which exemplified poor judgment, indecision, ineffectiveness, and finally, antipathy.

NOTES

1. Spector, *Advice and Support*, 337n.

2. Although formalized in December 1960, the NLF first began in 1954 when a group of ten people formulated its bylaws at the Saigon-Cholon Peace Committee. In Pike, *Viet Cong*, 82.

3. Ibid., 78.

4. This is evidenced by the amount of time that ARVN/U.S. military units spent after 1965 seeking out North Vietnamese infiltration routes into South Vietnam. See, for example: Jeffrey J. Clarke, *Advise and Support: The Final Years, 1965–1973* (Washington, D.C.: CMH, 1988), 233–41, 472–76; McChristian, *The Role of Military Intelligence*, 131–32; Tolson, *Airmobility*, 25, 165, 234–52; Tran Dinh Tho *Pacification* (Washington, D.C.: CMH, 1980); Douglas Kinnard, *The War Managers* (Hanover, N.H.: University Press of New England, 1977), 142–47.

5. This suggests that the southern subversives were more prepared than ever to move into the next phase of the insurgency. Tanham suggests that Le Duan may have journeyed to South Vietnam in order to see for himself the level and competence of the southern organization, in *Communist Revolutionary Warfare*, 126–29. It is probably more likely that, after the events of 1957 and 1958, Le Duan was hoping to get Hanoi involved before the conflict escalated any further. This was a mixed blessing for the southern subversives, who were still fighting against Diem on the nationalist plank and preferred the outcome to be an independent southern government. What the south got was a committed NLF and promises from Hanoi. Also see Pike, *Viet Cong*, s.v. Ho Chi Minh and the NLF.

6. The idea that guerrilla war began in earnest during the 1957 to 1958 period is supported by most sources, in particular by both those individuals who

were in South Vietnam and those that were involved in policy and analysis in Washington. See especially Hilsman, *To Move a Nation*, 418–19 and passim.

7. Fall provides an excellent account of the kinds of terrorist acts perpetrated by the southern insurgents leading up to the guerrilla phase in *The Two Viet-Nams*, 359–61.

8. *The Pentagon Papers*, Gravel ed., 1:333.

9. See discussion in Thompson, *Defeating Communist Insurgency*, 41–44. It should be recalled that, during the Malayan insurgency, the MCP also maintained both a separate terrorist arm, the Min Yuen, and a guerrilla force, the MRLA (see Chapter 2).

10. *The Pentagon Papers*, Gravel ed., 1:314.

11. Pike, *Viet Cong*, 102.

12. Ibid., 61–62.

13. Ibid., 59–60.

14. Fall deprecates the process as a "plebiscite [that] was only a shade more fraudulent than most electoral tests under a dictatorship. . . . In the Saigon-Cholon area, for example, 605,025 votes were cast by 450,000 registered voters, and mountain or deep-swamp areas patently not even under control of the government reported as heavy voting participation as the well-controlled urban areas." In *The Two Viet-Nams*, 257.

15. A concise look at GVN pacification operations during this period can be found in, Nighswonger, *Rural Pacification*, 6–9 and passim.

16. Pike, *Viet Cong*, 54. Mao stated that there are three types of political activities that support revolutionary guerrilla war: those directed toward the enemy (largely efforts to convert), those directed toward the people (agit-prop work), and those directed toward the guerrilla forces and supporters (indoctrinational). See Ibid., 36, 126–32.

17. A point of clarification should be made about Thompson's statement that a guerrilla phase has been reached when the subversive insurgent can initiate "division level" offensive operations (*Defeating Communist Insurgency*, 41–42). It would appear to be more dangerous to government forces if the insurgent were able to attack divisional targets with smaller, battalion-size guerrilla units and then disengage after inflicting maximum damage. The guerrilla force would then recede into the countryside, dispersing with greater efficiency when pursued by the government army. This was precisely the scenario in South Vietnam, as it had been in Malaya and the Philippines. Hence, the later development of government battalion combat teams (CTs) that could more easily chase the guerrilla forces, providing the much-needed maneuverability which the government had lacked when in a defensive posture. Guerrillas at divisional strength, though often on the defensive during the guerrilla phase, become necessary when the guerrilla force is preparing to move from primary to secondary insurgency.

18. Spector, *Advice and Support*, 314–15.

19. Ibid., 315.

20. Ibid.

21. It is interesting to note, from a CIA report on the 1956 to 1968 period, that North Vietnam wanted little to do with a "renewed war" in South Vietnam, preferring instead to "build socialism" in the north. In ibid., 312.

22. Tanham, *Communist Revolutionary Warfare*, 138–39.

23. Ibid., 140–41.

24. For later organizational charts of the political echelon of the Viet Cong, see Pike, *Viet Cong*, 211, 215.

25. Spector, *Advice and Support*, 316.

26. Ibid., 317.

27. Thompson, *Defeating Communist Insurgency*, 85. For problems of this kind faced by the British mission in Malaya, see Clutterbuck, *Conflict and Violence*, 178–79.

28. Spector, *Advice and Support*, 319–20.

29. Ibid., 320.

30. *The Pentagon Papers*, Gravel ed., 2:22.

CHAPTER 7

Secondary Insurgency and the American Reaction

In an explanation of the National Liberation Front, Douglas Pike states that it "was not simply another indigenous covert group, or even a coalition of such groups. It was an organizational steamroller, nationally conceived and nationally organized, endowed with ample cadre and funds, crashing out of the jungle to flatten the GVN."[1] While the effects on the ARVN forces were more gradual than Pike's statement might suggest, by the end of 1959 the GVN must have realized that it had suffered a truly destructive blow. That blow was delivered by the Viet Cong in a series of terrorist acts which showed a decisive increase in its capability to wage insurgency war.

Guerrilla-force operations were also enlarged so as to more decisively engage GVN military targets and army units in the field. Estimated patrol ambushes increased to over one hundred a month. As the insurgent campaign intensified, the ARVN sustained a number of reverses after initiating conventional search-and-destroy operations in Kien Phong Province near the Cambodian border. In one operation conducted in September, an ARVN patrol consisting of some six companies totaling over 360 men, and combined with a company of Civil Guard troops, was quickly ambushed by a battalion-size Viet Cong unit. The damage to the ARVN patrol included 12 men killed, 14 men wounded, and 9 missing or captured, while VC losses were negligible. The damage and embarrassment was carried further when two weeks later, in the same province, a company of ARVN infantry was attacked by a small Viet Cong patrol. Much to the surprise of the VC patrol, all the ARVN soldiers surrendered almost immediately after shooting broke out.[2]

Twice during October and November, ARVN "sweep" missions were turned away, forced to retreat when ambushed by Viet Cong units. While patrolling engagements were becoming common-place, they did not simply represent the ARVN going out and getting into trouble. Indeed, the Viet Cong were now aggressively seeking guerrilla engagements with the ARVN. In Quang Ngia Province during the same period, detachments of between twenty-five and fifty Viet Cong regularly entered military-controlled areas to conduct sabotage missions against defended targets. The loss of communication centers, bridges, and munitions depots was on the rise. Viet Cong units also seemed to enter at will any number of villages and towns in order to destroy or capture various military installations. The problem got so bad that Diem was forced to admit to the National Assembly that the southern provinces in the Mekong delta were under a "state of siege."[3]

Diem and the National Assembly responded by passing a series of harsh new measures, generally contained in what was known as Law 10-59. The law empowered certain government units in Viet Cong–controlled provinces to carry out punishment of suspected VC and their sympathizers. When the district commanders began complaining that they were losing even more control over their areas and populations, Diem announced a plan to relocate isolated villagers into fortified hamlets, soon to be known as agrovilles. But the program ran into early difficulties, none more damaging than the fact that many peasants were not inclined to uproot themselves and leave perfectly good ancestral land. What was more, these peasants were often forced to provide the labor to build their own agroville centers. Incentives, such as financial gain and greater government support, were merely dangled in front of the peasants as teasers and were never intended to be awarded. Funds provided by the government for the centers were never adequate. Needless to say, the agroville program did not achieve the socioeconomic goals it started out to achieve. What it did do was create a greater Viet Cong response—aggressive guerrilla operations which made it nearly impossible for the government to maintain any reasonable security during the building of settlements and after they had been established. By early 1961 the program skidded to a halt.[4]

If there were ever a friend to a subversive insurgency, it was Ngo Dinh Diem. In a January 1960 message to Admiral Radford, Diem noted that he had begun a program of antiguerrilla training, saying that "the Communists have given up all hope of controlling the countryside because of the presence of young men trained in guerrilla tactics."[5]

Diem's bravado illustrates the sad state of affairs within a government that was doing what it could to avoid reality. As Lansdale so aptly points out in his memoirs, "the Vietnamese have a strong touch of Potempkin [*sic*] in them and are as ready to put up false fronts as he was to build fake villages for Catherine the Great to view."[6] One questions whether the U.S. advisory mission, too, possessed some of the same disagreeable foibles as the government it was pledged to help. General Williams indicated that the overall problem facing the GVN was military, that if the ARVN were better trained and better led, its efficiency would improve in its engagements with Viet Cong units. Subsequently, Williams proposed the lifting of a ban on allowing U.S. advisors into combat situations with the ARVN units they were responsible both for training and helping to plan missions. But when such approval was granted, it was limited.[7] South Vietnamese military officers have since criticized the fact that U.S. "combat" advisors were only allowed in the field for up to six months before being rotated elsewhere. General Cao Van Vien wrote in 1980, "the fact that an ARVN battalion commander had to accommodate several different advisors during this time of command did not help build the kind of working relationship conducive to steady progress and improvement."[8]

No one in MAAG or in the Saigon government appeared to be conscious of the fact that government programs and military operations in the rural areas only aggravated the situation with the peasants. Continuing on such a road only increased antigovernment sentiment, driving many more angered peasants to the Viet Cong rather than to agrovilles. At one point in 1959, the CIA reported that in the Ca Mau region at the southern most portion of the country, the Viet Cong had achieved "virtual control" over the entire district and its villages.[9]

For the South Vietnamese government and its U.S. advisors the conflict was played down, as if its seriousness was all in the minds of those "few" perpetrators who would soon be annihilated. This position must have been laughable to the peasant farmer who witnessed the Viet Cong cadre among the villagers exhibit such ardent beliefs toward the struggle. To the Viet Cong, as Pike relates, *struggle* is the "pale translation of the Vietnamese term 'dau tranh.'" This was a term which represented an almost spiritual quest, one which absorbed one's entire being. "His life, his revolutionary work, his whole world is 'dau tranh.' The essence of his existence is 'dau tranh.'"[10] NLF/Viet Cong cadre thus concentrated on converting unsure peasants into fighters. GVN programs and actions made their efforts all the more easy. By 1960, full-time NLF cadre and Viet Cong regular troops were estimated to number nearly five thousand.[11] This was undoubtedly a questionable estimate, since it reflected an unlikely decline from the accepted estimate in 1954 of some twelve thousand Lao Dong cadre that had reportedly infiltrated across the parallel. Moreover, regional units left out of the estimate, those farmer-by-day, guerrilla-by-night soldiers, were believed to be much higher in numbers than the full-time cadre. A good measure of just what the GVN and its U.S. advisors were up against can be noted from the casualty reports offered in after-action reviews. Authors who have made a study of these reports disagree tremendously with the official GVN reports sent to Washington.[12] What it amounted to was a pretty face being put on an otherwise ugly set of figures.

Beginning in January 1960, and continuing for nearly six months, the Viet Cong hit successfully at a series of southern provinces with the specific purpose of leveling blows against the ARVN military capability. In Tay Ninh, Kien Giang, An Xuyen, Binh Duong, and Phuong Dinh Provinces, the Viet Cong achieved overwhelming success, throwing the ARVN into what was essentially a defensive posture.[13] Because Diem wanted to hear nothing of ARVN failures, his officers provided nothing but success stories, mostly fabricated. His Can Lao Party informants retrieved information from line-unit commanders that must have been disturbing, but they only gave Diem what he wanted to hear. Spector reveals that "the deliberate falsification of operational reports plus the lack of any reliable and precise method for advisers to assess the effectiveness of their units may account for the failure of Americans in the advisory group to recognize the progressive breakdown of South Vietnamese units."[14]

Because of the severe setbacks received by the South Vietnamese in the first half of 1960, ARVN training centers—their procedures and curriculum—came under direct fire from MAAG. General Williams and his subordinates often responded that ARVN failures were not due to improper training, but to the lack of training. Subject to criticism were the length of courses, the ratio of training centers as opposed to the number of actual qualified instructors (eventually thirty-three ARVN training centers existed in South Vietnam), and the communication gap between the Vietnamese and their American counterparts. Douglas Kinnard expands on the first two problems outlined above. He states that, without question, the most significant obstacle to effective training was the poor leadership offered at the school level. "Frequently, the training posts were filled by officers who had been relieved of combat commands for being ineffective—a natural tendency, but over time damaging to the training effort. . . . Training became a business-as-usual affair, five days a week, eight hours a day."[15]

Criticizing the lack of effective communication, Spector indicates:

> Separated by a wide gulf of culture and language, the American adviser could have only the vaguest idea of the effect his guidance and suggestions were having on the unit he advised. Advisers found their counterparts affable, highly accessible, and always willing to listen to advice. But that seldom produced significant results, for even when South Vietnamese commanders issued new orders or directives, they were reluctant to compel their subordinates to comply with them.[16]

Indeed, much of the communication problem that developed, particularly early on, stemmed from the view that many American advisors had of the Vietnamese in general. In a U.S. Army Command and General Staff College study, deficiencies in the South Vietnamese army were attributed to "the long-standing nature of the Vietnamese people:

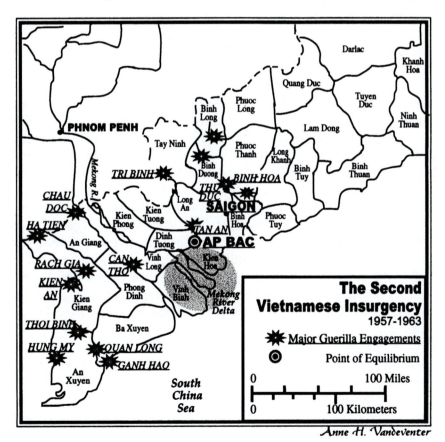

Anne H. Vandeventer

passive, submissive, fatalistic, accustomed to being led . . . pastoral and non-mechanical."[17] Americans routinely, referred to Vietnamese soldiers as "the natives" until the term was officially banned from use in 1957. One is struck by the sharp contrast between the American advisor in Vietnam and the American soldier fighting alongside Karen and Kachin tribesmen in Burma during the Second World War. In the latter case, Americans respectfully refrained from using derogatory terminology to describe their Burmese allies. Asprey provides a concise summary of American advisors in the region, stating that while there were exceptions, the advisors "came [to Vietnam] with confidence instead of caution; they started teaching before they had learned."[18] But the attitude that some U.S. advisors displayed was more than a simple lack of respect for a foreign people due to overconfidence, it was the symptom of a lack of respect for themselves. The "conventionalist" approach to their job as related to the daily inadequacies such an approach yielded, was not the fault of the student, but that of the teacher. These advisors began to realize, sometimes in horror, that their own training was not sufficient enough, particularly as the war progressed and the Viet Cong grew in strength. What is more, the South Vietnamese began to wonder just who the real "experts" were.

The deteriorating security situation in South Vietnam during the early part of 1960 also led to the institution of new, rather sweeping measures. The well-publicized Counterinsurgency Plan (CIP) was first inaugurated, not by President John F. Kennedy, but by his predecessor. President Eisenhower, just months before leaving office, initiated several Defense Department studies that undertook the provision of an official military doctrine of counterinsurgency war. The problem of the day was South Vietnam, so the studies isolated that particular region in providing analyses of possible countermeasures. Preliminary advice called for an American force increase as well as the need for civilian reforms. The basic structure of the plan met little if any resistance among analysts in either the Defense Department or the intelligence community. Consequently the stage was set for the coming U.S. presidential administration, one that would take a firm and controversial departure from known waters.

Although a complete review of the CIP is unnecessary, it is sufficient to note that the CIP became the hallmark initiative of South Vietnam strategy for Kennedy after he took office in January 1961.[19] Probably the most concise reason for the CIP's development was that no one really knew what else to do. The situation in South Vietnam was worsening each day for the GVN. President Kennedy was a known champion of the "counterinsurgency" cause, although the larger part of the U.S. military believed he was severely misguided. Nevertheless, the response was vigorous on the part of the military, from the adoption of the CIP to the development of "counterinsurgency doctrine," and the building of "new" special operations force units to carry on the task.

However, one must question the actual intent of such a plan. Not only was the majority of the military openly against such a strategy, it had received no support from the U.S. military advisory mission in South Vietnam, the one group that had supposedly been on top of the situation since 1955. General Williams was one soldier who protested regularly against the idea of a counterinsurgency strategy for the U.S., pointing to studies already conducted by MAAG incountry.[20] His findings were that antiguerrilla tactics existed within the framework of current army doctrine. A review of specific antiguerrilla doctrines during the period indicates that Williams's approach was purely conventional, and that the doctrines themselves merely echo that conventional belief. However, Williams vehemently denied the contention that the advisory group developed an ARVN conventional force around divisional units too large and cumbersome to maneuver effectively around guerrilla units.[21] Few military officers held the view that they needed to be concerned with political and social aspects of combating a guerrilla war. Spector states that it was only after President Kennedy assumed office that the Special Forces School at Fort Bragg introduced a course of lectures related to the social, economic, political, and psychological elements that make up revolutionary conditions.[22]

The Department of the Navy states that even while "fighting" communist insurgency in South Vietnam,

> . . . the Kennedy administration and the Navy accelerated efforts begun in the late 1950s to rebuild the conventional warfare strength of the U.S. Fleet, especially its capability to project power ashore. Although high-priority items in the defense budgets of 1961–1964 limited funding for a number of important programs of naval readiness, the Navy's ability to conduct a limited, non-nuclear war improved significantly. This was particularly true of the Pacific Fleet, which prepared to counter aggressive Communist military actions in Southeast Asia.[23]

At the very heart of this effort was the question of whether the country could afford to send the necessary conventional military strength to fight in South Vietnam. It was common knowledge that budgetary problems in the early 1960s presented a justifiable constraint on an overt military mission to Vietnam. This is perhaps one significant reason why the

Departments of the Navy and Air Force were engaged in the study of operational aspects related to the CIP, especially of the effect such a strategy would have on their ongoing global strategic commitments. It was the army, however, that was being asked to supply the manpower, resources, and policy changes needed on a vast level to accommodate the major portion of the CIP strategy. The army was looked to for its long standing excellence in versatility, resource management, and organizational structure. And, indeed, the army began instituting a series of investigations to explore the feasibility of the new strategy and needed changes based upon its accomplishments in South Vietnam. The army was in for a shock.

Perhaps the best critique came from an internal army report submitted to the Chief of Staff General George H. Decker in October 1961. Brig. Gen. Richard Stilwell was summoned to investigate and write a report analyzing the American military efforts in the area of "sublimited warfare," specifically that which was being conducted in South Vietnam. Stilwell found that three major areas needed attention. First, the executive branch lacked a comprehensive understanding of what U.S. Army capabilities and limitations were. While the army had a desire to initiate and maintain a sublimited strategy that conformed to CIP requests, it could not effectively do so without a thorough restructuring of its educational and operational system directed toward sublimited war. Just simply initiating a branch of special operations forces would not adequately meet the threat. Instead, the report stated, a "vigorous educational program, both inside and out of the Executive Branch, is a must; and the basic text for such a program could well be the Chief of Staff's speech."[24]

Next, Stilwell voiced concern over intelligence efforts and competing intelligence agencies intheater. Combined CIA and U.S. military intelligence efforts had failed up until 1961 because of a lack of "empathy" toward unified goals. Relating to MAAG's desire to assume the intelligence reins for paramilitary operations, which had previously been under CIA control, Stilwell indicated concern. "It is one thing to be authorized or directed to assume responsibility; it is quite another matter to be adequately prepared to discharge that responsibility without disruption of the tempo or continuity of operations." In a stinging pronouncement, Stilwell found that "how well we do in the field of joint planning and mutual reinforcement vis-à-vis CIA is in large measure a function of the qualified people who can be harnessed to this task. Such individuals are not now on hand."[25]

Ultimately, there existed an organizational vacuum within which few, if any, concrete changes to foster counterinsurgent planning could be successfully undertaken. Just the amount of work dumped on the Special Warfare School, one isolated venue, was evidence of the lack of interest or understanding on the part of senior army leadership in producing compatible sublimited war strategy, training, and execution. There were some positive changes occurring in the force structure and at the school levels, but, as of late 1961, these changes were seen as inadequate to accomplish the "vague" mission of counterinsurgent strategy established by the president.

Along with his strong criticism about the Military Assistance Program (MAP) and its bureaucratic constraints on the advisory group in Saigon, Stilwell took great exception to the conduct of counterinsurgent operations on the part of MAAG officers. Stilwell believed, as Lansdale certainly did, that the essential conduct of a MAAG officer must be to shun protocol, live where his counterpart lives, and be operationally oriented and directly involved in the problems faced by his allies. Stilwell summarized in late 1961 something that could have been summarized in 1957, or even 1967:

> Conceptually, these new Army [counterinsurgent] programs are alien to the MAP as it exists today. The average MAAG unit centers in the capital city; the administrative and logistic aspects of the aid program predominate; liaison is principally at the ministerial and senior officer level; and the scale of living accords with that of the diplomatic community. Grass roots contact is minimal or non-existent. The MAAG observes but stands aside from the local military problems.[26]

Stilwell suggested that U.S. advisors in Vietnam should roll up their sleeves, "sharing the same privations and working as equals alongside their Allies . . . [in order to] develop new understandings and identity of interests. This is a far cry from the pure advisor; but that word and the concept behind it appear to have outlived their usefulness."[27]

As if the organizational, material, and philosophical problems imposed by the military in the early 1960s were not enough, the very essence of the CIP was wrong for three basic reasons. First, as was stated in Chapter 1, to be successful at defeating a subversive insurgency, the government cannot be *countering* anything, as the mere thought of countering insurgency is reactionary and therefore produces a defensive posture which allows the subversive organization to initiate all principal political and military moves. Even Stilwell's report emphasizes the need for the army to take the war to the enemy homeland, to use the CIP, not to defend, but to attack the Viet Cong outright by turning their own resources against them. The problem was that the United States saw its CIP as a reaction to further Viet Cong incursions in the South. This fostered the erroneous attitude that a subversive insurgency can be engaged and defeated at anytime in its development, nullifying the very phases the CIP rationalized.

Second is the notion of *counterinsurgency* as being similar to, if not the same as, *counterguerrilla* war. As explained in Chapter 1, guerrilla operations are a tactical portion of the overall insurgency, which is not a military conflict as much as it is a political, economic, and social engagement. A thorough look at the portion of the CIP provided in *The Pentagon Papers*, indicates that U.S. policymakers were really using the term *counterinsurgency* to mean *counterguerrilla*. This illustrates that the emphasis remained on a known military solution, and that the Viet Cong were, in the end, accepted as being primarily a military target. In a CINCPAC memorandum on counterinsurgency operations, it is stated:

> The majority of the population in South Vietnam and Laos live in rural areas and have little or no interest in political ideologies. They are neither extreme nationalists nor dedicated Communists but rather they are apathetic toward each, willing to support whichever side is in momentary local control but only to the degree necessary to avoid inciting the wrath of the other side toward them.[28]

Thompson writes that the art of strategy in conflicts of intervention rests with the ability to "assess the weaknesses and assets on both sides," and rests also "in applying the means so as to improve the assets and eliminate the weaknesses on your own side and exactly the opposite on the side of the enemy. Victory, almost irrespective of battles, is then a foregone conclusion."[29] The reason for the comparison is to show the obvious lack of a notion of insurgent (counterinsurgent) strategy in the above CINCPAC memorandum and to illustrate that the strategy of a conventional military solution appeared to be predetermined, even as reflected in the CIP.

The third basic problem with the CIP was that it was conceived far too late to make any real difference in the already established Viet Cong insurgency, which, with increasing support from the North, was in phase two reaching for equilibrium. A competent and strong government headed by Diem was thought to be central to a successful implementation of the CIP. Despite Lansdale's continued endorsement of Diem, the GVN president was too far gone to salvage in the view of many South Vietnamese, with the exception of a few close family and friends who saw something in him beyond the decadence, corruption, and ineptitude which were easily exploited by the NLF.[30]

Lansdale, who had acted as Eisenhower's assistant secretary of defense for special operations, was called upon by Kennedy as a special assistant to report on the situation in Vietnam. In direct relation to the proposals of the CIP, Lansdale strongly attempted to reconfirm Diem's validity in the eyes of the then-current generation of U.S. policymakers. Lansdale seems to have succeeded in this attempt, stating that "Diem is still the only Vietnamese with executive ability and the required determination to be an effective President."[31]

Regardless of how many special missions were carried out, committees formed, reports made, the insurgency in South Vietnam became unstoppable by 1961. General Cao Van Vien of the South Vietnamese army later wrote of his experiences in a work about the U.S. advisor. General Vien indicated that a definite change within the insurgency occurred in the twelve-month period leading up to May 1961. During this period, over four thousand GVN officials were killed by the Viet Cong. In a Viet Cong assault upon the provincial city of Phoc Thanh in September, "the Communists employed a concentrated force of several battalions. It was obvious that the war of insurgency being waged by the Communists in South Vietnam had taken on a double edge: that of guerrilla warfare augmented by conventional attacks."[32] In our understanding of insurgency war, this change would indicate that the insurgents moved into secondary insurgency as early as fall 1961. However, other evidence would seem to show that a Viet Cong move this early was not likely since a point of balance, or equilibrium, had not yet been achieved.

In fact, it is unlikely that the Viet Cong were able to achieve equilibrium before the Battle of Ap Bac (to the Vietnamese, the Battle of My-Tho), which was waged from December 1962 to January 1963. Here, consistencies can be drawn between Ap Bac and the Battle of Hoa Binh ten years before, when Giap and the Viet Minh had been in a similar balance-of-force posture facing the French. In both fights, neither side was expecting to engage in a set-piece battle, and neither side proved overwhelmingly victorious at the end. At Ap Bac, the Viet Cong found themselves surrounded by GVN units but managed to breach one flank in broad daylight to avoid capture. The GVN held onto its position for a short while, and after licking its wounds from the large number of casualties taken, claimed a hollow victory with the possession of territory. While the Viet Cong employed guerrilla forces, their tactics matched the GVN in conventional wisdom step for step. Although the

GVN possessed U.S. advisors on the battlefield and brought in tanks, personnel carriers, artillery, and aircraft, the struggle indicated that the GVN was not willing to trade blood for land as the Viet Cong were, and as the Viet Minh had been willing to do in fighting the French.[33] A momentum shift, if there needs to be one, occurs well before the point of equilibrium is achieved, and no amount of military force and hardware will change the eventual outcome. Nevertheless, the South Vietnamese and their U.S. advisors continued to treat Ap Bac as a GVN victory throughout 1963, almost oblivious to the gains made by the Viet Cong in the ensuing months. Moreover, Diem was already wrapped up in another program to defend the South from further insurgent gains.

By the time of the Battle of Ap Bac, the U.S. advisory mission to South Vietnam had changed commanders twice. In August 1960, Lt. Gen. Lionel C. McGarr replaced General Williams as MAAG commander. McGarr was more sympathetic to the U.S. counterinsurgency effort than Williams would ever be, viewing insurgency strategically as a separate "species of warfare requiring development of special doctrine and techniques." But McGarr believed that the Viet Cong insurgency had already reached such a level that it necessitated an enlarged military force. "Under current conditions, . . . social and political reforms were of secondary importance, and pressuring Diem to undertake them might undermine Diem's confidence and trust in the United States."[34] However, as it would appear from the record, Diem's confidence in American support had already declined.

A memorandum of an April 1960 conversation between General Williams and President Diem reveals that Diem believed that the problem with the Viet Cong had become primarily a military matter and that it was important to now seek a military solution. When asked by General Williams the length of time it would take to "pacify" the country, Diem's reply was vague at best, only suggesting that an increase of another four to five thousand Civil Guardsmen would be needed to train the local villagers to protect themselves. What Diem was leading up to was a request for more financial and advisory support from the United States to boost his own conventional military designs for thwarting the Viet Cong.[35] It was obvious from this conversation that Diem had thoroughly bought into the conventional military posture sold to him by Williams. A conventional GVN force was necessary to some degree, but not as a one-way strategy in countering Viet Cong insurgency, which was by then confidently operating in the guerrilla phase. A conventional military response to the Viet Cong would only prove counterproductive.

This 1960 decision on the part of Diem and the U.S. advisory group to follow a conventional military strategy should be remembered for two specific reasons. First, the decision was bound to negatively affect every government program during the Diem administration that attempted to deal with the Viet Cong insurgency on a limited basis. More specifically, any future efforts related to counterinsurgency planning during Diem's tenure could not possibly have been taken seriously. The political and emotional commitment was for a conventional force structure. Williams stated that he was pleased with the decision by Diem to reduce the original increase in ARVN paramilitary units suggested earlier by Ambassador Durbrow.[36] Any subversive activity on the part of the Viet Cong to discredit the Diem government was believed to be subordinate to any military objectives maintained by North Vietnam, hence the need for a definite conventional military solution.

Second, after all of this convincing by the advisory group, the United States appeared equivocal in backing its philosophy of conventional military defense with financial support. It was found, in an analysis conducted by Diem's secretary of state, Nguyen Dinh Thuan, that actual U.S. monetary support to field such a large conventional GVN force had been steadily reduced by the United States over the previous four years.[37] Since Diem had been sold by the Americans on the necessity of such a large force posture, he felt it only right that the United States pay for a good portion of it. Plainly, Diem, now backed into a corner by the Viet Cong and the United States, was deferring entirely to American conventional wisdom. His country needed money, he needed protection, and to aquiese was the quickest way to get it. Rightly so, Diem was feeling increasingly vulnerable.

Still, the U.S advisory group understood, as did Diem, perhaps instinctively, that there was a need to pacify the countryside. Because the Viet Cong guerrillas remained the most visible threat, it was believed a more resolute and controlled attempt at pacification might help to settle things with regard to village defense, at least until aggressive military action could be mounted. Pacification efforts in the countryside would be intended both to frustrate the VC while providing a diversion from a conventional force build up. But past attempts had failed miserably. The need was for a new "pacification expert," a consultant in pacification matters who might provide the success formula that had repeatedly eluded the Saigon government.

When Robert Thompson arrived in Saigon in 1961, Diem was greatly relieved. Thompson had already proved successful in helping to develop British operations against the MCP insurgent forces in Malaya, a process which eventually brought about the famed strategic hamlet program. Although this program had received popular attention in the Diem camp, many American observers remained dubious in their outlook. The only way to defeat the insurgent, according to Thompson, was to systematically remove him from his base of support, the people. This was certainly not a new idea for the Diem government, harking back to agrovilles and the like, and familiarity was probably a key reason for Diem's warm reception of Thompson. It was obvious from the beginning, however, that Thompson brought something else to the situation that was lacking in the Diem experience—technique.

The strategic hamlet program was really a system of highly organized and interconnected fortified villages that maintained a strong defensive posture coupled with a series of military tasks. While the hamlets were heavily armed to discourage Viet Cong activity within their perimeter, the main GVN forces were to engage in what Thompson called "clear and hold" operations. As with Captain Latimer's plan in Malaya (see Chapter 2), the "clear and hold" mission of the GVN forces constituted the most important part of destroying the insurgent threat. Viet Cong were to be cleared out of the district and held at bay so that civic action teams could complete the necessary work to ensure the development of hamlets as self-contained villages. In other words, the hamlets would continue to multiply at such a rate that holding operations would quickly lead to other clearing operations. The succession was intended to be rapid, and the insurgent was to be constantly pursued where he lived, both inside and outside of the villages.

Contrary to much of the criticism leveled at this program, Thompson did believe that a large number of villages could be properly fortified in place, and those that did need to be moved would only be temporarily relocated. Thompson never saw the relocation of villages as mandatory, nor as permanent. He did see their need to be strategically fortified and secured against Viet Cong infiltration. As part of this plan, he also grasped the obvious differences between Malaya and Vietnam, particularly those differences associated with Vietnamese heritage and ancestral land. Time and distance of relocated villages all depended on the given tactical situation, something he realized would differ from province to province. What was most important, however, was the need for a government apparatus that had developed the finesse for employing the complicated hamlet program he wanted to institute. It was the reason he had been hired. What he quickly found, however, was an inept, corrupt, and decaying government machine being supported and advised by the United States. What is more, the insurgency they faced was maturing with force daily, and the allied advisory group paying his way seemed in denial about what was happening to them. Thompson understood something that few have understood about insurgency war, that there exist certain and various strategic principles that are consistent no matter the situation. What may vary, though quite little, is the implementation of tactical concepts specific to the area or region. As Sun Tzu well understood, just as in all aspects of war and politics, strategic principles represent constancy, while tactical concepts embody fluidity. In his later writings, Thompson did not hesitate in voicing his grave concerns over a situation that was futile if changes were not made, and even then there was no guarantee. But his American contractors wanted a guarantee, and he was giving them no such assurances.

Consequently, Thompson had a steady stream of detractors while in Saigon, particularly from the U.S. advisory group, and specifically from General McGarr.[38] One might have wondered if Lansdale had not reappeared, perhaps in different form? Thompson, as Lansdale did, brought new meaning to the word "antagonism." Begrudgingly, Thompson often had to explain the concept of *defense* versus that of *offense* within the hamlet security structure. He later wrote about the accusation that his hamlets were "too defensive," stating:

> This shows a lack of comprehension. Certainly the first object of the programme is the protection of the population, and each hamlet must therefore be capable of defending itself. But the concept as a whole is designed to secure a firm base and then to expand from that into disputed, and finally enemy-controlled, territory. If the programme is strategically directed, and supported by the armed forces, it becomes an offensive advance which will wrest the military initiative from the insurgent.[39]

Operation Sunrise, the code name for the strategic hamlet program, got under way in Binh Duong Province on 22 March 1962. According to GVN estimates, the number of completed strategic hamlets, or New Life Hamlets as they would later be called, reached over three thousand by the end of 1962, and there were another two thousand planned or already under construction throughout the Mekong Delta. Although it sounded great, it was a lie. By November 1963, at the moment at which the coup against the Ngos toppled the regime, the number of completed strategic hamlets was inflated by successors to the government to some eight thousand.[40] The predominant U.S. view was that the strategic hamlet program had failed, mainly because the hamlets had been extended into essentially "unsecured" areas. But Thompson had warned against just that sort of uncontrolled proliferation of hamlets, particularly when being operated, indeed tested, by a novice political group that actually placed greater emphasis on other programs remote in strategic concept and design to insurgent operations. Diem's background of failure in land development programs, especially the agrovilles, did not make him an expert handler on the subject of strategic hamlets. It turned out that many of the "completed" hamlets were nothing more than empty shells, or had been established in such exposed areas that they were easily overrun by the Viet Cong.[41] In fact, hamlet numbers were known to be inflated, by conservative estimates, some 900 percent. Like Lansdale, Thompson had been brought to Saigon on the pretense of conducting larger operations than actually occurred. After a few short months of watching powerlessly as his programs systematically failed, Thompson too would leave Saigon, continuing his analysis of the war from home.

By late 1962, General McGarr was finishing his tour of duty in South Vietnam. Although McGarr had won some influence within the counterinsurgent school, his beliefs about the situation in South Vietnam were typically molded by his predecessor. McGarr accepted the validity of guerrilla war operations, but he also accepted the idea that a breaking point had occurred in South Vietnam, one that put the GVN on exceedingly dangerous ground. Given the maturity of the subversive insurgency he faced, his conclusions are difficult to fault. The circumstances were, by summer 1962, as desperately critical for the Saigon government as they would ever be in the future. It was appearing to U.S. leaders back in Washington that maybe a Korea-styled military conflict in Vietnam was closer to occurring than they originally thought. Initially, it seems odd that President Kennedy's choice for a successor to McGarr, a man who would be charged with seeing to the undertaking of the president's own sponsored counterinsurgent program, would be left to the selection committees made up of regular army officers. Not only did these officers follow a conventional school of thought, but they opposed almost everything Kennedy was attempting to do with the army through the CIP. But, perhaps even Kennedy by then was doubting himself.

Roger Hilsman, a man outside the realm of conventionalist thinking, relates that "there would, quite obviously, be enormous advantages if [McGarr's] replacement could be chosen from among the younger officers who shared the conviction that guerrilla warfare was as much a political as a military problem."[42] He even offered a suggestion in Brig. Gen. William P. Yarborough, a special forces officer who was then commanding the Special Warfare Center. Stilwell, in his 1961 report, refers to Yarborough as "a remarkable soldier, brilliant and imaginative," qualities all too often overlooked in the military.[43] Also with a compatible background was Colonel William R. Peers, an officer with extensive

OSS guerrilla experience, who Hilsman himself had served with in Burma during the Second World War.[44] But the suggestions were never pushed through as "a part of policy," and MAAG, soon to be revised as the Military Assistance Command, Vietnam (MACV), would receive its new commander in General Paul D. Harkins. Unfortunately for the process of combating the Viet Cong insurgency, General Harkins was a throwback to General Williams, possessing extensive experience in fighting the set-piece battle but having had little opportunity to fight the fluid political-military combat of insurgent warfare. Indeed, it would be Harkins who would eventually find himself shamefully promoting the Battle of Ap Bac as a GVN victory.

It is ironic, at last, that both Thompson and Lansdale, for all of their grounded experience in quelling past subversive insurgencies, were left without successes in Vietnam. Their difficulties can be explained in several ways. It is clear that both men were overrun or undercut, not by the Viet Cong, but by the people in Washington and in Saigon who had elicited their services from the beginning. Neither man was utilized by authority to implement his ideas as part of an entire program, something both men had been able to do in their previous successes. Such autonomy and commitment had proved to be essential. In Vietnam, both Thompson and Lansdale were forced to relate their concepts to working programs that were, for the most part, already failing. What remained of their programs after they left Vietnam were either altered or administered by others who were completely unaware of the extent of the insurgent threat facing them. Moreover, the expertise exemplified by both men was never fully grasped by those who were part of the government machine overseeing operations. Strangely, Thompson and Lansdale were never really included as part of that machine, and those operating the machine knew that they could parcel out what they as "non-experts" believed to be the crucial details of their policies—a sure prescription for disaster.

It is also clear from their individual writings that both Thompson and Lansdale questioned themselves. This led inevitably to progress in their own thinking about insurgency. Later, as the deputy secretary of defense for special operations, and after Thompson had left Saigon, Lansdale openly questioned whether the British experience in Malaya was the correct model to apply in South Vietnam. He stated that the Malayan insurgency was "sharply different" in many ways from the problems faced by the Saigon government.[45] No doubt this is true. However, similarity did exist in one vital area. Lansdale's experience in the Philippines represented success over an indigenous insurgency, while Thompson's experiences in Malaya were strategically closer to what was being faced in South Vietnam.

What began in South Vietnam during 1954 as a quasi-internal insurgency, became an externally (or foreign) sponsored insurgency within four years. It is often stated that because the Lao Dong, and later the NLF, maintained an open flow of supply with North Vietnam, a situation was created that lessened any real similarities with the MRLA in Malaya. This is thought to be particularly true since border conditions favored the South Vietnamese insurgency in geographical ways that provided an advantage the MRLA never possessed. The reader will recall from Chapter 2 that one of the key reasons for the failure on the part of the MRLA was their inability to establish firm logistical lines of support with China. However, in such translations it is often easy to forget that these objectives were military targets and only possible to neutralize after political objectives were secured.

Consequently, the British experience with regard to strategic hamlets in Malaya is observed to have had little crossover effect in South Vietnam due to the level of support provided by North Vietnam from early 1960 onward. There is no question, particularly in light of our discussion on the larger strategic concerns about subversive insurgencies, that logistical matters must be dealt with differently than they are in conventional forms of warfare. Often, as in conventional engagements, they are perceived as the obvious strategic military targets of opportunity, to be exploited and destroyed as quickly as possible. However, in an insurgency, this approach creates an overemphasis on secondary targets, and only distracts from the principal non-military objective of decreasing the political subversive need for logistical support, rather than attempting to destroy military lines of supply.

The strategic conditions of insurgency war do not change because geographic and demographic circumstances change. In other words, the guerrilla logistical route of supply, no matter how apparent, should never be the overriding concern to a government endeavoring to halt insurgent conflagration. Instead of trying to destroy subversive supply routes as the first order of business—as in chasing down guerrilla units—the government's focus should be on increasing the paucity for political demand by decreasing the subversive means of recruiting personnel and garnering attention from the populace.

In Malaya, although border conditions had been much more favorable to the government than in South Vietnam, the division between the Chinese and Malay populations was so distinct, and the endorsement from Red China so thorough, that it might as well have been an ideological model for the Viet Cong. Though southern revolution against a U.S. presence was unlikely during the tenure of American involvement, the only real strategic difference between the British-Malayan colonial regime and the U.S.-Saigon regime in South Vietnam, certainly by 1965, was about five years. The "non-indigenous" quality of the NLF subversives in the south existed because of open, and very real, sponsorship from North Vietnam. Moreover, the insurgency in South Vietnam had little to do with U.S. involvement other than the fostering of a government in Saigon. Since the southern insurgency became part of the nationalist movement that would help to eventually unify the country, Americans must begin to understand how little the conflict had to do with them, or with perceived communist aggressions.

Before leaving Vietnam, Thompson spoke directly to MAAG officials, as well as to Diem, about the state of affairs in South Vietnam. As a realist, Thompson advocated harsher measures than many Americans, including Lansdale, were prepared to use. Thompson once stated that the public will tolerate "remarkably tough measures" provided that they are taken under the law of the land and duly enforced by accepted officials.[46] The statement was probably more Maoist in its terse tone than most Americans were ready for. It also appeared as an attempt to expose elements within the Diem government as representing something less than "accepted officials." Perhaps more than anything else, however, it was Thompson's warning that the conflict in Vietnam was going to be more protracted than the struggle in Malaya was, and probably more protracted than anyone was willing to admit—that is, except for the Viet Cong.

Finally, one speculates about the ability of either Lansdale or Thompson to carry their past successes over to the Vietnam problem. It is apparent, in hindsight, that neither faced favorable circumstances. While the Diem government insisted on following corrupt policies, the U.S. advisory group continued to believe that the Viet Cong represented primarily a military obstacle. Given the state of affairs in South Vietnam by 1960, even with the advent of slightly tougher measures, Thompson was incapable of succeeding. In purely strategic terms, the Viet Cong had reached phase two of their insurgency well before 1960, and, by 1961, were preparing for secondary insurgency against the Saigon government. The fact that very few policymakers in South Vietnam knew what was going on, let alone cared to make themselves aware of the insurgent process, only complicated possibilities of stopping the Viet Cong. Desperate, and not having any real understanding of the threat or how to succeed against it after the battle at Ap Bac, both Washington and the U.S. advisory mission concurred that it was necessary to push for a change in the rules of engagement.

Although the United States would attempt pacification endeavors in the future, like some nightmare they were unable to awake from, the opportunity for successful implementation of able government insurgent measures had passed. Once the pace of Viet Cong progression through secondary insurgency began to quicken after Ap Bac, in many respects culminating with the coup against the Ngo's in November 1963, the United States believed it was left with no other recourse but to escalate the conflict. Almost instinctively, the United States knew it had lost the insurgency. With the insurgent base of support relatively secure throughout a good portion of South Vietnam by 1964, the escalation of U.S. conventional forces in 1965 was undertaken as a way to simply change the rules of engagement, adding nothing to counter the already established insurgency.[47] As Pike so aptly states:

> The end of 1964 was the end of an era in Vietnam, and there would be no going back to the old revolutionary guerrilla warfare that had marked the previous five years. . . . The American escalation, the massive influx of American troops into South Vietnam, the air strikes against North Vietnam were all of a new order. An old war had ended and a new war begun, one with new rules and new participants, with new tactics and new strategies, and with new definitions of victory and defeat, whose outcome could more easily be surmised.[48]

The move into secondary insurgency on the part of the Viet Cong was helped along by direct military support from North Vietnam. This was especially emphasized during 1964 when North Vietnamese army units moved into South Vietnam in direct support of the Viet Cong. It appeared to U.S. advisors that the North Vietnamese guerrilla campaign in the South had ceased, and a new conventional war of takeover had begun. Many now felt exonerated in their belief that a "Korea-styled" invasion would occur from the north. This proved a dangerously false assumption on the part of American political and military leaders, causing them to engage militarily with a "phantom" conventional threat. It is ironic that the NVA was nearly always used in support of the southern insurgent forces, and not the other way around. The only thing the American army of the 1960s could hope to do was stop the NVA from conventional invasion. Hanoi knew this, as did the leaders of the NLF. Subsequently, the insurgency in the south, reaching a point of equilibrium in 1964, was able to continue almost indefinitely. Even if NVA support receded, the southern insurgency had the ability to continue hindering U.S. policy efforts throughout South Vietnam, almost indefinitely.

Thompson finds that even in the later part of the war, when whole North Vietnamese regular units entered South Vietnam, the majority of them were still infiltrators because they came onto the logistic supply of the insurgent base within the country. It is interesting to note that, even up until the end of 1967, the percentage of North Vietnamese forces within South Vietnam was still equivalent to about 20 per cent of the whole insurgent strength—roughly 60,000 out of some 300,000.[49] Thompson's point, that the war always remained an insurgency, boosted by infiltration and aided to a limited extent by raids from the North, becomes clearer when one realizes the lack of strategic effect the American military effort had on the strength of the Viet Cong. Just how badly the NVA was beaten on battlefields of the Central Highlands had little to do with how Viet Cong were functioning politically in the Lower Delta. It took a long time for American military leaders to understand this. After 1964, the United States headed down a road of strategic conventional military commitment from which it would do its utmost to never back away.

In relationship to the Korean model of limited war policy, it might be said that the United States fought the North Vietnamese with political and military ambivalence, even timidity. A conventional force posture was not represented by conventional force objectives. There was no permanent occupation of territory, no conquest of enemy governments, no projection of absolute power. If a nation is to wage conventional war within the context of a limited war policy, fear of expanding the conflict in an undesired manner permeates all decisionmaking. Such fear creates political hesitation at best, strategic paralysis at worst—no doubt the gravest of concerns for limited war policymakers.

A notion of that kind would appear to go against all strategic precepts, from Sun Tzu's to Jomini's and beyond, to match the wrong force with the wrong objectives. Many within the conventional school have stated that the only real problem with the American experience in Vietnam was that if a conventional force was committed, then conventional force objectives should have been vigorously pursued. Instead, while the broad political goal of attaining a sovereign and secure border between the two Vietnams remained, there was no single strategic direction anyone knew to follow. Because the questions were militarily cast, the solutions and outcomes were bound to be represented in military terms. The war in Vietnam after 1965 became a hodgepodge of U.S. military and political policy, trial and error brought on by fighting a complicated secondary, phase two insurgency with the wrong tools.

General Curtis LeMay's well-known suggestion to bomb the North Vietnamese into the "stone age" was unrealistic, not because the United States was unable to accomplish such a feat, but because the United States did not want to occupy Hanoi or get into a potential war with the Chinese. Even the use of tactical nuclear weapons against North Vietnam was considered as an outside option, but was rationalized as something that defeated the entire purpose behind limited war strategy. Destabilization of the region in such a catastrophic manner was never intended as part of a policy of containment. Of course, neither were the ensuing ten years of American military involvement, proving equally that a policy of containment was meaningless without implementing the correct political and military strategy.

Throughout all of this, the subversive political threat of the NLF remained the real enemy to the Saigon government. Overt military solutions were doomed from the beginning. Although competent in a limited tactical sense, American conventional military operations were completely unsuccessful in accomplishing the strategic goal of obtaining a secure southern border. By 1965, the United States perceived that it only had three options: to obliterate North Vietnam with the combined weight of its entire conventional and non-conventional military might; to completely withdraw from Southeast Asia, acceding to any potential military objectives established by the communists in the region; or, to do just as it did, allow itself to be sucked into the quicksand of a misguided, misled, and misunderstood policy of limited war strategy.

In the end, there was no strategic conventional military threat in South Vietnam during the ten-year period from 1954 to 1964. After 1965, with the exception of several incursions made by the North Vietnamese Army into the South, there remained no significant strategic military threat. However, in the eight years after 1965, with only minor exceptions, a strategic military threat was the principal focus of the American-led mission. All of this folly eventually became, in the eyes of U.S. policymakers, a North Vietnam versus America war after the Diem government fell in November 1963. When the conflict was firmly escalated by the United States in 1965, the subversive insurgency had gradually and fully developed, and was then able to take on a role that complemented the use of North Vietnamese regular army units against U.S. conventional forces. It had become a successful secondary, phase two insurgency. The problem for the United States was that it continued to believe after 1965 that quelling the insurgent activity of the firmly established Viet Cong could be accomplished, and what is more, it could be accomplished through overt, conventional-force methods. The political situation in South Vietnam was always the most critical element to the equation of halting the subversive insurgency. This all-important political struggle never stabilized before the point of equilibrium was reached by the subversive insurgents, and was never going to stabilize given the large U.S. conventional military buildup. The objectives of the North Vietnamese regular army units remained subordinate to Viet Cong activities until after U.S. withdrawal. It was not before 1975 that civil war would break out in earnest between North and South Vietnam. The insurgency was thus able to evolve, making way for new conflict development, and eventually, new government.

NOTES

1. Pike, *Viet Cong*, 76.
2. Spector, *Advice and Support*, 331.
3. Ibid., 331–32; Also see Fall, *The Two Viet-Nams*, 332–35.
4. Pike, *Viet Cong*, 63–64; Spector, *Advice and Support*, 332–34.
5. Quoted in Spector, *Advice and Support*, 335.
6. Lansdale, *In the Midst of Wars*, 344.
7. This was marginally lifted by Admiral Harry D. Felt, CINCPAC, in May 1959, when U.S. advisors were allowed to accompany regimental units into the field as long as the advisors did not engage in combat; in Spector, *Advice and Support*, 332.
8. Cao Van Vien et al., *The U.S. Advisor* (Washington, D.C.: CMH, 1980), 190.
9. Spector, *Advice and Support*, 332.
10. Pike, *Viet Cong*, 85.
11. This was an official MAAG estimate of VC strength in the south. In Robert F. Futrell, *The United States Air Force in Southeast Asia: The Advisory Years to 1965* (Washington, D.C.: Office of Air Force History, 1981), 53.
12. See chart entitled "Civilian Assassinations and Kidnappings in South Vietnam," GVN Quarterly Report to U.S. Embassy, in *The Pentagon Papers*, Gravel ed., 1:336; cf., Pike, *Viet Cong*, 102–3; Fall, *The Two Viet-Nams*, 360–68.
13. An excellent and concise account of these operations can be found in Spector, *Advice and Support*, 337–48.
14. Ibid., 344.
15. Kinnard, *The War Managers*, 96.
16. Spector, *Advice and Support*, 346.
17. Ibid., 286.
18. Asprey, *War in the Shadows*, 2:1030.

19. A good overview of development of the CIP can be found in *The Pentagon Papers*, Gravel ed., 2:23–55 and passim; also see Spector, *Advice and Support*, 361–68; Douglas S. Blaufarb, *The Counterinsurgency Era: U.S. Doctrine and Performance, 1950 to Present* (New York: The Free Press, 1977), 52–88 and passim; Richard A. Hunt, *Pacification: The American Struggle for Vietnam's Hearts and Minds* (Boulder, Colo.: Westview Press 1995), 16–44 and passim.

20. In an article written after he left the advisory group in Saigon, General Williams outlined some of the problems that continued to face ARVN units, in both their training and field operations. None of it reflected any acceptance or even acknowledgment of the then current CIP doctrine and the push for its military-wide acceptance. See Lt. Gen. Samuel T. Williams, "The Practical Demands of MAAG," *Military Review* 41 (July 1961): 2–15. As a follow-on, see the article by General Harold K. Johnson, "Subversion and Insurgency: Search for a Doctrine," *Army* 15 (November 1965): 40–42.

21. Spector, *Advice and Support*, 352.

22. Ibid., 353.

23. Edward J. Marolda and Oscar P. Fitzgerald, *The United States Navy and the Vietnam Conflict: From Military Assistance to Combat, 1959–1965* (Washington, D.C.: Naval Historical Center, 1986), 277.

24. Richard G. Stilwell, "Army Activities in Underdeveloped Areas Short of Declared War" (report to U.S. Army War College, Carlisle Barracks, Pa., 13 October 1961), 3. Reference can be made to Army Chief of Staff, Gen. George H. Decker, "The Military Aspects of the Cold War" (lecture to U.S. Army War College, Carlisle Barracks, Pa., 8 June 1961). Much of this research activity led to the establishment, during 1962, of the Special Operations Research Office (SORO).

25. Stilwell, "Army Activities," 15, 18.

26. Ibid., 49–50.

27. Ibid., 44.

28. Quoted in Spector, *Advice and Support*, 361. Also see, "The Counterinsurgency Plan," in *The Pentagon Papers*, Gravel ed., 2:23–25 and passim. These conclusions can be compared to those provided by SORO during a later period.

29. Thompson, *No Exit from Vietnam*, 122.

30. Lansdale was a reluctant part of the Taylor-Rostow mission to Saigon in the autumn of 1961. Hilsman, who knew Lansdale at the time, indicates that Lansdale did voice concerns to Diem about his brother and special assistant, Ngo Dinh Nhu. "Diem's unwillingness to delegate authority to anyone but Nhu was having its consequences in overwork for themselves and inefficiency in the operation of the government. Both were defensive and increasingly isolated. Diem seemed especially cut off, since he apparently got this information only through Nhu." In Hilsman, *To Move a Nation*, 421–22.

31. *The Pentagon Papers*, Gravel ed., 2:26. For total concurrence with Lansdale's view of Diem, see Taylor, *Swords and Plowshares*, 401 and passim.

An August 1960 letter from Lansdale to General McGarr reflects continued support for Diem. Lansdale still believed the problem was not Diem, but a combination of the vexing issue of the Viet Cong and the poor behavior exhibited by ARVN troops in the field. In Spector, *Advice and Support*, 361.

32. Cao Van Vien et al., *U.S. Advisors*, 123–24.

33. For greater insight into the battle at Ap Bac, as well as of the U.S. military's politicization and complete misperception of the early conflict in Vietnam, read MACV, Lt. Col. John Paul Vann, "Senior Advisor's Final Report," 1 April 1963, CMH. One of the more intriguing accounts of the battle can also be found in Neil Sheehan's, *A Bright Shining Lie: John Paul Vann and America in Vietnam* (New York: Random House, Inc., 1988), 201–65 and passim. Also see Dave Richard Palmer, *Summons of the Trumpet: U.S.-Vietnam in Perspective* (San Rafael, Calif.: Presidio Press, 1978), 27–38; Hilsman, *To Move a Nation*, 447–49; Fall, *The Two Viet-Nams*, 381; Duiker, *The Communist Road to Power in Vietnam*, 230–35.

34. Spector, *Advice and Support*, 368. This is the inception of the army's false belief that if an insurgency can be militarily beaten back, even in a later phase, then the counterinsurgents will have new life. Such strategy implemented in South Vietnam after 1965 proved futile at overcoming the steady erosion of popular government control as opposed to acceptance of the subversive insurgency. As long as the political infrastructure of the subversive insurgency does not weaken, the government remains in grave danger.

35. Department of State, *Foreign Relations of the United States, 1958–1960*, vol. I (Washington, D.C.: GPO, 1986), 374.

36. Ibid., 374. Also see, Spector, *Advice and Support*, 276–77, 370–71.

37. Financial backing fell sharply from $171 million in 1956 to $124 million by 1960, a point at which the military commitment of the Viet Cong was on the rise. In *Foreign Relations of the U.S.*, 1:361.

38. See "Initial Reaction of U.S. Advisors," in *The Pentagon Papers*, Gravel ed., 2:140–42.

39. Thompson, *Defeating Communist Insurgency*, 126.

40. These figures were inflated under the New Life Hamlet program, a quickly thrown together copy of the original strategic hamlet program that died when Diem and Nhu were killed. See summary in *The Pentagon Papers*, Gravel ed., 2:153–58; cf., Nighswonger, *Rural Pacification*, 63.

41. Hilsman, *To Move a Nation*, 462.

42. Ibid., 426.

43. Stilwell, "Army Activities," 33. For more contemporary views by Stilwell, see "U.S. Counterinsurgency: Political and Psychological Dimensions," in *Guerrilla Warfare and Counterinsurgency: U.S.-Soviet Policy in the Third World*, ed. Richard H. Shultz, Jr., et al. (Lexington, Mass.: Lexington Books, 1989), 299–308.

44. Hilsman, *To Move a Nation*, 426. Also see Hilsman, *American Guerrilla*, for experiences with Peers during World War II. It might also be important to note

that the rank of these men at the time of developing a CIP was not indicative of their respective levels of expertise, but rather the military's lack of tolerance for officers who thought outside the normal confines of old paradigms. Also, see contemporary views by Yarborough, "Counterinsurgency: The U.S. Role—Past, Present, and Future," *Guerrilla Warfare and Counterinsurgency: U.S.-Soviet Policy in the Third World*, ed. Richard H. Shultz, Jr., et al. (Lexington, Mass.: Lexington Books, 1989), 103–14.

45. Spector, *Advice and Support*, 356.
46. Thompson, *Defeating Communist Insurgency*, 53–54.
47. Thompson, *No Exit from Vietnam*, 163–78.
48. Pike, *Viet Cong*, 165.
49. Thompson, *No Exit from Vietnam*, 45.

Summary Notes on Lessons of a Failed Strategy

An explanation of America's involvement in Vietnam is, at the very least, a complicated task. It is a task made even more complex by the tangled web of misinterpretations which have compiled as a result of the U.S. military's "rebuilding" efforts since 1975. If anything, this study of insurgency war and its relationship to the American experience in Vietnam, is not comprehensive enough. The American failure, which occurred well before 1965, was directly related to an inability and an unwillingness to understand insurgency as a unique part of political-military strategy. Unfortunately, as this book goes to publication, the trend continues. There is little doubt that this trend can only negatively affect America's future role in maintaining global security. If this study can help clarify the ongoing debate, and cause the reader to penetrate the strategic question further, then it has succeeded.

In Chapter 1 it was first necessary to show the divergence and confusion related to insurgency war analysis in existing sources before a working definition could be presented. Within the parameters of the working definition of insurgency an attempt was made to explain the principles of insurgency from both a tactical and strategic perspective. In doing so, it was important to also show how insurgencies gain in momentum from a bottom up, rather than a top down approach. This grass roots development of subversive insurgent organizations is important to political entities such as the Communists, but only because of their ability to soundly organize strong-willed, disenfranchised nationalists. Communism never was a prerequisite for insurgent organizations to exist, nor was it a founder of the strategic design of insurgency war. As well, the revolutionary principles of Mao Tse-tung, Vo Nguyen Giap, and Ho Chi Minh lend support to the strategic design of insurgency war, but cannot lay claim to its invention. Due to a void in the development and understanding of insurgency as a *method* and as a *type* of warmaking, separate in strategic design from previously accepted polemical influence, the proposed working definition and explanation was necessary before an ensuing review of the American experience in Vietnam could be fully understood. This is not to say that insurgencies did not exist elsewhere. Indeed, after 1945 a number of insurgent threats existed globally, many of which still exist today, and may continue into the next millennium. But it is still Vietnam that provides the best contemporary lessons for United States policymaking, and therefore provides the subject for practical application in this study.

Before Vietnam took center stage in U.S. policymaking, however, certain events in Southeast Asia demanded attention. Chapter 2 provided examples of insurgencies in both the Philippines and in Malaya, subversive threats that were successfully quelled by their respective governments. These insurgencies were representative of a growing strategic problem in the region. What was mistakenly viewed by American policymakers as some bold Communist plan for world dominance after 1945, was in reality the exertion of separate subversive insurgent groups in areas that were susceptible to revolutionary/civil movements, i.e., political and economic vacuums which begged for the resurgence of competent self-government, free from the colonial traditions of the past. The communist backdrop was merely an organizational wheel in which the separate subversive groups found common principles that helped to mask real internal grievances related to postwar politics.

The American and British experiences exemplified success with two different types of insurgencies, described as *indigenous* and *non-indigenous*. Although separately pursued, they possessed common lessons. It was proven necessary for a sound governing apparatus to exist, one that was sympathetic to the needs of the people, an intelligence and psychological warfare scheme that represented common goals and objectives, and a non-corrupt military and police force that was trained specifically to engage subversive insurgent political and military threats. Importantly, this force needed to be large enough to over-match the insurgent guerrilla capability, yet never sway from the intent to be an insurgent force itself. This, therefore, becomes one of the key maxims, that insurgencies cannot effectively be countered, but must be opposed by other insurgencies.

The emergence of Edward Lansdale and Robert Thompson, two men that brought with them similar irregular war experiences from World War II, were overwhelmingly successful in their respective missions. Both brought expertise and a flair for the creative approach to insurgency techniques. Both men would also involve themselves in the American advisory mission to Saigon in the mid-1950s and early 1960s. While their personal sagas are better told elsewhere, these individuals provide a distinct character to this story, helping to illuminate the humanism of such struggles that face nations. Too often, in field manuals and subcommittee reports, the human character of war is lost among the complexity of bureaucratic decisionmaking, and quite typically among the treatises of previous generations. Representing the battlefield today in terms of being "technological" also helps to further a perceived lack of humanism regarding modern conflict, and establishes a false sense of personal security, the notion that somehow war has become clean. Americans have always looked for a way to avoid or soften their connection to global responsibility, often preferring an unrealistic appraisal of future solutions when faced with contrary facts. Recent American wars provide a facade which help to advance the myth that the world is now basically safe, a fantasy that America has somehow become untouchable.

Chapters 3 through 7 can therefore be taken together since they explain circumstances in Vietnam after the Second World War in relation to the insurgency model proposed in Chapter 1. The importance of the events which led to Viet Minh victory over the French in the first Vietnamese insurgency, occurring roughly from 1945 to 1954, help to also explain the defeat of the Diem government and the American advisory mission. This happened as a result of the second Vietnamese insurgency, running from its inception in 1954, to the point of attaining equilibrium ten years later. The southern insurgency's final evolution to civil war occurred only after the U.S. military withdrew from Saigon in 1973, and culminated with the fall of Saigon to northern troops in 1975.

Despite the lack of defined political purpose the American soldier fought tenaciously. But no matter how tenacious the American soldier may have been, or how purposeful the American political will may have gotten, it was not going to turn the tide against a subversive insurgency that had reached equilibrium. Not grasping this fact, not understanding the principles of insurgency war, the United States, as many nations before it, proceeded along a path that exacted an unreturnable price.

There is no question that the American inability to understand the earlier French debacle led to the disastrous policies implemented during the tenure of the U.S. Military Assistance Advisory Group. When the Diem government was toppled in November 1963, less than two years later the United States introduced large conventional land forces, providing the false sense that it had changed the conflict to something understandable, and, therefore, winnable. The Vietnamese insurgents had succeeded at everything but the removal of U.S. political influence in South Vietnam, something that was bound to happen given the confused state of American political and military affairs. Escalating the war from low to middle intensity was not only an act of frustration, but an open admittance of failure on the part of the Saigon government and the U.S. advisory mission to successfully wage insurgency war. American leaders failed to correctly diagnose the problem in South Vietnam from the beginning, instead turning to a familiar form of military policy that had proved successful in previous wars. The fact that the struggle in Vietnam did not lend itself to proven conventional war strategies was never fully realized by the official decisionmakers in Washington. It is questionable whether any headway has been made nearly half a century later.

However, warnings of problems that lie ahead for the U.S. military are abundant. With the overt conventional threat from traditional cold war enemies now declining, increased economic volatility in the United States appears to outline the need to rethink much of its current military policies. Lessons from the U.S. experience in Vietnam are far from learned; indeed, confusion about strategies employed by and against the U.S. military continues to cause controversy and debate. The rise of both the conventional and insurgency schools of thought are no doubt healthy for this continued debate and analysis. But the debate has yielded little satisfaction, and those strategists in the "other than conventional camp" have been unable to persuade status quo thinkers that their strategic paradigm is obsolete for the new millennium. The complex realities of an insurgent strategy are not to be avoided if global American security interests are to be met. Make no mistake, conventional and nuclear deterrent policies, combined with the tremendous industrial capacity that the United States maintains, are part of the equation for providing a dominant insurgent strategy. The combined elements of military doctrine, political policy, national security, allied strategies, and the principles of insurgency war must also go into making up a concerted, unified strategic design.

Despite these realizations, American security continues to be threatened in low-intensity regions, perhaps more than ever before. Third World subversive insurgent regimes have little to fear from a post-Vietnam America, and even less to fear from a post–Gulf War America.

The occasional use of large conventional forces in the future will only be economically feasible when part of an international effort, made increasingly meaningless in today's undulating riptide of Third World demands where allied intentions become more capricious. As strategic polarity dissipates, it is clear that the majority of America's future battles will be low-intensity in nature. Whether one likes it or not, insurgency is a strategic fact of life in America's future. The idea of a strong United Nations peacekeeping force, able to respond unilaterally and globally to meet all conventional force needs, is something that a potentially unstable U.S. economic climate will foster and, therefore, be forced to accept. Yet, at the same time, the United States can ill afford to be the sole police force in the world. If, then, many of America's political and military policy objectives are to be achieved without the intervention of foreign powers and the collision of large conventional armies, they will most likely be achieved within an insurgency framework. The level of achievement may well depend on how clear U.S. policymakers are about the strategic concepts of insurgency war. Though implementation of insurgency war strategy cannot be seen as a panacea for all security problems facing the United States, it can help keep eventual operational costs low and prevent such security problems from becoming overt military conflicts.

As W. W. Rostow stated in his notable speech at Fort Bragg some years ago, the best way to win an insurgency war is to prevent it from happening in the first place. In fact the best way to prevent any war is to make clear policy decisions in a way that allows national security objectives to be achieved with a minimum amount of force and persuasion. Sun Tzu maintained throughout his own writings that anyone who saw his own reflections on war as a means to prescribe rather than as a means to prevent, understood little and was doomed to perish. Under such conclusions, much work should then lay ahead for the U.S. strategic planner, provided that future policymakers do not copy the same disastrous policies that were pursued a half century ago in Vietnam. However, a brief look into current U.S. military doctrine and strategic understanding leaves considerable room for worry.

Steven Metz, in an article published by the U.S. Army War College, states:

A frightening contradiction dominates the counterinsurgency environment: there is little indication that U.S. skill in this type of conflict has grown as rapidly as the strategic relevance of insurgency. This dangerous gap between capabilities and the extent of the threat, which first became evident during counterinsurgency's post-Vietnam Dark Ages, can be traced to a number of factors. Among the most pressing is the lack of coherent planning processes to link strategic, operational, and tactical responses and bring order to the erratic, ad hoc way that the United States currently approaches counterinsurgency.[1]

Charles Maechling, Jr., perhaps reflecting the heart of America's lack of resolve, states that subversive insurgent movements are "more protracted in duration than the counterinsurgency programs of the United States, which tend to be reactive and decisionseeking. Unless these revolutionary strategies are understood, the United States will face a series of Vietnam-like defeats, smaller in scale but more devastating in cumulative impact."[2]

America's lack of a diverse strategic military understanding is representative of a nation that is bound by conventional military perspectives and lacks the social and political fabric to institute new designs for a future political-military strategy that can ably combat subversive insurgency. General Stilwell supported this point in 1961 when he stated:

> Attempts to generate positive, coordinated forward plans may continue to flounder as they have in the past by reason of running counter to the American character. As a nation we are adept at dealing with specific, concrete, one-time issues; we have the greatest of difficulty gearing ourselves to problems which are open-ended as to time, obscure as to issue and substantively of less than critical importance.[3]

For America, the lessons about Vietnam are probably more subtle than anything yet encountered in its political-military history, and present a far greater dilemma for a nation struggling with globalism. An attempt to develop a capable and efficient security policy during a time of extreme paradigm shift is undoubtedly at the heart of that dilemma. While all this might have something to do with what social thinker Alvin Toffler refers to as a transition from a "Second Wave" to a "Third Wave" society, it probably has more to do with America's strategic position in the world after 1945, a position that continues to necessitate a working knowledge of insurgency it does not currently demonstrate. Indeed, America's global political role has changed more dramatically than most Americans know, as did Rome after the Republic for most Romans. Insurgencies are historically ancient occurrences and the lack of understanding them has helped to provide a foundation for the erosion of nations—the benchmark of which is represented by a growing loss of political purpose and awareness, a penchant for entrenched strategic ideology.

Robert Thompson illustrates an aspect of the American character which cannot be avoided. The "traditionalist" view of war, the Clausewitzian perspective that has become so popular in recent analysis, finds little solace in Thompson's writings:

> The training and indoctrination seem to have led to a view of strategy which at best is getting there 'firstest with the mostest,' which makes a little sense, and at worst is 'find 'em and fight 'em,' which makes no sense at all. One of the reasons for this approach may be that the mechanical and technological advances of recent years (together with the logistic problems which they have raised) have led to a new computerized attitude to war in which men are themselves merely one of the machines.[4]

Insurgency war is therefore best understood, not as a science to be quantified and mastered in some mechanical fashion, but rather as a strategic art to be revealed, studied, and integrated over time. Current U.S. doctrine indicates that America is still politically and militarily well behind the learning curve. It cannot afford to remain that way.

> The most difficult things in the world
> must be done while they are still easy,
> the greatest things in the world
> must be done while they are still small.
> —The *Tao-te Ching*

NOTES

1. Steven Metz, "Counterinsurgent Campaign Planning," *Parameters* 19 (September 1989): 60. More recently, from his position as associate research professor of national security affairs at the Strategic Studies Institute (SSI), Dr. Metz elaborates on a need to further evaluate insurgencies in terms of being "spiritual" or "commercial." See Steven Metz, *The Future of Insurgency* (Carlisle Barracks, Pa.: Strategic Studies Institute, U.S. Army War College, 1993), especially his conclusion, 24–5; Steven Metz, "A Flame Kept Burning: Counterinsurgency Support After the Cold War," *Parameters* 25 (autumn 1995): 31–41.

2. Charles Maechling, Jr., "Insurgency and Counterinsurgency: The Role of Strategic Theory," *Parameters* 14 (autumn 1984): 32. For further treatment, see John M. Gates, "People's War in Vietnam," *The Journal of Military History* 54

(July 1990): 325–44; Edward N. Luttwak, "Notes on Low Intensity Warfare," *Parameters* 13 (December 1983): 11–18; Max B. Manwaring, "Toward and Understanding of Insurgent Warfare," *Military Review* 68 (January 1988): 28–35; Rod Paschall, "Low-Intensity Conflict Doctrine: Who Needs It?" *Parameters* 15 (autumn 1985): 33–45;   Krepinevich, *The Army and Vietnam*, 268–75. For a fascinating and still contemporary critique of military bureaucracy and planning, see Cincinnatus, *Self-Destruction*, 165-89 and passim.

   3.   Stilwell, "Army Activities," 20.

   4.   Thompson, *No Exit from Vietnam*, 130. For further treatment of the post-1945 era as related to this study, see Thompson's, *Revolutionary War in World Strategy, 1945–1969* (New York: Taplinger Publishing Company, 1970).

Abbreviations

AFP	Armed Forces of the Philippines
ARVN	Army of the Republic of Vietnam
BCT	Battalion Combat Team
BUDC	Barrio United Defense Corps
CAO	Civil Affairs Office
CAT	Civil Air Transport
CIA	Central Intelligence Agency
CINCPAC	Commander-In-Chief, Pacific
CIP	Counterinsurgency Plan
CMH	Center for Military History
DA	Department of the Army
FM	Field Manual
FMFM	Fleet Marine Field Manual
GPO	Government Printing Office
GVN	Government of Vietnam
JCS	Joint Chiefs of Staff
JUSMAG	Joint United States Military Advisory Group
LIC	Low-Intensity Conflict
MAAG	Military Assistance Advisory Group
MACV	Military Assistance Command, Vietnam

MCP	Malayan Communist Party
MDAP	Mutual Defense Assistance Program
MIS	Military Intelligence Service
MPAJA	Malayan People's Anti-Japanese Army
MRLA	Malayan Races' Liberation Army
NATO	North Atlantic Treaty Organization
NLF	National Liberation Front
NSC	National Security Council
NVA	North Vietnamese Army
OPC	Office of Policy Coordination
OSS	Office of Strategic Services
PSYWAR	Psychological Warfare
SEATO	Southeast Asian Treaty Organization
SMM	Saigon Military Mission
SOE	Special Operations Executive
SORO	Special Operations Research Office
TRADOC	Training and Doctrine
VC	Viet Cong

Selected Bibliography

UNPUBLISHED DOCUMENT SOURCES

U.S. Army Center for Military History (CMH), Washington, D.C.
U.S. Army Military History Institute (MHI), Carlisle Barracks, Pa.

PUBLISHED DOCUMENTS

U.S. Congress, State Department, and Department of Defense

House Committee on Armed Service. *United States-Vietnam Relations 1945–1967: Study Prepared by the Department of Defense*. (The Pentagon Papers). 12 Vols. Washington D.C.: GPO, 1971.

U.S. Congress. House. *United States Defense Policies in 1960*. House Doc. 207. 87th Cong., 1st sess., 1961.

Senate Committee on Foreign Relations. *The United States and Vietnam: 1944–1947*, by Robert M. Blum. 92d Cong., 2d sess., 1972. Washington, D.C.: GPO, 1972.

Department of the Army. *FM 31-15 Operations against Irregular Forces*. Washington, D.C.: GPO, 1961.

———. *FM 31-16 Counterguerrilla Operations*. Washington, D.C.: GPO, 1963.

———. *FM 31-20 Operations against Guerrilla Forces*. Washington, D.C.: GPO, 1951.

———. *FM 31-21 Guerrilla Warfare and Special Forces Operations*. Washington, D.C.: GPO, 1953.

———. *FM 31-21 Guerrilla Warfare*. Washington, D.C.: GPO, 1955.

———. *FM 31-21 Guerrilla Warfare and Special Forces Operations*. Washington, D.C.: GPO, 1958.

———. *FM 31-21 Guerrilla Warfare and Special Warfare Operations.* Washington, D.C.: GPO, 1961.

———. *FM 31-21A (SECRET) Guerrilla Warfare and Special Warfare Operations.* Washington, D.C.: GPO, 1961.

———. *FM 31-22 Army Counterinsurgency Forces.* Washington, D.C.: GPO, 1963.

———. *FM 31-22A (SECRET) U.S. Army Counterinsurgency Forces.* Washington, D.C.: GPO, 1963.

———. *FM 33-5 Psychological Operations.* Washington, D.C.: GPO, 1963.

———. *FM 100-20 Field Service Regulations, Counterinsurgency.* Washington, D.C.: GPO, 1964.

———. U.S. Army Infantry School. *Operations against Guerrilla Warfare.* USAIS Special text 31-20-1. Fort Benning, Ga.: USAIS, 1951.

———. U.S. Army Intelligence Center and School. *The USAICS Handbook on Urban Terrorism.* Sup. Rev., 03317-1. Fort Huachuca, Az.: USAICS, June 1978.

———. U.S. Army Special Warfare School. *Readings In Counterguerrilla Operations.* Fort Bragg, N.C.: USASWS, 1963.

———. U.S. Army Special Warfare School. *Counterinsurgency Planning Guide.* USASWS Special text 31-176. Fort Bragg, N.C.: USASWS, 1963.

———. *TRADOC PAM 525-44 U.S. Operational Concept for Low-Intensity Conflict.* Washington, D.C.: GPO, 1988.

Department of State. *American Force Policy, 1961: Viet-Nam.* Current Doc., nos. 537-547. Washington, D.C.: GPO, 1961.

Department of State. *American Foreign Policy, 1962: Viet-Nam.* Current Doc., nos. 9-83 to 9-91. Washington, D.C.: GPO, 1962.

Department of State. *Foreign Relations of the United States, 1958–1960.* Vol. 1. Washington, D.C.: GPO, 1986.

Joint Chiefs of Staff. *A Dictionary of United States Military Terms.* Washington, D.C.: Public Affairs Press, 1963.

Joint Pub 3-07. *Joint Doctrine for Military Operations Other Than War.* Washington, D.C.: 16 June 1995.

Marine Corps. *FMFM-21 Operations Against Guerrilla Forces.* Washington, D.C.: GPO, 1962.

Public Papers of the Presidents of the United States: Harry S. Truman, 1945–1953. Washington, D.C.: GPO.

Public Papers of the Presidents of the United States: Dwight D. Eisenhower, 1953–1961. Washington, D.C.: GPO.

Public Papers of the Presidents of the United States: John F. Kennedy, 1961–1963. Washington, D.C.: GPO.

Public Papers of the Presidents of the United States: Lyndon B. Johnson, 1963–1969. Washington, D.C.: GPO.

U.S. Intelligence Reports, Messages, and Communiqués

Central Intelligence Agency. CIA Research Reports: Vietnam and Southeast Asia, 1946–1976. *The Crisis in Indochina.* (10 February 1950): 1–10. Frederick, Md.: University Publications of America, 1983, text-fiche.

———.*Consequences to the U.S. of Communist Domination of Mainland Southeast Asia.* (13 October 1950): 1–13. Frederick, Md.: University Publications of America, 1983, text-fiche.

———. *Probable Developments in Indochina through mid–1954.* (4 June 1953): 1–10. Frederick, Md.: University Publications of America, 1983, text-fiche.

CINCPAC. *Message to the Secretary of State.* (5 December 1963): 1. Frederick, Md.: University Publications of America, 1983, text-fiche.

Joint Chiefs of Staff. *Message to CINCPAC.* (2 December 1963): 1. Frederick, Md.: University Publications of America, 1983, text-fiche.

———. *Message to the President.* (6 December 1963): 1–2. Frederick, Md.: University Publications of America, 1983, text-fiche.

National Security Council. Documents of the National Security Council, 1947–1977. *U.S. Policy Toward Asia.* NSC Doc. 48. (10 June 1949): 65. Washington, D.C.: University Publications of America, 1980, text-fiche.

———. *The Position of the U.S. with Respect to Asia.* NSC Doc. 48/1. (23 December 1949): 40. Washington, D.C.: University Publications of America, 1980, text-fiche.

———.*Collaboration with Friendly Governments on Operations against Guerrillas.* NSC Doc. 90. (26 October 1950): 1–4. Washington, D.C.: University Publications of America, 1980, text-fiche.

———. *U.S. Objectives and Courses of Action with Respect to Communist Aggression in Southeast Asia.* NSC Doc. 124. (13 February 1952): 1–19. Washington, D.C.: University Publications of America, 1980, text-fiche.

———. *U.S. Objectives and Courses of Action with Respect to Southeast Asia.* NSC Doc. 124/2. (25 June 1952): 1–22. Washington, D.C.: University Publications of America, 1980, text-fiche.

———. *U.S. Policy and Courses of Action with Respect to Southeast Asia.* NSC Doc. 177. (30 December 1953): 1–31. Washington, D.C.: University Publications of America, 1980, text-fiche.

———. *U.S. Policy and Courses of Action with Respect to Southeast Asia.* NSC Doc. 177, Special Annex. (31 December 1953): 1–20. Washington, D.C.: University Publications of America, 1980, text-fiche.

———. Minutes of the Meetings of the National Security Council, with Special Advisory Reports. *U.S. Psychological Strategy with Respect to the Thai Peoples of Southeast Asia.* (2 July 1953): 1–47. Frederick, Md.: University Publications of America, 1982, text-fiche.

OSS/State Department Intelligence and Research Reports. Postwar Japan, Korea, and Southeast Asia. *Biographical Information on Prominent Nationalist Leaders in French Indochina.* Indochina, no. 11. (25 October

1945): 1–99. Washington, D.C.: University Publications of America, 1977, text-fiche.

————. *The Role of Communists in Malaya*. (16 March 1947): 1–145. Washington, D.C.: University Publications of America, 1977, text-fiche.

————. Supplement, 1950–1961. *North Vietnam Increases Pressures on South Vietnam*. (7 June 1960): 1–3. Washington, D.C.: University Publications of America, 1977, text-fiche.

OFFICIAL MILITARY HISTORIES

Cao Van Vien, Ngo Quang Truong, Dong Van Khuyen, Nguyen Duy Hinh, Tran Dinh Tho, Hoang Ngoc Lung, and Chu Xuan Vien. *The U.S. Advisor*. Washington, D.C: CMH, 1980.

Clarke, Jeffrey J. *Advice and Support: The Final Years, 1965–1973*. Washington, D.C.: CMH, 1988.

Collins, Brig. Gen. James Lawton, Jr. *The Development and Training of the South Vietnamese Army, 1950–1972*. Washington, D.C.: GPO, 1975

Fulton, Maj. Gen. William B. *Riverine Operations: 1966–1969*. Washington D.C.: GPO, 1973.

Futrell, Robert F. *The United States Air Force in Southeast Asia: The Advisory Years to 1965*. Washington, D.C.: Office of Air Force History, 1981.

Hunt, Richard A. "The Challenge of Counterinsurgency." In *The Second Indochina War: Proceedings of a Symposium Held at Airlie, Virginia 7–9 November 1984*, 121–142. Edited by John Schlight. Washington, D.C.: CMH, 1986.

Kelly, Col. Francis J. *U.S. Army Special Forces: 1961–1971*. Washington, D.C.: GPO, 1973.

Komer, Robert W. "Commentary." In *The Second Indochina War: Proceedings of a Symposium Held at Airlie, Virginia 7–9 November 1984*, 161–165. Edited by John Schlight. Washington, D.C.: CMH, 1986.

Marolda, Edward J. and Fitzgerald, Oscar P. *The United States Navy and the Vietnam Conflict: From Military Assistance to Combat, 1959–1965*. Washington, D.C.: Naval Historical Center, 1986.

McChristian, Maj. Gen. Joseph A. *The Role of Military Intelligence, 1965–1967*. Washington, D.C.: GPO, 1974.

Ngo Quang Truong. *RVNAF and U.S. Operational Cooperation and Coordination*. Washington, D.C.: CMH, 1980.

Pike, Douglas. "Conduct of the Vietnam War: Strategic Factors, 1965–1968." In *The Second Indochina War: Proceedings of a Symposium Held at Airlie, Virginia 7–9 November 1984*, 99–119. Edited by John Schlight. Washington, D.C.: CMH, 1986.

Schlight, John, ed. *The Second Indochina War: Proceedings of a Symposium Held at Airlie, Virginia 7–9 November 1984*. Washington, D.C.: CMH, 1986.

Spector, Ronald H. *Advice and Support: The Early Years of the U.S. Army in Vietnam, 1941–1960.* Washington, D.C.: CMH, 1983.

Tolson, Lt. Gen. John J. *Airmobility, 1961–1971.* Washington, D.C.: GPO, 1973.

Tran Dinh Tho. *Pacification.* Washington, D.C.: CMH, 1980.

PERIODICALS AND ARTICLES

Army Information Digest. 1951–1962.

Arnold, S. L. and Stahl, David T. "A Power Projection Army in Operations Other Than War." *Parameters* 23 (winter 1993–94): 4–26.

Buzzanco, Robert. "Prologue to Tragedy: U.S. Military Opposition to Intervention in Vietnam, 1950–1954." *Diplomatic History* 17 (spring 1993): 201–22.

Clutterbuck, Col. Richard L. "The SEP–Guerrilla Intelligence Source." *Military Review* 42 (October 1962): 13–21.

Cullather, Nick. "America's Boy? Ramon Magsaysay and the Illusion of Influence." *Pacific Historical Review* (August 1993): 305–38.

Currey, Cecil B., USAR. "Edward G. Lansdale: LIC and the Ugly American." *Military Review* 68 (May 1988): 45–57.

Downey, Edward F., Jr. "Theory of Guerrilla Warfare." *Military Review* 39 (May 1959): 45–55.

Elting, John R. "Jomini: Disciple of Napoleon?" *Military Affairs* 28 (spring 1964): 17–26.

Filbert, Maj. Edward J. "The Roots of U.S. Counterinsurgency Doctrine." *Military Review* 68 (January 1988): 50–61.

Gates, John M. "Indians and Insurrectos: The U.S. Army's Experience with Insurgency." *Parameters* 13 (March 1983): 59–68.

———. "People's War in Vietnam." *Journal of Military History* 54 (July1990): 325–44.

Hampton, Col. Ephraim M. "Unlimited Confusion Over Limited War." *Air University Quarterly* 9 (spring 1957): 28–47.

Htaik, Maj. Thoung, "Encirclement Methods in Antiguerrilla Warfare." *Military Review* 41 (June 1961): 90–95.

Johnson, Harold K. "Subversion and Insurgency: Search for a Doctrine." *Army* 15 (November 1965): 40–42.

Luttwak, Edward N. "Notes on Low-Intensity Warfare." *Parameters* 13 (December 1983): 11–18.

Maechling, Charles, Jr. "Insurgency and Counterinsurgency: The Role of Strategic Theory." *Parameters* 14 (autumn 1984): 32–41.

Manwaring, Max G. "Toward an Understanding of Insurgent Warfare." *Military Review* 68 (January 1988): 28–35.

Metz, Steven. "Counterinsurgent Campaign Planning." *Parameters* 19

(September 1989): 60–68.

―――. "A Flame Kept Burning: Counterinsurgency Support After the Cold War." *Parameters* 25 (autumn 1995): 31–41.

Paschall, Rod. "Low-Intensity Conflict Doctrine: Who Needs It?" *Parameters* 15 (autumn 1985): 33–45.

―――. "Marxist Counterinsurgency." *Parameters* 16 (summer 1986): 2–15.

Qiang Zhai. "Transplanting the Chinese Model: Chinese Military Advisors and the First Vietnam War, 1950–1954." *The Journal of Military History* 57 (October 1993): 689–715.

Rattan, Lt. Col. Donald V. "Antiguerrilla Operations: A Case Study From History." *Military Review* 40 (May 1960): 23–27.

Rostow, W. W. "Vietnam and Southeast Asia: The Neglected Issue." *Parameters* 13 (March 1983): 2–14.

Sarkesian, Sam C. "American Policy on Revolution and Counterrevolution: A Review of the Themes in the Literature." *Conflict* 5 (February 1984): 137–184.

Summers, Harry G., Jr. "A Strategic Perception of the Vietnam War." *Parameters* 13 (June 1983): 41–46.

―――. "Vietnam Reconsidered." *The New Republic* (12 July 1987): 25–31.

Ward, Lt. Col. James R. "Vietnam: Insurgency Or War?" *Military Review* 69 (January 1989): 14–23.

Williams, Lt. Gen. Samuel T. "The Practical Demands of MAAG." *Military Review* 41 (July 1961): 2–15.

BOOKS AND PAPERS

Asprey, Robert B. *War in the Shadows: The Guerrilla in History.* 2 vols. Garden City, N.Y.: Doubleday and Company, 1975.

Averch, Harvey and Koehler, John. *The Huk Rebellion in the Philippines: Quantitative Approaches.* Santa Monica, Calif.: The Rand Corporation, 1970.

Baclagon, Uldarico S. *Lessons from the Huk Campaign in the Philippines.* Manila: M. Colcol & Co., 1960.

Blaufarb, Douglas S. *The Counterinsurgency Era: U.S. Doctrine and Performance, 1950 to Present.* New York: The Free Press, 1977.

Bowman, Stephan Lee. "The United States Army and Counterinsurgency Warfare: The Making of Doctrine, 1946–1964." M.A. thesis, Duke University, 1981.

Brinton, Crane, Craig, Gordon A., and Gilbert, Felix. "Jomini." In *Makers of Modern Strategy.* Edited by Edward Meade Earle. Princeton, N.J.: Princeton University Press, 1966.

Cable, Larry E. *Conflict and Myths: The Development of American Counterinsurgency Doctrine and the Vietnam War.* New York: New York University Press, 1986.

Calvert, Michael. *Prisoners of Hope*. London: Jonathan Cape, 1952.

Cincinnatus [Cecil B. Currey]. *Self-Destruction: The Disintegration and Decay of the United States Army During the Vietnam Era*. New York: W. W. Norton, 1981.

Clausewitz, Carl von. *On War*. Edited and translated by Michael Howard and Peter Paret. Princeton, N.J.: Princeton University Press, 1976.

Clutterbuck, Richard. *Conflict and Violence in Singapore and Malaysia, 1945–1983*. Boulder, Colo.: Westview Press, 1985.

Currey, Cecil B. *Edward Lansdale: The Unquiet American*. Boston: Houghton Mifflin Company, 1988.

————.*Victory at Any Cost: The Genius of Viet Nam's Gen. Vo Nguyen Giap*. New York: Brassey's, (US) Inc., 1997.

Dallek, Robert. *Franklin D. Roosevelt and American Foreign Policy, 1932–1945*. London: Oxford University Press, 1979

Duiker, William J. *The Communist Road to Power in Vietnam*. Boulder, Colo.: Westview Press, 1996.

Elliot-Bateman, Michael. *Defeat in the East: The Mark of Mao Tse-tung on War*. London: Oxford University Press, 1967.

Endicott, John E. and Strafford, Roy W., Jr. *American Defense Policy*, 4th ed. Baltimore, Md.: The Johns Hopkins University Press, 1977.

Fall, Bernard B. *Street Without Joy: Indochina at War, 1946–1954*. Harrisburg, Pa.: Stackpole Company, 1961.

————. *The Two Viet-Nams: A Political and Military Analysis*. New York: Frederick A. Praeger, 1963.

Galula, David. *Counter-Insurgency Warfare: Theory and Practice*. New York: Frederick A. Praeger, 1964.

Greene, T. N., ed. *The Guerrilla and How to Fight Him*. New York: Frederick A. Praeger, 1962.

Halperin, Morton H. *Limited War: An Essay on the Development of the Theory and An Annotated Bibliography*. Cambridge, Mass.: Center for International Affairs, Harvard University, 1962.

Hanrahan, Gene Z. *The Communist Struggle in Malaya*. New York: Institute for Pacific Relations, 1954.

Heilbrunn, Otto. *Partisan Warfare*. New York: Frederick A. Praeger, 1963.

————. *Warfare in the Enemy's Rear*. New York: Frederick A. Praeger, 1963.

Hilsman, Roger. *To Move a Nation: The Politics and Foreign Policy in the Administration of John F. Kennedy*. Garden City, N.Y.: Doubleday and Company, 1967.

————. *American Guerrilla: My War Behind Japanese Lines*. New York: Brassey's, (US) Inc., 1990.

Ho Chi Minh. *Ho Chi Minh on Revolution: Selected Writings, 1920–1966*. Edited by Bernard B. Fall. New York: Frederick A. Praeger, 1967.

Howard, Michael. "Jomini and the Classical Tradition in Military Thought." In *The Theory and Practice of War*, edited by Michael Howard. New York:

Frederick A. Praeger, 1965.

Hunt, Richard A. *Pacification: The American Struggle for Vietnam's Hearts and Minds.* Boulder, Colo.: Westview Press, 1995.

Johnson, Chalmers. *Revolutionary Change.* Boston: Little, Brown and Company, 1966.

Jomini, Baron Henri de. *The Art of War.* Translated by G. H. Mendell and W. P. Craighill. Philadelphia: J. B. Lippincott and Company, 1862.

Kinnard, Douglas. *The War Managers.* Hanover, N.H.: University Press of New England, 1977.

Kissinger, Henry A. *Nuclear Wapons and Foreign Policy.* New York: Harper & Bros., 1957

Kitson, Frank. *Low-Intensity Operations: Subversion, Insurgency, Peace-Keeping.* Harrisburg, Pa.: Stackpole Books, 1971.

Krepinevich, Andrew F., Jr. *The Army and Vietnam.* Baltimore, Md.: The Johns Hopkins University Press, 1986.

Lachica, Eduardo. *Huk: Philippine Agrarian Society in Revolt.* Manila: Solidaridad Publishing House, 1971.

Lacouture, Jean. *Ho Chi Minh: A Political Biography.* Translated by Peter Wiles. Translation edited by Jane Clark Seitz. New York: Random House, 1968.

Lansdale, Edward Geary. *In the Midst of Wars: An American's Mission to Southeast Asia.* New York: Harper & Row, 1972.

Liddell Hart, B. H. *Strategy.* New York: Praeger Publishers, 1967.

Mao Tse-tung. *Mao's Primer on Guerrilla War.* Translated by Samuel B. Griffith. In *The Guerrilla and How to Fight Him,* edited by T. N. Greene. New York: Frederick A. Praeger, 1962.

———. *On Guerrilla Warfare.* Translated by Samuel B. Griffith. Foreword by B.H. Liddell Hart. London: Cassell, 1962.

———. *Mao Tse-tung on Revolution and War.* Edited with an introduction and notes by M. Rejai. New York: Doubleday & Company, Inc., 1969.

Marr, David G. *Vietnam 1945: The Quest for Power.* Berkeley, Calif.: University of California Press, 1995.

Matloff, Maurice, ed. *American Military History.* Washington, D.C.: GPO, 1969.

McCuen, John J. *The Art of Counter-Revolutionary War.* Harrisburg, Pa.: Stackpole Books, 1966.

Metz, Steven. *The Future of Insurgency.* Carlisle Barracks, Pa.: Strategic Studies Institute, U. S. Army War College, 1993.

Meyer, Col. Harold J. "Jack." *Hanging Sam: A Military Biography of General Samuel T. Williams, From Pancho Villa To Vietnam.* Denton, Tx.: University of North Texas Press, 1990.

Mitchell, Edward J. *The Huk Rebellion in the Philippines: An Econometric Study.* Santa Monica, Calif.: The Rand Corporation, 1969.

Mockaitis, Thomas R. *British Counterinsurgency, 1919-60.* London: The Macmillan Press Ltd., 1990.

Murray, J. C. "The Anti-Bandit War." In *The Guerrilla and How to Fight Him*, edited by T. N. Greene. New York: Frederick A. Praeger, 1962.

Neumann, Sigmund. "The International Civil War." In *Why Revolution? Theories and Analysis*, edited by Clifford T. Paynton and Robert Blackey. Cambridge, Mass.: Schenkman Publishing Co., Inc., 1971.

Nighswonger, William A. *Rural Pacification in Vietnam*. New York: Frederick A. Praeger, 1966.

O'Ballance, Edgar. *The Indo-China War, 1945–1954: A Study in Guerrilla Warfare*. London: Faber and Faber, 1964.

O'Neill, Bard E. "Insurgent Strategies: An Examination of Four Approaches." In *American Defense Policy*, 4th ed., edited by John E. Endicott and Roy W. Strafford, Jr. Baltimore, Md.: The Johns Hopkins University Press, 1977.

———. *Insurgency and Terrorism: Inside Modern Revolutionary Warfare*. New York: Brassey's (U.S.) Inc., 1990.

Osgood, Robert E. *Limited War: The Challenge to American Strategy*. Chicago: The University of Chicago Press, 1957.

———. *Limited War Revisited*. Boulder, Colo.: Westview Press, 1979.

Paget, Julian. *Counter-Insurgency Operations: Techniques of Guerrilla Warfare*. New York: Walker and Company, 1967.

Palmer, Dave Richard. *Summons of the Trumpet: U.S.-Vietnam in Perspective*. San Rafael, Calif.: Presidio Press, 1978.

Paret, Peter. *French Revolutionary Warfare from Indochina to Algeria: The Analysis of a Political and Military Doctrine*. New York: Frederick A. Praeger, 1964.

Paret, Peter and Shy, John W. *Guerrillas in the 1960's*. New York: Frederick A. Praeger, 1962.

Patti, Archimedes L. A. *Why Vietnam? Prelude to America's Albatross*. Berkeley, Calif.: University of California Press, 1980.

Paynton, Clifford T. and Blackey, Robert. *Why Revolution? Theories and Analysis*. Cambridge, Mass.: Schenkman Publishing Co., Inc., 1971.

The Pentagon Papers: The Defense Department History of United States Decisionmaking on Vietnam. Senator Gravel ed. 4 vols. Boston: Beacon Press, 1971.

Pike, Douglas. *Viet Cong*. Cambridge, Mass.: M.I.T. Press, 1966.

Plano, Jack C., Greenberg, Milton, Olton, Roy, and Riggs, Robert E. *Political Science Dictionary*. Hinsdale, Ill.: The Dryden Press, 1973.

Pustay, John S. *Counterinsurgency Warfare*. New York: The Free Press, 1965.

Pye, Lucian W. *Guerrilla Communism in Malaya: Its Social and Political Meaning*. Princeton, N.J.: Princeton University Press, 1956.

Rostow, W. W. "Guerrilla Warfare in Underdeveloped Areas." In *The Guerrilla and How to Fight Him*, edited by T. N. Greene. New York: Frederick A. Praeger, 1962.

Sarkesian, Sam C., ed. *Revolutionary Guerrilla Warfare*. Chicago: Precedent Publishing, 1975.

————. *Nonnuclear Conflicts in the Nuclear Age.* Westport, Conn.: Praeger Publishers, 1980.

Sarkesian, Sam C. *Unconventional Conflicts in a New Security Era: Lessons from Malaya and Vietnam.* Westport, Conn.: Greenwood Press, 1993.

Scott, Andrew M., with Clark, Maj. Donald P., Ehrman, R. Bruce, Salmon, John W., Jr., Shill, Harold B., and Trapnell, Cpt. Frank W. *Insurgency.* Chapel Hill, N.C.: The University of North Carolina Press, 1970.

Scruton, Roger. *A Dictionary of Political Thought.* New York: Harper & Row, Publishers, 1982.

Sheehan, Neil. *A Bright Shining Lie: John Paul Vann and America in Vietnam.* New York: Random House, Inc., 1988.

Sheehan, Neil, Smith, Hedrick, Kenworthy, E. W., and Butterfield, Fox. *The Pentagon Papers: As Published by the* New York Times. New York: Bantam Books, Inc., 1971.

Short, Anthony. *The Communist Insurrection in Malaya: 1948–1960.* New York: Crane Russak & Company, Inc., 1975.

Shultz, Richard. "Strategy Lessons from an Unconventional War: The U.S. Experience in Vietnam." In *Nonnuclear Conflicts in the Nuclear Age,* edited by Sam C. Sarkesian. Westport, Conn.: Praeger Publishers, 1980.

Shultz, Richard H., Jr., Pfaltzgraff, Robert L., Jr., Ra'anan, Uri, Olson, William J., Lukes, Igor, eds. *Guerrilla Warfare and Counterinsurgency: U.S.-Soviet Policy in the Third World.* Lexington, Mass.: Lexington Books, 1989.

Shy, John. "Jomini." In *Makers of Modern Strategy: From Machiavelli to the Nuclear Age,* edited by Peter Paret. Princeton, N.J.: Princeton University Press, 1986.

Shy, John and Collier, Thomas W. "Revolutionary War." In *Makers of Modern Strategy: From Machiavelli to the Nuclear Age,* edited by Peter Paret. Princeton, N.J.: Princeton University Press, 1986.

Stilwell, Richard G. "U.S. Counterinsurgency: Political and Psychological Dimensions." In *Guerrilla Warfare and Counterinsurgency: U.S.-Soviet Policy in the Third World,* edited by Richard H. Shultz, Jr., Pfaltzgraff, Robert L., Jr., Ra'anan, Uri, Olson, William J., Lukes, Igor. Lexington, Mass.: Lexington Books, 1989.

Summers, Harry G. *On Strategy: A Critical Analysis of the Vietnam War.* Novato, Calif.: Presidio Press, 1982.

————. "A War Is a War Is a War Is a War." In *Low-Intensity Conflict: The Pattern of Warfare in the Modern World.* Edited by Loren B. Thompson. Lexington, Mass.: Lexington Books, 1989.

————. *On Strategy II: A Critical Analysis of the Gulf War.* New York: Dell Publishing, 1992.

Sun Tzu. *The Art of War.* Translated and with an introduction by Samuel B. Griffith. London: Oxford University Press, 1963.

Taber, Robert. *The War of the Flea: A Study of Guerrilla Warfare Theory and Practice.* New York: Lyle Stuart, 1965.

Tanham, George K. *Communist Revolutionary Warfare: From the Vietminh to the Viet Cong*. Santa Monica, Calif.: The Rand Corporation, 1961; rev. ed., New York: Frederick A. Praeger, 1967.

Tarr, David W. "The Strategic Environment, U.S. National Security and the Nature of Low Intensity Conflict." In *Nonnuclear Conflicts in the Nuclear Age*, edited by Sam C. Sarkesian. Westport, Conn.: Praeger Publishers, 1980.

Taruc, Luis. *He Who Rides the Tiger*. New York: Frederick A. Praeger, 1967.

Taylor, Maxwell D. *Swords and Plowshares*. New York: W. W. Norton & Co., 1972.

Thompson, Loren B., ed. *Low-Intensity Conflict: The Pattern of Warfare in the Modern World*. Lexington, Mass.: Lexington Books, 1989.

Thompson, Robert. *Defeating Communist Insurgency*. New York: Frederick A. Praeger, 1966.

———. *No Exit from Vietnam*. New York: David McKay Company, Inc., 1969.

———. *Revolutionary War in World Strategy, 1945–1969*. New York: Taplinger Publishing Company, 1970.

Valeriano, Col. Napoleon D., and Bohannan, Lt. Col. Charles T. R. *Counter Guerrilla Operations: The Philippine Experience*. New York: Frederick A. Praeger, 1962.

Vo Nguyen Giap. *People's War, People's Army*. Foreword by Roger Hilsman. Profile of Giap by Bernard B. Fall. New York: Frederick A. Praeger, 1962.

Weigley, Russell F. *History of the United States Army*. New York: The Macmillan Company, 1967.

———. *The American Way of War: A History of United States Military Strategy and Policy*. New York: The Macmillan Company, 1973.

Yarborough, William P. "Counterinsurgency: The U.S. Role—Past, Present, and Future." In *Guerrilla Warfare and Counterinsurgency: U.S.-Soviet Policy in the Third World*, edited by Richard H. Shultz, Jr., Pfaltzgraff, Robert L., Jr., Ra'anan, Uri, Olson, William J., Lukes, Igor. Lexington, Mass.: Lexington Books, 1989.

Zasloff, Joseph J. "Origins of the Insurgency in South Vietnam, 1954-1960: The Role of the Southern Vietminh Cadres," RM 5163. Santa Monica, Calif.: The Rand Corporation, March 1967.

Index

About the Author

DONALD W. HAMILTON is Professor of History at Mesa College and serves as a reserve officer in the U.S. military.